FOUR WORDS FOR FRIEND

Marek Kohn

FOUR WORDS FOR FRIEND

Why Using More Than One Language
Matters Now More Than Ever

YALE UNIVERSITY PRESS
NEW HAVEN AND LONDON

For information about this and other Yale University Press publications, please contact:
U.S. Office: sales.press@yale.edu   yalebooks.com
Europe Office: sales@yaleup.co.uk   yalebooks.co.uk

Set in Adobe Caslon Pro by IDSUK (DataConnection) Ltd
Printed in Great Britain by TJ International, Padstow, Cornwall

Library of Congress Control Number: 2018962174

ISBN 978-0-300-23108-3

A catalogue record for this book is available from the British Library.

10 9 8 7 6 5 4 3 2 1

For Sue and Teo

Contents

CHAPTER ONE

Other Words Are Possible

*If we are to make the most of languages, we
have to recognise that they are there to obstruct
communication as well as to enable it.*

I have written this book in my second language. I would not be able
to write it in my first, Polish, which I never finished learning before I
went to school and moved decisively into the English speech community. Millions of migrants' children follow the same trajectory, leaving
the home language behind, and merging into the dominant one.
Having lost touch with my first language for many years, before developing a more recent commitment to repair the remaining ramshackle
structure and build upon it, I am an entirely typical 'heritage speaker'.
My vocabulary is limited, my grammar improvised and to a large
extent guesswork. Yet the language is mine, and it is part of me.

Less typical, perhaps, is my conviction that my language history
makes me a particularly suitable author for a book on this subject. I
am very aware that not being able to do something properly is an
unusual attribute to claim as a qualification for writing about it. An
effortless polyglot might seem a more obvious person to go to for
insights into the plural use of languages. You should certainly go to

one if what you are interested in is high-performance polyglotism. That is indeed fascinating, but I feel it is a world of its own. Mathematical and musical genius are likewise fascinating, but they are not the phenomena to focus on if we're more concerned about how ordinary people can count or hold a tune.[1]

My claim is based not on expertise but on another kind of knowledge: often tenuous, fragmentary or occluded, but always present. One of the most influential ideas in the science of bilingualism is that both languages are continuously activated in a bilingual's brain. The awareness that arises from knowledge of more than one language may also be continuously active. It forms part of one's basic understanding of the nature of language, expression, thought and meaning. Although it may go unrecognised in everyday life, it is still there, embedded in one's cognitive constitution. It colours the way one apprehends the world. That is what I mean and try to explain when, if someone asks, I say I'm bilingual.

This has been on my mind for almost my entire life. It's why I can't take languages for granted. There's nothing like losing something to make one appreciate its value (though what that provides me with is a motivation, rather than a qualification, for writing about this subject). And there's something compellingly strange about the enduring presence of 'that language of the past that withers without ever leaving you'. It leaves the sense that it is still up to something. You feel you might manage to glimpse it at work if you could only turn round quickly enough. That, I think, is why tropes about the pursuit of occult or encrypted knowledge appear at certain points in this book.[2]

Not all of the first language's effects are enigmatic. One in particular is clear to me. I know, from a lifetime's experience, that even a limited, unreliable and defective purchase on a language can provide insight into the meaning contained in another language. It creates a background awareness that knowledge and expression are always contingent upon the particular framework of whatever language happens to be their vehicle. Any degree of familiarity beyond tourist phrases will supply examples to sustain the recognition that words in different languages rarely occupy exactly the same space of meaning, even if they are reasonable translation equivalents. Their boundaries do not align tidily, and they combine in different ways. Even a very basic level of competence will be enough to highlight suggestive structural differences in emphasis between languages, such as the way that English capitalises the first-person singular pronoun, whereas many other European languages prefer to capitalise second-person pronouns. And it promotes a tacit awareness of the truth crystallised by the linguist Roman Jakobson in his observation that 'Languages differ essentially in what they *must* convey, not what they *may* convey.' English speakers learning Russian will discover that when referring to a friend, they can't simply call the person 'my friend', but have to choose from among several words – four, typically, give or take – that denote different degrees of closeness. They are obliged to testify about how warm their friendship is. Languages set different distances between people.[3]

Contrasts like these cast each language in a different light. One language provides a perspective on the other. It heightens the constant awareness that there is no one single way of saying something, or understanding it: that whatever words are chosen, other words are possible.

✳ ✳ ✳ ✳

Languages exist both to enable communication and to obstruct it. They establish perimeters inside which information is free to circulate, but across which it is unable to pass. This two-sided character makes it impossible to take languages for granted. The relationships between them need work, or at least thought, just as the relationships between their speakers do. And all these relationships are intertwined.

If we can get languages to work together, to flourish in each other's company, we will help their speakers to do the same.

Their speakers, ourselves: integrating languages, within communities or within individual minds, is a way to turn competition into co-operation, suspicion into trust, antagonism into conviviality. It's not the only way, but it is a special one. At the most fundamental level, it confounds the division between 'us' and 'them'. It helps us get the best out of human nature, and the most out of human culture.

Although languages can't be taken for granted, many people are able to use more than one without giving the matter a thought. Babies whose carers speak two languages to them, or more, acquire each with equal ease. Countless millions of people switch effortlessly between languages throughout the course of every day, according to where they are and whom they encounter. India, where languages flow into each other and people move routinely between them, may be more representative of language practices around the world than the United States, in which English is dominant and monolingualism prevalent. Even the United States may be more multilingual than it appears, since although the Census Bureau records that about 20 per cent of the population speak a language other than English at home, it does not ask about any of the other ways and settings in which different languages can be used. Bilingualism is as normal and natural as monolingualism. Yet for many people who speak English and only English, it seems little short of miraculous.[4]

One of the reasons for this is that they misunderstand the meaning of fluency and are overawed by a bilingual ideal, that of the 'balanced' speaker who is equally fluent in each language. People tend to think of fluency as a yes-or-no category – you are either fluent in a language or you are not – rather than the continuum implied by the source of the word. Flow may be smooth or restricted or interrupted; so may fluency. It is a matter of degree. 'Balanced', or 'symmetrical', bilinguals are the exception, not the norm. Bilingualism should not be defined by them –

and especially not when people talk of 'true' or 'genuine' bilinguals, implying that the vast majority are 'false' or, as one researcher labelled them many years ago, 'pseudo-bilinguals'. The linguist François Grosjean defines bilinguals as 'those who use two or more languages (or dialects) in their everyday lives'. There is no need to specify the balance between those languages, the extent to which each is used, or the user's proficiency in them. They are just part of everyday life.[5]

Pragmatic and open-sounding as it is, this definition cannot help but tangle with other understandings of bilingualism. The most familiar one sticks to the meaning of 'bi' and reserves the term for the use of two languages. Any more than that is multilingualism, though the word is most often used to describe the presence of a variety of languages in nations, cities or communities, whether or not individuals within them can speak more than one. 'Plurilingualism' has been proposed as an etymologically sound term for the use of two or more languages. It has also been invested with a significance that is similar in spirit to Grosjean's definition, but much more ambitiously inclusive. Rather than posing the question of whether a person meets the criteria necessary to be categorised as bilingual (and everyday use is a criterion that discounts many deep seams of bilingual resources) it asks what they are able to do with different languages. Instead of looking towards 'mastery' of two or more languages, it looks at the entire portfolio of language abilities that the person has at their disposal. They may be able to sustain a conversation in one, employ some useful basic phrases in another, understand what somebody is saying in a third language despite being unable to reply in it, and draw upon their overall body of linguistic knowledge to make inferences about meanings in hitherto unfamiliar languages. In short, the idea is to appreciate the value of all linguistic resources, however imperfect or limited, and to make the most of them.[6]

This approach has been adopted by the Council of Europe for language education across the continent. It is also the one I take in this book, although I prefer simply to talk about using more than one language. There are many ways to use language, all of which may be significant and valuable. You may use one just for exchanging pleasantries, but the importance of pleasantries should not be underestimated. You may be spoken to in one language and reply in another: it still adds up to a conversation. (This works best with languages that are to some extent mutually comprehensible, such as Danish, Norwegian and Swedish.) Particular forms of language use don't have to be regular or frequent to be important in a person's life. Some people read novels or follow movie dialogue in languages they are unable to speak. Others correspond with relatives abroad in languages they have no occasion to speak out loud. Making the most of languages is not a matter of becoming able to conduct one's entire life in alternative tongues, but of drawing upon languages that come to hand in particular settings.

It takes more than a positive attitude, though. In many settings, limitations loom larger than capacities, and perhaps nowhere more so than in families, where languages are subject to the most intense emotional demands. Answering a question in a different language from that in which it is asked is one thing between strangers, quite another between close kin. Among strangers, it represents makeshift understanding; among family, fundamental division. 'Family meals are utterly disjointed,' admits one mother, describing how she speaks Bengali to her daughter, who replies in English, which is the only language spoken in the home that her husband understands. In a TV soap about Polish migrants in London, the nastiest character is the adult daughter who answers her warm-hearted mother in English. Interested only in money, the younger woman has turned her back not only on her mother tongue but also the values that were embedded in it. One thing about soap opera characters is that they convey simple truths: in this case, the sense of rejection that is impossible to altogether avoid when somebody answers you from the other side of a language border.[7]

These mood swings are inherent in the use of languages. The possibilities are endless, and so are the difficulties. An infant has the potential to enter any language; a child may feel obliged to choose one over others. Adults remain perfectly capable of learning new languages, but life's other demands pile up on their desks and get in the way. Many children and adults are highly fluent in a language, but are discouraged from using it because it lacks prestige or economic value, or because too few people around them understand it, or because it provokes hostility from speakers of other languages, or because there are laws restricting where and how it may be spoken. Using more than one language involves not just gaining languages but also hanging on to them. It involves choices not just for individuals but for the communities and nations of which they are part. Grammar, vocabulary and pronunciation aren't the half of it.

In order to make the most of languages, to use them fruitfully, and to pursue the ideal of their integration, we have to find paths that take us around these obstacles and across these borders. This book doesn't provide maps. It picks a way through the terrain, looking out for the intriguing and the unexpected, but does not survey the whole of the landscape. It doesn't offer guidance on optimal ways to learn languages or to raise children in bilingual homes, though it makes observations on these matters. Many excellent sources of such advice are readily available. Instead, it offers ideas and information intended to help readers think about the use of languages, and to understand their relationships with languages better. *Four Words For Friend* is not intended to give direct answers to questions like whether taking a language course is a good use of one's time, or whether to send bilingual children to Saturday schools where they are taught in the languages they don't hear in their weekday classes. It is, however, written with the hope that the perspectives and context it provides might be of some value to people facing such questions, and of interest to a much larger circle of people drawn to the compelling contradictions of language use.[8]

Finding paths through language territories may not require maps, but it does require guiding principles. This book follows several; one is that paths are worth finding. The use of more than one language is a good thing: not always, not necessarily, not inherently, but in most circumstances and in spirit, it is good. There are many reasons for this, but the underlying one is that it favours a complex of goods: openness, interconnection, inclusion, mutual exchange and the sharing of knowledge.

Another is that the two-sided character of language must always be recognised. It is the place from which the path has to start. We will get hopelessly lost if we lose sight of the truth that language exists as much to prevent communication as to make it happen. This is not really a paradox: the design logic of enabling information to circulate within a group, while restricting its ability to enter or leave, is all too easy to grasp. There you have it: the two sides of human nature, inward community and outward exclusion, the latter the engine of the former. Sympathy is generated by drawing limits around it. To transcend this design, to liberate those better angels of our nature, we need to treat the dual character of language as a contradiction that must be resolved, or at least mitigated.

The third basic principle, that all of a person's linguistic resources should be valued, helps to ease the conflict. Under this principle, languages are treated with due respect, but not with undue deference. A language is regarded not as an edifice within which a community is housed and to which individuals may aspire to gain admission, but as an assembly of elements which individuals are free to use as they wish. This does not mean that maintaining its integrity and sustaining its vitality are unimportant. Quite the reverse: the better shape a language is in, the more use its elements will be. A healthy language will keep its identity while encouraging a rich variety of relationships to flourish across its boundaries, in different combinations, balances, modes and registers, at different levels of proficiency. Its perimeter will not be a dumb fence; it will be a complex and productive interface, like the membrane of a living cell. Yet the key to this complexity is the simple principle that we should make the most of whatever we can grasp. It is a practical, everyday way to reduce the inherent tensions of language use.

The first steps are simple too. Make what you can of the words you hear and see, spoken, written or signed. Start speaking, and keep going.

* * * *

Extensive tracts of this book are haunted by the ghost of Johann Gottfried Herder, the thinker whose ideas about the intimate relationship between peoples and languages helped to kindle the fires of nineteenth-century Romantic nationalism. Though he did not hold all the views that have come to be associated with his name, he represents the ambivalent impulses that come from treating language as identity: the championing of languages spoken by common folk, the belief that languages constitute peoples and that sustaining a people requires the preservation of its defining language, the tendency to regard other languages as competitors rather than partners, and an inclination to take selective views of what counts as linguistic or cultural heritage. Today he is channelled by people like Máirtín Ó Muilleoir, a member of the Northern Ireland Assembly and of Sinn Féin, the Irish nationalist party whose goal is a 'new republic' covering the entire island of Ireland. 'A language is the soul of a people,' Ó Muilleoir declared, speaking against the background of his party's call for an Acht na Gaeilge, an act guaranteeing Irish language rights in Northern Ireland. The Democratic Unionist Party, which stands for the opposite of Sinn Féin but is required to share power with it, seemed to agree. It chose to remain out of power, leaving Northern Ireland governed from London, rather than accept Sinn Féin's demand.[9]

The idea that languages are the souls of nations took hold in the continental European imagination during the very period in which, on their north-western island, the Irish people gave up their own language and accepted that of their British rulers. In the Republic of Ireland, only about 1.5 per cent of the population speak Irish daily, other than in school; in Northern Ireland, it is the main language for only 0.2 per cent of the province's residents. Once a people has renounced its language – its soul, in Ó Muilleoir's terms – it falls to the state to incorporate the language into the fabric of national institutions. The state speaks the language so the people don't have to. An admixture of the heritage language in everyday discourse has a significant symbolic effect, though. It is not a trivial thing that the leader of the Irish government is known as the Taoiseach and the police are called the Garda Síochána. Linguists refer to instances of a word in speech or writing as 'tokens', copies from the template. Scattered throughout conversation, official discourse and public space, Irish tokens matter.[10]

When a state takes upon itself the role of language protector, it takes on decisions about how far to permit alterations to the language's standard form. Nowadays many such adjustments arise through social change, when significant layers of opinion come to the view that certain usages do not adequately reflect society's needs or values. In English, the absence of satisfactory gender-neutral pronouns has led to the ad hoc co-option of 'their' as a singular pronoun, first to refer to an unspecified person of unspecified gender, and more recently to specific persons who do not identify as male or female. On one side, individuals are asserting their right to specify which pronouns should be used in reference to themselves: 'My pronouns are they, their and them.' On the other, the idea that people can choose their own pronouns is anathema to institutions charged with authority over language. So-called 'inclusive' language, warns the Académie française, puts French in 'péril mortel'.[11]

Not having a Romantic vision of language or nationhood, I don't believe that a people has a soul. Believing instead that languages should help individuals flourish, and that language should serve society, not the other way round, I'm pleased to see pronouns being repurposed in the cause of inclusiveness. When there are no clear considerations of fairness or respect, however, and it is more a question of grammar for grammar's sake, I have a deep-rooted sense of order. I bristle when I see a misplaced apostrophe in the same way that I bristle when a driver fails to signal a turn. I understand the importance of consistency and house style.

I'm all the more grateful, therefore, to my editor and his colleagues for agreeing to let this book depart from Yale's style guide in one particular respect. The normal practice in English-language publishing is to put non-English words in italics. That would hardly be in the spirit of this book, though, and would run counter to one of its central themes. I want to encourage people to make the most of all the linguistic resources at their disposal, whether those are just a few words in a particular language or a fully-equipped grammar. They should feel that all the words they know are part of their own domain, not that certain ones don't really belong in it – and that they themselves don't really belong in the domains where those words come from. The less foreign they feel foreign languages to be, the better. Italics signify limitations on the free movement of language and the inhibition of fluidity in its use. They smack of othering, the practice of exclusion from in-groups by the use of labels or rhetorical artifice. Applying italics in the following pages would have seemed like making the immigrant children in the class wear different-coloured blazers.

Integration is more than just combination, though. Although it is necessary to be able to treat languages as assemblies of elements, it is also necessary to understand that they are more than the sums of their parts. People implicitly recognise this. When they cherish a language as their own, their emotions are invested in the system as a whole, as a structure extensive, strong and flexible enough to support the rest of the culture that goes with it. To acknowledge this is to acknowledge that there is an important truth enshrined in the idea that a language is the soul of a people.

That idea is also what people affirm when they claim languages they do not speak as their own. The special relationship between the Irish people and their language has echoes on the other side of the world, in the northern Australian region of Arnhem Land, where local people may confuse anthropologists by identifying their languages as the ones their ancestors spoke, rather than the languages they themselves use. (Their declarations are based on their hereditary claims to lands in which particular languages are believed to have been installed by ancestral beings: the language comes with the territory.) The character of the relationships between languages and peoples will vary from place to place, but they are always special.[12]

If a language is to remain capable of supporting its associated culture, the integrity of its structure must be maintained in the face of changing environments. Linguistic nationalists in Europe met the challenges of modernisation by compiling dictionaries and consolidating standardised forms of their languages. In doing so they accentuated the contrasts between them, sometimes introducing differences that had not previously existed. The historian Timothy Snyder notes how Lithuanians adopted Czech characters to 'make their language look less Polish'. Those characters had been designed by Czechs who wanted to make their own language look less German (and also to avoid the clutter of double consonants such as 'cz' – possibly because the Polish language's insatiable demand for the letter 'z' caused shortages throughout eastern Europe).[13]

Standardisation reduces diversity by elevating one dialect above others, which may then be left to decay in obscurity along with the villages in which they are spoken. But it enlarges the range of domains in which the language can find a voice, allowing it to enter literature and official discourse. In doing so, standardisation expands the community that the language draws together. The language thereby acquires new responsibilities, which illustrate just why it is necessary to value conformity as well as flexibility in its use. As in driving, so in speaking and writing. Signalling turns and other sideways moves is most importantly a safety issue, but more often and more broadly it is a matter of community. Most failures to signal do not create any real risk of collision or injury. Their offence is a lack of consideration for other people going along or across the road. Traffic rules are the basis of a system that constitutes road users as a co-operative community, establishing procedures intended to promote efficient travel by reducing the conflicts of interest between the members of the community as fairly and practically as possible. A driver or a cyclist who doesn't bother to signal a turn is signalling a lack of commitment to the rules, and therefore to the community itself.

Similarly, questions of grammar are never just for grammar's sake. You may be indifferent to apostrophe offences because you do not have the kind of personality that feels threatened by tiny infringements of order, or you may be affronted if you do, but either way, your usage has implications for your attitude to the language system, which may in turn have implications for your attitude to the language community. Apostrophe attitudes are the epitome of excessive pedantry (and referring to them is a handy way for pedants to signal that they are not entirely devoid of self-awareness) but they illustrate the point. A wrongly inserted apostrophe creates a momentary ambiguity that perturbs the course of comprehension – 'just a moment, is this actually a new verb; do I need to revise my working hypothesis about the meaning of what I've read so far?' On its own, its effect is minimal, but similar errors can rapidly mount up and make statements genuinely hard to understand. They impair the shared system of communication and create inconvenience for the community it supports. Among writers, adherence to literary standard forms is a sign of commitment not just to their craft, but to the cultural community in which they claim membership.

The inescapable truth of the matter is that relationships with languages are complicated. We need to make them work for us, and at the same time we need to support them. We need to respect their standards, but also appreciate their flexibility. Much of the art of language use, and language choice, lies in matching language to context. Monolinguals as well as bilinguals do this all the time. People speak in different ways to babies and to grown-ups, teachers and classmates, superiors and servants. In multilingual societies, the different registers are often different languages – with English typically occupying the most privileged rank. English also enjoys privilege around the world as the default lingua franca, a situation which reveals the limits of language sensitivity among English-speaking monoglots. Among foreigners, native English speakers often forget the idea of attuning their speech to that of their hearers. They fail to notice that they are baffling their interlocutors with their idioms, and intimidating them with their unreflective fluency. It probably never occurs to many of them that non-native speakers may suspect the natives of using their superior language skills to deceive them. Excessive fluency can lead to distrust.

Conversely, limited fluency can bring people together. Talking about the use of English as the lingua franca in a multinational European company, one member of staff described the collective creation of a new speech community: 'When we are talking English with Spanish, Italian, and German people, we are creating our own language in a way … we are emerging a new kind of English.' Non-native speakers of English felt comfortable speaking with each other, despite their mistakes, but ill at ease with native speakers. The reason was that the non-natives had their limitations in common. Mistakes did not create divisions among them; inequalities did. And if mistakes in communication are shared, they will cease to be mistakes:

people will converge on them and adopt them as proper usages. Mainland Europeans may well develop new speech communities that will add to the already abundant variety of 'World Englishes'. It might become grammatically as well as factually correct to say that they are emerging a new kind of English.[14]

Native English speakers are able to take their language for granted because of its prestige and power. They have the luxury of being able to regard relationships with non-native speakers as straightforward. Being inconsiderate to their interlocutors, by discounting the need to find an appropriate style of speech, is likely to work to their own advantage. Since the world has decided that English is to be its lingua franca, it is natural enough for native speakers to have a sense of entitlement. And it is also natural enough that they may find it difficult to appreciate why other languages are so important to their native speakers, especially when there are strong rational arguments for shifting to English.

These merge without resistance into a thicker soup of arguments based on values and beliefs about what the relationships between peoples should be. Pragmatic arguments – migrants should speak English to avoid misunderstandings in the workplace, or to make friends in the playground – shade into demands of a more dogmatic cast: this is the language of this country, so if you want to live here, you had better speak it.

There is plenty of truth in the proposition that to become part of the national community you must become part of the national language community. Membership implies the capacity to converse with any other member, to understand the speech and writing encountered in everyday life, to share in the enjoyment of popular culture, and to follow public affairs – though not all of these capacities need to be exercised. If that were all there was to the issue, it would be simple. Learning a country's most prevalent language offers manifold benefits for the learner, and also for the nation. But when somebody says 'we speak English in this country' to somebody they overhear speaking a foreign language on a bus, they are not indicating a route to membership of a national community. They are demanding that the person obeys what they assert to be the rules for the conduct of the collective, because they consider that speaking a foreign language in public shows disrespect for the 'host' society. Responses such as 'I'm on the phone to my mother in Germany' are unlikely to cut any ice with them. (Consistently applied, the principle would seem to require that the bus passenger speaks English and their mother replies in German.)[15]

The pressure to silence a family language often comes from within the family itself. Dina Mehmedbegovic worked to help victims of ethnic cleansing in Bosnia who were brought to Britain as refugees in the 1990s. Some of them told her that within a few months of starting to resettle, in London and Essex, children were telling their parents: 'When you pick me up from school, don't speak to me in our language.' The hidden costs of resettlement were beginning to appear. 'People who had lost their homes were now fearing loss of language, identity, self and family ties.'[16]

People who have been driven from their homes will fear such losses more than people who have chosen to leave theirs; children who have been forced out of one community may be even more anxious than children in general to fit into their new one. Yet the consequences are far-reaching among migrants of whatever circumstances, and their descendants, even if they are not painful. Belonging becomes a zero-sum game: strengthening ties to the new community means weakening ties to the old one.

This may seem obvious, but it is not. It may seem inevitable, but it need not be. Bilingualism is potentially a unique form of integration, enabling a person to be part of two cultures and flourish in both. It offers the possibility of belonging to two communities instead of having to sacrifice membership of one in order to secure a place in the other. More profoundly, it creates conditions that may allow two cultures to integrate within a single mind. Instead of posing a zero-sum problem, bilingualism need not require loss, and may be an opportunity for mutual gain. It's not a trick. You can have both.

The catch is that you may not be able to get them on your own. For some individuals it might be a successful solo project, but for most people bilingualism requires collective consent and effort. Relatives, neighbours, colleagues, teachers, peers, officials, policy-setters, law-makers and strangers on buses all have their part to play. Agreements will need to be reached and balances struck: it is desirable that everybody should be able to use the dominant language, and it may not be desirable to encourage multilingualism in all settings. Sometimes it will be more important to place the weight on unity rather than diversity; sometimes it will be necessary to establish unity before diversity can be fruitfully cultivated. Organisations will need to work out rules and guidelines. Individuals will have to cultivate the art of using more than one language, in ways that are appropriate to the time, the place and the people with whom the languages are being used.

Given goodwill, the use of more than one language can help resolve the tension between unity and diversity. It can help people to maintain their identity without being confined by it, by productively confusing the boundaries between 'us' and 'them'. But that is precisely why the necessary goodwill may not be forthcoming: why using more than one language is widely regarded as threatening, suspicious and subversive. Bilingualism is an affront to nativists who insist that each nation ought to comprise a single people and speak a single language. As well as demonstrating that being part of one community does not have to mean that a person belongs any less fully to another, it proves that people can be cosmopolitan and have roots too. It is the deepest form of integration, and the subtlest.

All this makes it the antithesis of the growing agitation to close borders, build walls and impose a resentful simplicity upon the world.

Using more than one language is not simply associated with qualities such as openness and understanding. It stands for them, against hostility and mistrust. And because it is inseparable from values that are bitterly contested, encouraging it involves standing up for those values.

In this book I'm pursuing a particular kind of integration, between science and social questions. That does not mean confusing facts and values, but creating a dialogue between their respective estates. My intention has been to find a path between the scientific, personal and political domains of language, piecing together a story about how languages are gained, how they are lost, how they are encouraged, how they are inhibited, and how they might be better used. It's only one of many possible trails – and certainly not the most obvious one, routed as it is through Rīga in Latvia and Hyderabad in India. But I'm glad I picked it out, and I hope readers will be too.

The trail moves through the learning of languages, the loss of languages, the possible effects of bilingualism upon mental function, the possible effects of language on thought, and the subjective experience of being bilingual or multilingual. It proceeds from how children first enter language to how people learn languages later in life, and how the children of migrants lose their heritage languages, to the controversial question of whether bilingualism confers mental advantages in other domains besides that of language itself. It explores a trio of intriguing phenomena that cast light upon the relationship between languages and thought, as well as stopping to consider how languages shape relationships, and the effect of entering different languages upon one's sense of oneself. It then turns from questions about individuals' encounters with languages to the question of how societies respond to the presence of different tongues among them. Here it visits a small country, Latvia, in which is encapsulated an extraordinary concentration of some of the most significant themes in European language politics and history. As elsewhere in the book, the path here avoids well-trodden areas and picks out a zone where unexpected insights can be found. For contrast and comparison, it takes in India and Singapore as well.

It ends up with the wider world in view. There is an account of what is likely to happen, including the effects of technology on the relationships between languages, and there is a hint of what could happen, if we were to embrace the power of using more than one language. Although the path passes from individuals to groups, it begins the other way round. Before we consider individuals, we have to consider communities. First of all we must face the great contradiction, between sharing information and concealing it, upon which languages are founded. That's where this all starts.

CHAPTER TWO

Babel: The Conspiracy Theory

*Languages are badges of belonging; accents are
answers to the question 'Where are you from?'*

In 1951 the government of Costa Rica welcomed Teodoro Castro
Bonnefil to its diplomatic corps. In 1952 it appointed him Minister
Plenipotentiary to Italy, and then to Yugoslavia. In 1953 the Order of
Malta bestowed a knighthood on him, admitting him to a body of
'Catholics enlivened by altruistic nobleness of spirit and behaviour'
not far short of a thousand years old.[1]

He would not have been ennobled, or retained the confidence of
the Costa Rican government, had he succeeded in the project he had
planned earlier that year. The Soviet leader Stalin decided that he
wanted the Yugoslav leader Tito dead. Teodoro Castro volunteered
for the mission, offering not only convenient access, thanks to his
diplomatic privileges, but also a lengthy history of relevant experience. He suggested several methods, including spraying Tito with
pneumonic plague bacilli, shooting him at a diplomatic reception and
escaping in a cloud of tear gas, or presenting him with jewellery in a
box that would release poison gas when opened. None of these

schemes were attempted, and it was not Tito but Stalin who died in March 1953.[2]

Don Teodoro had been a Soviet agent for decades before he became a Costa Rican diplomat. Iosif Romualdovich Grigulevich was born Josifas Romualdovičius Grigulevičius in what is today the Lithuanian capital Vilnius, in 1913. His mother was Russian and his father was a member of Lithuania's small Karaite ethnic community; the townspeople mostly spoke Polish or Yiddish. As a young man he became a communist militant, spending a year in prison for subversive activities. His father emigrated to Argentina and Josifas followed in 1934, taking with him orders from OGPU, the Soviet secret police, and the first of his many code names and aliases, ARTUR. In Argentina he learned Spanish, adding to a portfolio of tongues said to number up to ten. He used it in Spain during the Civil War, and later in Mexico, where he nearly succeeded in assassinating another of Stalin's bêtes noires, the former Bolshevik and Red Army commander Leon Trotsky. By the end of the Second World War he had made his way to Chile, where he obtained Costa Rican documents. He acquired his Costa Rican diplomatic passport after befriending the country's president, José Figueres. The former Soviet intelligence officer Boris Volodarsky speculates that Figueres may have believed he and Don Teodoro were distantly related.

Grigulevich's feat of national infiltration is all the more remarkable for the fact that he did not learn Spanish until he was an adult. Although monolingual Anglophones often marvel at the grammatical perfection and idiomatic fluency of people who have learned English in college or afterwards, the tell-tale accent nearly always seems to remain, instantly noticeable however faint it is. Beyond infancy, when the set of sounds recognised as speech is compiled, other sounds are irredeemably foreign. Older learners will struggle to pronounce them, as in the stereotypical French 'ze' for English's 'the', and may be oblivious to distinctions that seem obvious to native speakers, as when Japanese speakers hear no difference between the English 'r' and 'l'. People approaching a language as adults will hear its sounds as those of similar ones in their native tongues, rather than hearing their differences in an objective fashion – a subtle but fundamental kind of ethnocentrism.

Even adolescence may be too late. A study conducted in Stockholm recruited nearly two hundred people who fancied they could pass as native in Swedish, though their first language was Spanish, and subjected their confidence to scrutiny. Most of those who learned Swedish as children convinced a panel of native speakers that they were fellow natives, but only five of the eighty-eight late learners did – and all of those five had begun to learn the language before they were eighteen. When their skills were examined more closely, none of the adolescent learners were up to native standards. The highest performer among them reached native levels on seven out of ten measures. It was her accent that let her down.[3]

Iosif Grigulevich was an exceptional individual in many ways, a natural with the cloak and willing with the dagger, but he was not an exception to the accent rule. In Santiago de Chile, a confederate persuaded Costa Rica's consul that Teodoro Castro Bonnefil was the illegitimate son of a prominent Costa Rican. If Don Teodoro had grown up outside the country, that would explain the foreign cast of his accent – which, conveniently for his cover, had been taken for Brazilian when he was in Argentina. No doubt his supposed father's name also helped to open the door for him. Prestige and kinship cast powerful spells.

Even if the Costa Rican establishment had been a little less credulous, it would have been vulnerable to Soviet penetration. The USSR was a major power whose appetite for ruthless subterfuge knew no bounds; Costa Rica was a small country whose army President Figueres had just abolished. In the wake of a recent civil war, the Central American republic had plenty of pressing concerns: communist agitation was one of them, but the risk of being used as a front for clandestine activities by a Soviet agent presumably was not. In other circumstances, the first question would have been 'is he one of us?'

In other places and times, pronunciation is the diagnostic test. People are challenged to utter words that distinguish 'us' from 'them', friends from foes, often with fatal consequences. The prototype is the biblical story of how the men of Gilead smote their enemies and blocked their escape by seizing the passages of Jordan:

> and it was so, that when those Ephraimites which were escaped said, Let me go over; that the men of Gilead said unto him, Art thou an Ephraimite? If he said, Nay; Then said they unto him, Say now Shibboleth: and he said Sibboleth: for he could not frame to pronounce it right. Then they took him, and slew him at the passages of Jordan: and there fell at that time of the Ephraimites forty and two thousand.[4]

'Shibboleth' is how the King James Bible renders the Hebrew word for an ear of corn. In Lebanon, in the bloodshed of the 1970s, it is said that the shibboleth was the Arabic word for tomato. A story from the time tells how a bus was boarded by armed men, one of whom held a tomato and demanded each passenger tell him what it was: those who said it was a 'banadura', identifying themselves as Lebanese, were ordered off the bus; those who called it a 'bandura', revealing themselves to be Palestinians, remained on the bus and were slaughtered. The motif was familiar not just from the Bible. Stories from the Dominican Republic tell of how soldiers massacring Haitian settlers in 1937 carried sprigs of parsley, perejil in Spanish, and killed those who did not roll the 'r' in the word, revealing that their native tongue was Creole. When the Peasants' Revolt tore through London in 1381, dozens of Flemings were slaughtered. Geoffrey Chaucer alluded to the episode in the *Canterbury Tales*, remarking that Jack

Straw's mob 'Ne made nevere shoutes half so shrille / Whan that they wolden any Flemyng kille.' The results of their bloodlust were seen in the pile of thirty or forty headless corpses outside a church near where the northern end of Southwark Bridge is today. In this case too it was the naming of everyday foodstuffs, bread and cheese, kaas en brood in Middle Dutch, that spared them or condemned them.[5]

Why they were attacked is less clear. The historian Erik Spindler suggests that it may have been because the only thing the rebels had in common was their Englishness, 'and to kill a Fleming in June 1381 was to become a little more English'.[6]

To challenge someone with a shibboleth and a weapon is to ask with the most extreme of prejudice the most ordinary of questions: 'Where are you from?' Under ordinary circumstances an accent provides an immediate, honest and reliable answer before the question even has to be asked. Like an electronic identification transponder on an aircraft, it emits a continuous signal of trustworthiness: 'I am not trying to deceive you about who I am.' By retaining traces of their accents, a Dutch businesswoman with grammatically immaculate English or a Swedish scientist perfectly at home in American idiom enjoy an optimised ability to communicate with English speakers. Having minimised the snags and stutters in the fluency of their speech, they also minimise the ripples of unconscious suspicion that may impede the fluency with which their listeners take in what they say.

A signal is reliable if it is hard to fake. Biologists illustrate the principle by pointing to the tail of the peacock and the antlers of the stag, encumbrances that can't be sustained if their bearers are not in good condition. Splendid tail fans and arboreal crowns of antlers act as reliable signals that the males displaying them are fit prospects as mates. Accents are honest in a different way: not because they are costly to acquire or maintain, but because they are ingrained so early in life, before an individual is capable of forming a deliberately deceptive intent, and because it is so hard to erase them completely. A trace of an accent signals trustworthiness precisely because the speaker cannot shed it, and so can't help but be honest about where they are from.

As signals, accents are also convenient for their receivers, who can process them with very little effort. Listeners decide within a few seconds whether or not a speaker's mother tongue is the same as theirs, and their decisions are generally sound. Indeed, they may be able to tell almost as soon as the speaker opens their mouth. Finding that a group of American English speakers had no trouble detecting traces of a French accent in single phrases, 'two little birds' or 'two little dogs', one researcher cut the utterances into shorter and shorter units, and found that the Americans could often still spot the foreign accent in the first thirty milliseconds of the 't' sound.[7]

If people can place the accent, they can be confident about where a speaker is from, and if they can't, they can at least be confident that the speaker is not from where they themselves are from. They can't be certain, though. A small proportion of people are able to sound like natives in languages they have learned after childhood. One Dutch study identified a number of particularly high-performing English teachers, none of whom had learned the language before the age of twelve. Like the procession of American actors who cross the Atlantic and manage to sound as though they have been in Britain all along, and their British counterparts who have crossed in the opposite direction, they had incentives and coaching. They told the researchers that it was very important for them professionally to speak English without a noticeable Dutch accent, and they had been intensively schooled in Received Pronunciation, the traditional accent of the BBC. A panel of judges from the north of England failed to distinguish the teachers from a group of native speakers from the south of England; and even when the tests were repeated with judges and native speakers who all spoke standard British English without a regional accent, some of the teachers were rated as more native-like than some of the natives.[8]

Motivation is necessary, and so is extensive practice, either through formal training or through immersion in a society of people speaking a different language, but even together they may not be sufficient. Evidence suggests that somebody who starts to learn a language after they have left childhood behind will not become able to pass as native without an unusually high degree of linguistic aptitude. Niclas Abrahamsson and Kenneth Hyltenstam, who recruited the 200 people in Stockholm who thought they might pass as native Swedish speakers, found that among those who had learned the language after childhood, even the ones who did pass had inferior grammatical intuition to that of natives. They all, however, had high levels of aptitude for learning languages. Abrahamsson and Hyltenstam consider that aptitude is the key to achieving what they call 'nonperceivable nonnativeness'. Individuals with a talent for languages can make up for a late start by developing a facility for it that sounds like that of a mother-tongue speaker, but is not quite as good as the real thing. They can suppress the signal that identifies where they are from, leaving clues that can only be detected under laboratory conditions.[9]

Life can erase that signal too. Emigrés returning to their homeland after a long absence may find their compatriots sceptical about their origins. When Germans in Germany listened to German emigrants describing a Charlie Chaplin film, they decided that a quarter of the speakers were not native, even though all had left their homeland in their teens or as adults.[10]

Nearly half a century earlier, in 1955, a German linguist had encountered similarly discriminating ears when he toured the country of his birth and observed the effects of the great displacement, in which many millions of Germans were driven west by the Red Army and the regimes that followed in its train, to be dispersed within Germany's divided, occupied and reduced territory. Werner Leopold had himself left Germany as a young man, to escape the economic crisis that enveloped his country after its defeat in the First World

War, and spent several years in Costa Rica before settling in Milwaukee. Returning to Germany after its second catastrophic defeat, he found a land crowded with displaced persons hastily shedding their dialects and adopting standard German in their efforts to be accepted by their new neighbours, who for their part were also shifting towards collo-quial versions of the standard form. The latter was a mutually accept-able common speech, whereas attempts to use dialects met resistance from both sides. Children might find themselves punished by their classmates for speaking their familiar dialect at school, and by their parents for speaking the dialect of their new surroundings at home.[11]

People who adopted a local dialect ran the risk of being regarded as bogus, especially in the countryside. Leopold met a man in Stuttgart who spoke the Swabian dialect at work. Herr Schreiber had been with the firm for twenty-four years and his colleagues accepted his Swabian as genuine, but an old woman in a village just five kilometres from the city had scornfully told him that 'You are not even from Stuttgart.' And indeed she was right: he was originally from Alsace.[12]

Such attitudes may be encountered within city limits too. A.M. Bakalar is a writer from Poland who has lived abroad for many years. She writes in English and thinks in it too; she speaks it with an accent that is hard to place, since it has been shaped by a succession of different places. Her Polish speech and manner have altered corre-spondingly, to the extent that on a return visit to the city in which she grew up, Wrocław, she was told by a local that she couldn't possibly be from there. In Poland a judgement like that is an implied reproach, for losing touch with one's roots. It is all the more striking in this instance because people's roots in Wrocław are hardly deep. Formerly called Breslau, the city is the capital of Lower Silesia, one of those central European heartlands whose German population was expelled after the war. Many of the Poles who took their place had themselves been expelled from eastern territories annexed by the Soviet Union, as their accents revealed.[13]

The deductions about belonging that people make from speech offer a clue to the first question we face if we want to understand how and why people speak more than one language: why are there so many different languages in the first place? Six to eight thousand exist today, depending on how you draw the lines between languages and dialects. Linguists tend to edge away from such distinctions, which are hard to specify and frequently political. Danish and Norwegian are classed as distinct languages, but their speakers understand each other better than do speakers of Mandarin and Cantonese, which are often described as dialects of Chinese. A language is a dialect with an army and navy, the linguist Max Weinreich famously observed, speaking in Yiddish, a language tragically harnessed to fateful irony. Applying techniques used to model the evolution of living forms, the biologist Mark Pagel reckons that before there were such things as armies and navies, before people began to farm instead of gathering and hunting, twelve to twenty thousand languages may have been spoken around the world.[14]

In making comparisons between the evolution of languages and of species, Pagel is sustaining a train of thought started by Charles Darwin, who was powerfully impressed by the parallels between the two. The similarity in the process of isolation and divergence is compelling. When one population of a species becomes separated from another, it may alter so much that it can no longer interbreed with the other one. Likewise when one group of people speaking a particular language becomes isolated from another, the ways they speak may grow so different that the two groups can no longer understand each other. In the first case we consider that a new species and in the second that a new language has evolved.[15]

Yet there must be more to the evolution of language than mountains and rivers and suchlike obstructions, as the Australian linguist and anthropologist Donald Laycock came to realise during his many years of fieldwork in Papua New Guinea, where over 800 languages form the richest concentration of linguistic diversity on the planet. In certain circles Laycock is remembered not as an analyst of human tongues but as the lexicographer of an angelic one. He compiled the Complete Enochian Dictionary, documenting the tongue 'revealed' to Dr John Dee, the sixteenth-century mathematician and Astrologer Royal to Queen Elizabeth I. This was the linguistic equivalent of the philosopher's stone: the language Adam used to name the creatures in Eden; the language last spoken on earth by the prophet Enoch, and spoken still in heaven by the angels. Laycock himself was not a mystic but a Skeptic, a member of the rationalist movement that debunks pseudoscience and claims of paranormal phenomena. He prefaced the dictionary with a decidedly sceptical exposition of the similarities between Enochian and English, not that the believers' certainties were greatly troubled.[16]

Laycock detected linguistic tricks in New Guinean villages as well as in Dee's journals of magic. Papua New Guinea is not short of physical obstacles that could isolate communities and thereby allow their languages to drift apart. Its highlands are so inaccessible from the outside that Westerners had no idea they were extensively populated until the 1930s, when explorers became able to venture over them in aeroplanes. Yet Laycock found that the highlands were home to the languages with the most speakers, while mosaics of tiny language territories covered the more accessible terrain, where it was much easier for different communities to come into contact with each other. He calculated that in the Sepik area, the focus of his research, dialects had a maximum of 500 speakers each.

Sepik villagers gave him a simple explanation for what was going on. 'It wouldn't be any good if we all spoke the same,' he was told more than once. 'We like to know where people come from.'

Dialects and languages thus served as badges of belonging. Laycock came to the conclusion that in Melanesia – the arc of islands north and east of Australia from New Guinea to Fiji – language 'is, in its very diversity, being used constructively, to hold social groupings to a small and manageable level – and conversely, to keep other groups at a distance'. As the great linguist Wilhelm von Humboldt had observed more than a century before, 'every language draws about the people that possesses it a circle'.[17]

Laycock found that it was used not just constructively but inventively too. Buin, a language spoken in Bougainville Island to the east of New Guinea by around 25,000 people, has a dialect called Uisai, with about 2,500 speakers. Uisai's vocabulary is opposite in gender, across the board, to that of Buin. All the words that are masculine in Buin are feminine, and vice versa. The only explanation, Laycock figured, was that at some point in the past an influential Uisai speaker had 'announced that from now on his people were not to speak like the rest of the Buins'. In 1978 another anthropologist, Kenneth McElhanon, actually witnessed such a decision. The people of a village called Indu held a meeting where they agreed that in order to differentiate themselves from other communities that spoke the same language, Selepet, they would stop using the Selepet word for no, bia, and henceforth say 'buŋe' instead.[18]

Some villagers manage without such manipulations by perceiving differences where linguists can see none. In New Britain, an island that lies between Bougainville and New Guinea, the people of the village of Bolo speak what, as far as linguists are concerned, is a language called Aria – but people from other Aria-speaking villages say that what the Bolo folk speak is Mouk. This is denied by Mouk speakers from the village of Selkei, who say that the language spoken in Bolo is indeed Aria . . . which in turn is denied by the Bolo villagers themselves, who maintain that they still speak a quite distinct language called Anêm, although in fact they have by now forgotten it.[19]

As well as helping to illustrate why linguists are uncomfortable around distinctions between languages and dialects, Bolo shows how precious people feel language differences to be. Even if they do not actually exist, they have to be claimed or imagined. Bolo villagers retain Anêm as their badge of belonging although they have lost it as a medium of communication, rather as the Republic of Ireland has retained Irish after gaining independence from New Britain's namesake. People of other villages deny that the language actually spoken in Bolo is the same as theirs. The only agreement in all this is that Bolo is a distinct community, defined by how it speaks. Villagers are not just particular about language, they are more particular about it than linguists.

A number of scientists have considered why this should be. They begin with the observation that language diversity and biological diversity resemble each other in their distribution. The concentrations of each are greatest close to the equator and decrease with latitude. Daniel Nettle, a behavioural scientist and biologist, has identified two outstandingly diverse language zones, containing 60 per cent of the world's languages between them. One runs from Ivory Coast in West Africa eastwards and south into the Congo region. The other is an even more sweeping eastward and southward arc from southern India through south-east Asia and Indonesia to New Guinea and its retinue of Pacific islands. These zones, he points out, 'correspond almost exactly to the two great belts of equatorial forest which harbour so many of the Old World's species'.

A tropical climate is much the same in December and in July: hot and wet. Plants can persist all year round instead of dying in winter and returning in spring. The growing season for food plants is long, and so the risk of famine is low. Communities can be confident about being able to rely on their own resources. Such confidence diminishes with distance from the equator. At higher latitudes, growing seasons are short, and the risk of food shortages is correspondingly high. People are likelier to have to call on outside help – and are more likely to get it if they speak the same language as those to whom they are calling. Nettle argues that language diversity is lower at higher latitudes because people need bonds of mutual support that reach beyond their immediate neighbourhoods.[20]

This is more than simply a question of making oneself understood. A lingua franca will enable communication, but people who share a native language will feel a closer bond and be readier to help each other. In tropical regions, the longer growing seasons cause populations to grow and become denser, thus bringing communities into closer proximity. Although the risks of seasonal harm are lower, the risks from other people are higher. Nettle reaches the same conclusion as Laycock: under such conditions, linguistic diversity enables communities to remain small and detached from outsiders. Small communities are stronger because their bonds are closer, and so are better able to resist attacks, encroachment, theft or unwelcome ideas. Hunter-gatherer languages tend to keep themselves to themselves; those of the Amazon region are particularly reluctant to erode their differences by adopting words from each other.[21]

On the other hand, isolation is undesirable, and impossible in a crowded landscape anyway. Melanesian villagers reconcile their internal and external needs by speaking their parochial dialects among themselves while knowing at least one other language and often several. In the 1980s, Donald Laycock was confident that Melanesian village languages could be sustained in bundles with other tongues 'against all odds', even when spoken by just a few hundred people, or even a few score.[22]

Overoptimistic as it might sound, Laycock's claim has some indirect backing from Arnhem Land, across the Arafura Sea, in the Top End of Australia's Northern Territory. The four hundred people who live in Warruwi Community, on a small island just off the coast of the mainland, speak some eight languages between them. They sustain these languages both by speaking them and by declining to do so. Two people may hold a conversation in two languages, understanding what the other is saying and replying in their own tongue. Nancy Ngalmindjalmag and Richard Dhaŋalaŋal have been married for more than thirty years: Nancy speaks to Richard in Mawng, one of the main languages spoken in Warruwi; Richard speaks to Nancy in one of the others, Yolŋu-matha. Unlike, say, a Norwegian-Swedish couple, they are not speaking languages that are to a significant extent mutually intelligible, but ones that belong to different linguistic families. And unlike so many couples around the world with different native languages, they do not use English as a private lingua franca, although they speak it well. Placing boundaries around the use of both large, powerful languages and small neighbouring ones is a strategy that can help to sustain languages with very low numbers of speakers. Near the Arnhem Land coastal township of Maningrida, the Gurr-goni language was still being passed on to children in the early years of the twenty-first century, despite having had only thirty to eighty speakers during the previous fifty years.[23]

For Indigenous Australian languages in general, however, the story was one of decline, accelerating in the later years of the previous century. A survey published in 1990 estimated that seventy of Australia's ninety surviving Indigenous languages were threatened or severely endangered. And reports from Papua New Guinea offer only limited support for Donald Laycock's optimism. New Guinean languages are subject to the economic forces that are changing their speakers' ways of life. People who want to work in towns or speak with tourists will shift to widely spoken languages. In Papua New Guinea they mostly opt for Tok Pisin, a lingua franca that reveals its English roots in its name ('talk pidgin'). It has replaced local languages in many Sepik communities. One study documented the collapse of multilingualism over three generations. Older men spoke at least two and up to five languages besides their native tongue; children only spoke Tok Pisin.[24]

Some communities seem to be holding on to their distinguishing languages, though. The numbers of people speaking Buin and its Uisai dialect have increased since Laycock did his fieldwork, for example. He was probably right that bilingual pairs comprising a local language and a lingua franca are stable – but only as long as

33

people's ways of life remain traditional. Too much contact with people from elsewhere may overwhelm an exclusive language. The decline of the Sepik language Abu' Arapesh, which is yielding to Tok Pisin, was hastened because its speakers observed the custom of not speaking it in front of visitors, to avoid the suspicion that they were practising magic.

One reason why villagers are particular about language is that they have more to be particular about. Languages spoken across large areas by large numbers of people tend to be simpler than local languages confined to local people. The more widely spoken a language is, the less fussy it is likely to be about its grammar. As a lingua franca, Tok Pisin is a good example. It began as a pidgin, improvised on the spot between strangers who needed to make themselves mutually understood, and gradually acquired the structures that made it into a proper language. Although it is now many people's first language, simplicity is the key to its success. Tok Pisin needed to be simple enough for adults to pick it up.

Its main parent, English, may also be an example. Old English, spoken before the Norman invasion, was an inflected language with grammatical gender and a system of cases. A noun's ending depended on whether the thing it denoted was doing something, or was having something done to it, or was associated with something, and so on. Over time Old English whittled down its range of endings and emerged in the twelfth century as Middle English, the language of Chaucer. The endings disappeared particularly quickly in the east Midlands, where the Viking area of settlement met Saxon territory. This suggests a desire on the part of Anglo-Saxon and Norse folk to ease communication by removing grammatical hindrances that divided them. Since endings were the main respect in which the otherwise similar languages differed, discarding inflection was the natural way to enhance mutual understanding. Latin had already done the same, making it easier for the diverse peoples of the Roman

Empire to speak to each other. Vulgar Latin, as the lingua franca is known, subsequently gave rise to the Romance languages. Like English, they adopted a fixed word order, subject–verb–object, to indicate who did what to whom.[25]

Widely spoken languages may also be less particular about time than confined ones. Mandarin, which with 850 million speakers has the largest population of all, manages fine without tenses. By contrast Yagua, spoken by 6,000 people in the Amazon region of Peru, attaches different endings to verbs according to whether they describe something that happened today, yesterday, a few weeks ago, a few months ago, or in the more distant past.[26]

The thing about such punctilious grammatical marking is that it tends to be redundant. Subjects and objects can often be distinguished by their order in the sentence, or the verb that connects them, or both, so there is no overwhelming need, as far as comprehensibility is concerned, to put the subject noun in the nominative case and the object in the accusative. It may be reasonably easy to make yourself understood in an inflected language without inflecting it – and you may be understood more easily if you trade accuracy for fluency, rather than pausing to consult a fragmentary mental grammar at every turn. Grammatical accuracy is important as a test of belonging, or at least association, but standards can be relaxed if communication has to take priority. The more a language is learned by adults rather than children, the more likely it is to dispense with cases. A survey found none at all in any language learned in adulthood by more than half of its speakers.[27]

Altering the rules or setting them aside are ways to lower the barriers between groups. We might imagine that along the indistinct and intermittently contested line separating the Anglo-Saxon kingdom of Mercia from the Norse Danelaw, the tensions would have eased when Danes tackled Old English the easy way, without worrying about grammatical gender or the endings of adjectives, and Anglo-Saxon listeners accepted their usage. This would in part have been a matter of communicative efficiency, a way to reduce misunderstandings. But that might not have been its entire or even its primary purpose – especially since there was already a high degree of mutual comprehensibility between the languages. By discarding some of the linguistic badges signalling that people are members of one group and not members of another, it may also have been a means to strengthen affinity by trimming down the boundaries between the two. It would be nice at least to think that the various Englishes spoken today are partly founded upon a conciliation between neighbouring communities.[28]

The advantages of simplicity are obvious for a language that needs to be learned by adults. But why should languages learned from birth be any more complicated? Gary Lupyan and Rick Dale, whose survey of more than 2,000 languages established the tendency of the widely spoken ones to dispense with inflectional endings, suggest that complexity might actually make a language easier for very young minds to grasp. A child whose internal grammar is not yet fixed and tuned may be helped by multiple indications about what is going on in an utterance. Marking words by their endings confirms the inferences the child makes from their order and meaning. What to an adult learner is an infernal memory load is a welcome succession of helping hands to a child just entering into language. To a very young child repeated information is not redundant, but necessary.[29]

Whatever the reasons, children entering a language are admitted to a system that excludes outsiders, and adult ones especially. A number of evolutionary thinkers suspect that this may be much of its point. They suspect it because whenever they see co-operation, they are on the alert for cheats. The question of co-operation has been one of evolutionary theory's most contested and productive themes for more than half a century. Evolution is a process of competition, yet it produces abundant co-operation among all manner of living forms. Theorists have devoted countless hours and computer cycles to specifying the conditions under which natural selection can resolve this apparent paradox. They are acutely aware how easy it can be for a cheat to infiltrate a network of co-operators and prosper at the expense of the fair players. In their computer models, cheats leave more descendants than co-operators and the population fills up with the cheating kind. In human societies, cheats drive others to cheat, and if the rot isn't stopped everybody ends up having to fend for themselves.

Cheating, free-riding and deception are especially threatening to human groups because humans are so intensely and fundamentally groupish. Humans are also an intensely and fundamentally language-using species. For human society in general and language in particular, trust is of the essence. The evolutionary psychologists Peter Richerson and Robert Boyd suggest that because trust is always necessary but always vulnerable, 'syntax and semantics are the easy part of the evolution of language. The hard part is to figure out how humans could make use of language.' For a system of language to become established, people have to be able to trust what others say to them; and for it to be sustained, they have to maintain their guard against the subversion of trust.[30]

Richerson and Boyd argue that language differences serve to limit communication and the spread of ideas across groups. Language boundaries act as a barrier to two kinds of misleading communication: lies, and information that doesn't apply within the listener's particular group. They also help to ensure that non-applicable information continues not to apply, by keeping out ideas that could change the group's beliefs, customs, practices and own peculiar identity. On the outside, as Donald Laycock realised in New Guinea, they act as identification badges, marking the boundaries of community.

The evolutionary psychologist Robin Dunbar recognises their power as badges too. He is best known for Dunbar's Number, his calculation that the size of the neocortex in the human brain limits a person's meaningful social network to about 150 people, a figure in the same ball park as the numbers Laycock reported for dialect speakers in Sepik villages. Dunbar is impressed by the rate at which languages split off from each other – 500 to 1,000 years in Europe, by Mark Pagel's estimate – and the ability of dialects to emerge over the course of a generation or so. If language was simply a means to communicate, he argues, evolution would have curbed its exuberant ability to diversify. It looks to him as though evolution has done just the opposite, selecting language for its 'corruptibility'. For Dunbar, the basic purpose of language is to form bonds within groups, which entails keeping them apart from others.[31]

New languages certainly behave as though they are in a hurry to get away from their relatives. A third of the differences in vocabulary between Bantu languages and their source tongues in Africa arose at the time they split off or shortly after, as did equivalent differences among a fifth of European languages. The process is currently under way in former Yugoslav republics. As in the New Guinea village that decided to change its word for no, it is a self-conscious exercise in creating differences between neighbours whose actual differences are felt to be insufficient. Croatian linguists unearthed the word zrako-plov from a nineteenth-century dictionary and declared it to be an acceptably native replacement for 'avion', aeroplane, which continues to be used in Serbia. When they were unable to find a suitable term on even the dustiest philological shelves they coined new native words, such as doigravanje, a substitute for the foreign sporting import 'play-off'. And as in the New Britain villages that could not agree on what language was spoken in one of them, if differences do not actually exist, they are imagined. On landing at Sarajevo Airport in 1998, three years after the fighting in Bosnia was brought to an end, Robert D. Greenberg was complimented on how well he spoke Bosnian. A couple of days later a Bosnian Serb driver told a Serbian border guard to let the linguist through, because the driver considered him to be 'one of theirs'. Yet on both occasions Greenberg was speaking the same language, which had been called Serbo-Croatian when he learned it. He wondered how long it would be before a foreigner would run into a real language barrier at the boundary between the ethnic 'entities'.[32]

In this Darwinian light, the biblical story of the Tower of Babel begs to be rewritten. The Book of Genesis tells how people divided into nations with different languages, but then united and spoke a single common tongue. Thus combined and strengthened, they began to build a city with a tower that would reach heaven. God cut them back down to size by disrupting their language and scattered them across the face of the earth. The place became known as Babel, from the Hebrew word 'balal', meaning jumble. This was a top-down political intervention, neutralising challengers by splitting them up.

The story has an intuitive appeal because divide and rule is such a familiar strategy for the exercise of power. But from where evolutionists are standing, it is upside down. Humankind was divided not from above, by an all-powerful Lord, but from below, by small groups of separatist conspirators. People do intuitively recognise the conspiratorial character of language divisions, when they suspect that foreigners are practising magic or talking about them behind their backs.

That character is also implied in the Italian adage 'traduttore, traditore', 'translator, traitor'. Professional translators invoke it frequently, to affirm that translation can never be perfectly faithful, though it seems an overly dramatic way to describe what are generally well-intentioned compromises and approximations. The saying rings much truer as an expression of the resentment felt within a group when one of its number opens up a gap in its language perimeter, revealing the contents of its private talk to outsiders.[33]

Translators have a patron saint, Jerome, who translated biblical texts into Latin; translator-traitors have an ideal candidate as a patron anti-saint in Malintzin, La Malinche, Doña Marina, the Nahuatl interpreter to, and mistress of, the Spanish conquistador Hernán Cortés. Many of her myth-makers have deemed her a traitor to the native people of Mexico, and her name is the root of the term 'malinchism', which refers to the belief that the foreign is always better than the indigenous.

At the same time, Malintzin's mythology cannot help but recognise the fruitfulness of crossing language boundaries. Because she bore Cortés a son, she is celebrated as the founding mother of Mexico's mestizo (mixed) population. And thus it has always been. Evolution has shaped language not just for conspiracy and corruptibility, but for co-operation and coalitions as well. No matter how exclusive they are, languages remain learnable. Children can easily inhabit more than one speech community, speaking one language in the home and another outside. Adults can learn new languages to levels of fluency higher than those of many native speakers, while transmitting their origin signals through the ineradicable traces of their foreign accents.[34]

Those traces matter to people because the village disposition still persists among city dwellers and citizens of great nations. Even in the most complex and fluid societies, many people feel more comfortable if they can assign any given person to one group, and one alone. 'Where are you from?' means 'what group do you belong to?' An accent offers an honest answer, even if the question remains unspoken – and even if it is an answer that contradicts the questioner's opinions about whether a person of 'non-native' ancestry really belongs to the country in which they have grown up. It isn't always accepted, though, as I'm occasionally reminded when somebody in Britain asks me where I'm from. They seem to place more weight upon evidence of ancestry, my foreign name, than on evidence of upbringing, my southern English accent. Or perhaps they can hear some alien undertone in my speech of which I myself am unaware.

Cheats do sometimes prosper, of course. Iosif Grigulevich got away with it. He disappeared some months after Stalin's death and reappeared in Moscow, where he became a successful academic, publishing dozens of books on Latin America, religion and ethnography until his death in 1988. The state he served conspiratorially for so long only outlived him by three years, though; whereas Costa Rica, the smallest of the many states he deceived, is still on the map, and still without an army. By the time he died, the whole world had become a village. People around the globe employ the same language strategy that has always worked for those villagers in Papua New Guinea: a private language and a lingua franca, a screen and a channel.

There is one group, however, for whom the strategy cannot work: native English speakers, whose language is the global lingua franca. The Polish novelist Olga Tokarczuk has one of her narrators reflect on how lost English speakers must feel in a world where every last bit of information is in their language, and anybody anywhere is liable to understand them the moment they utter a word: 'There are already plans, I've heard, to bring them under protection, and maybe even assign them some little language, one of those extinct ones that nobody needs anymore, so that they can have something of their own.'[35]

* * * *

Languages are nets of belonging and exclusion, instruments of communication and concealment, systems of rules that permit endless possibilities. It's all a lot to take in. What do infants make of them, and how do they enter them? How do people learn new ones later in life?

CHAPTER THREE

The Rising Din

Babies are disposed to enter language, and can readily enter more than one. Adults, not so much.

When Elizabeth Barber, an American scholar, arrived at the Hermitage Museum in Leningrad, as it was then, she found that the curators with whom she was to work spoke only Russian. She was forced to speak the language as best she could, trying to disregard the trail of grammatical errors she left in her wake. 'Any self-respecting adjective in Russian gives you on the order of forty possible categories of forms to choose from, according to case, number, gender, and animacy, not to mention long and short forms and declension classes,' she later explained. 'If you have to dive into this labyrinth to select a form consciously, you find when you surface proudly with your hard-won morpheme that the conversation is ten miles down the road. Either that, or your interlocutor is sound asleep.'[1]

By the third day, her head began to fill with a 'rising din' of Russian, as her memory circuits played fragments of her new colleagues' speech back to her: 'words, sounds, intonations, phrases, all swimming about in the voices of the people I talked with'. After five days, the sounds 'became so intense that I found myself chewing on them ... to the rhythm of my own footsteps as I walked the streets and museums'. This din heralds the lowering of the barrier. When it enters your head, you are on the threshold of entering the language. As Barber observed, the constant repetition brings phrases closer to hand when one is trying to converse. It also provides a stock of ready-made expressions, already fitted with the correct grammatical forms. These make it easier to keep a conversation going and thereby encounter new examples of speech that will find their way into the din. The different voices play their part too, giving a sense of the variety of ways in which a language is spoken.

Above all, it is insistent. It commands attention for the new language, forcing other mental traffic into slow lanes and side roads. It claims a place on the inside for a phenomenon from the outside. Language entry goes both ways: if a person is to enter a language community, the language must enter their mind and integrate into it.

If it is intense for an adult, how much more overwhelming it must be for an infant, surrounded by voices in the open air for the very first time, and new to language altogether. We don't know that a din rises in the newborn's head, even though we have all been through the experience. Amnesia inclines us to assume that entry into language is painless, as does the apparent ease with which children typically become speakers. But many if not most skills require struggle to acquire, even if they seem effortless once mastered. We take language to be one of the most fundamental characteristics of being human. Why should we assume that entering into humanity is easy, any more than being born into the world is easy? Perhaps babies cry over words as well as milk and teeth.

Like the adult in whom the din arises, the infant finds itself in a world that is not entirely unfamiliar to it. Both already recognise some regularities. If the adult did not already have some knowledge of the structure of the language, the din would just be noise. Unless the hearer is able to discern elements within it such as sounds, words or phrases, their repetition will serve no constructive purpose. Typically developing infants emerge with two or three months' experience of hearing sounds, albeit muffled by maternal tissue and amniotic fluid. The most significant sounds they hear are their mothers' voices. Changes in foetal heartbeat indicate that, even in the womb, they come to distinguish between the voices of mothers and others. Although the insulation surrounding them filters out higher frequencies, the rhythms of speech get through. So do sufficient vowel sounds for newborns to notice a difference between native and non-native ones. They also have a sense of the melody of a language, which they reproduce in their crying. When a group of French newborns and a group of German ones were compared, the French babies' cries typically followed a rising melodic contour, increasing gradually in pitch and then falling away; the German cries traced a falling contour, rising at the beginning and then lowering gently. (German cries were also at their loudest soon after they began; French ones took longer to reach peak volume.) The differences followed the characteristic intonation of each language: in French, pitch tends to rise towards the end of words or phrases, before dropping right at the end; in German, pitch is more likely to peak on an accented syllable before gradually declining as the phrase is completed.[2]

Babies bring a preference for their mothers' voices out of the womb with them. Scientists gave newborn infants the means to exercise choices, in the form of an audio system connected to an artificial nipple that registered when it was sucked. The babies heard recordings of their mothers' voices and of other women, reading *And To Think That I Saw It On Mulberry Street*, the first Dr. Seuss book. They found that by spacing how frequently they sucked the nipple they could select which voices they heard, and they chose their mothers'. A newborn baby will lie more still, its heart beating more slowly, if it hears its mother's voice instead of an unfamiliar woman speaking.

Newborns prefer to hear their mothers' voices in the form familiar from the womb, with the higher frequencies filtered out.[3]

These preferences are aspects of a fundamental bias for speech, as opposed to other kinds of sound. Given a choice between syllables and sounds that are not speech but have similar acoustic forms, newborn babies incline to the syllables. They also prefer the rhythms of speech to which they became accustomed before they were born. Some languages, such as French and Spanish, give roughly equal time to each syllable; others, such as German and Dutch, make the intervals between stressed syllables the same length, and shorten the ones in between to fit. Newborn babies pay more attention to speech in their mother tongue than to speech in a language that has a different basic rhythm pattern. Babies who had two mother tongues, because they heard their mothers speaking both English and Tagalog during the last trimester of pregnancy, showed no preference for one over the other. They were, however, able to distinguish between the two. (Tagalog, a major language of the Philippines, is syllable-timed; English, like its German and Dutch cousins, is stress-timed.)[4]

The benefits that babies gain from the bias towards speech and the ability to distinguish its sounds are not confined to language learning. Preferences for the mother's voice and the mother tongue are aspects of the preference in which the infant's early life is enveloped, for the mother herself. By paying attention to the sound of her voice, and responding warmly to it, the infant will intensify the bond with her. That is probably the most effective way in which babies can help themselves to survive and flourish. An ear for differences in speech will also help a baby tune in to other caregivers. Language has a privileged place in development not because it is uniquely human, but because it is part of a complex through which infants secure their basic needs.[5]

To grasp language, an infant must be able to recognise that speech is made up not just of a particular set of sounds, but also of words.

That is not obvious without a prior disposition to find patterns in the sound stream and divide it up into segments. A machine recording speech will produce an image of a continuous waveform, not a succession of units resembling a written sentence. Pauses often occur in the middle of a word, so they are not reliable guides to where one ends and another begins. Infants, however, may be able to detect irregularities in patterns of speech that do not even occur in the language they hear around them. A number of languages, including Turkish, Yoruba, Swahili, Finnish and Hungarian, have a property known as vowel harmony. It imposes rules about which vowels may go together in a word. A Turkish word may contain either vowels produced with the tongue towards the front of the mouth or ones made with the tongue towards the back, but not both: 'i' can go with 'e', and 'o' with 'a', but 'i' and 'e' cannot go with 'o' or 'a'. In Finnish, vowels of a kind band together to produce words like Töölö, the name of a Helsinki neighbourhood, and a concentration of umlauts that might conceivably be a clue to the popularity of heavy metal in Finland. English imposes no such segregation on its vowels. Yet at the age of seven months, a group of babies growing up surrounded by English noticed vowel harmony in streams of meaningless syllables. Their acuity, which they will not be able to apply to their mother tongue, hints at the presence of further hidden depths to the perceptual infrastructure that guides infants into language.[6]

That infrastructure is visual as well as auditory. Infants learn by looking at speech as well as listening to it. A baby gets its eye in quickly: four-month-olds shown muted videos of people talking were able to distinguish French and English, with their distinctively different rhythmic patterns. Researchers observed a sequence of change in gaze among babies who were exposed to a single language (English, Spanish or Catalan). Between the ages of four and eight months, infants shifted their attention from speakers' eyes to speakers' mouths; it remained there for the next several months, before going back to the eyes by the end of the first year. Babies on a track to bilingualism were already paying more attention to the mouth at four months. They evidently found themselves having to draw upon more cues in order to tackle the extra challenges of the dual input.[7]

Babies' abilities to discriminate different features of speech appear to depend on maturity rather than experience. Being born three months prematurely gives an infant three months of exposure to open-air sounds by the time the original due date is reached, but the baby will not be able to recognise the characteristics of its mother tongue any sooner than if it had gone to full term. The likelihood that this is a process driven internally, rather than by external input, is illustrated by a study of babies whose mothers had taken antidepressants such as fluoxetine (Prozac) and paroxetine during pregnancy. Infants in their early months are open to any sound of any language, an inventory totalling 600 consonants and 200 vowels. They are able to recognise all that they encounter equally well, and discriminate between them. By the end of their first year, however, they only have ears for their mother tongues. They lose their ability to recognise the nuances of sounds that are not part of their native languages. At six months, a typical baby surrounded by the English language can distinguish between a 'd' sound of the kind heard in English and a Hindi 'dh', which ends with a puff of air. At ten months and onwards, the two will increasingly sound the same. For babies whose neurochemistry had been altered by exposure to antidepressants, however, the timetable was accelerated. By six months, they were already unable to tell the sounds apart. The shift started before they were born. Late in gestation foetuses can ordinarily distinguish between vowel sounds, but not consonants: foetuses exposed to antidepressants were already able to discriminate consonants as well.[8]

The researchers observed that these drugs appeared to have over-corrected the effects of maternal depression, which could be seen in babies whose mothers had been depressed but not medicated. For these infants, the timetable seemed to be slowed down. They were still able to distinguish between the Hindi and English sounds at the age of ten months. The process of attuning to the mother tongue may have been slowed because their depressed mothers spoke less to them, and less in the 'motherese' baby talk that accentuates the features of speech, making early learning easier.

The study combined two perspectives on how infants enter language, and what that implies for people learning languages later in life. One perspective is rooted in the idea of a critical period, determined by the development of the nervous system, during which entry into language is uniquely easy. During this period languages are acquired; after it, they have to be learned. The idea is intuitive, appealing to our sense of wonder at the ease with which small children seem to take up languages, and the contrast with the effort that learning a language demands when we are old enough to remember the process. It also chimes with the influential idea of an innate 'language acquisition device', proposed by Noam Chomsky, linguist and leader of the 'cognitive revolution' in psychology that began in the 1950s.

Chomsky has radically overhauled his theories over the years, however, and he casts less of a spell over empirical researchers than he once did. The idea of an internally programmed critical period has also been modified in the light of evidence and criticism. Some researchers prefer to emphasise the unique social circumstances of early life, in which the infant is the focus of an intensive linguistic induction programme conducted by its caregivers. This is yet another stretch of the fault-line that runs through the realm of ideas about how humans are made, with nature on one side and nurture on the other. Both shape a baby's language development, as the antidepressant study highlights: the effect of the drugs points to a developmental sequence that can be brought forward by neurochemical intrusion, and the effect of the mothers' mental state shows that carers' behaviour can also alter the timing.[9]

In its strictest sense, a critical period is a biologically determined window that closes when the brain and nervous system reach a certain level of maturity. Information from the outside world must be written into the system while it is still forming and open to impressions. If the window of opportunity is missed, it may be difficult or impossible to inscribe the knowledge later. The effect was highlighted by a comparison of deaf and hearing adults in Canada. Those who had been born deaf, but whose hearing parents did not sign to them in their early years, had severe difficulties with English grammar; those with early experience of language, whether spoken or signed, had none.[10]

Findings like these suggest that without early experience, a person's ability to learn language throughout life may be seriously impaired. Not all researchers report the sharp declines that resemble windows closing, though, and for those who do, the pattern has come to look more like a series of sensitive periods. First comes the learning of sounds, known as phonemes, the suite of units that comprise a spoken language. Phonemes create the differences between words, such as cat, sat and mat. Once these basic elements are in place, children go through phases of heightened sensitivity to more complex elements of language, strengthening their purchase on how to form, modify and combine words. Their ability to learn is at its peak during these sensitive periods, then declines steeply and flattens out. By puberty, the windows are closed, closing or about to close.[11]

The conjunction with puberty suggests that the installation of language structures may be part of the physical process of growing up, orchestrated by molecular switches that conduct body and brain towards their mature condition. Once maturity is attained, the system is in its optimal form. Altering it to any great extent would undo the progress, so it is time to close the windows. If this account is broadly correct, the loss of language-learning abilities is one effect of a grand developmental design.

Or it could be a product of experience, the effect that languages themselves have upon the neural systems in which they are installed. As a language beds into a young brain, it defines the characteristics of language in general. New languages, having different characteristics, may then be difficult to fit into the established organisation, because the first to move in has taken control of the space.

To test this hypothesis, two researchers in Sweden recruited people whose first language could not interfere with subsequent ones, because they had lost it in childhood. Gunnar Norrman and Manne Bylund compared abilities to discriminate Swedish vowel sounds from each other across three groups: native-born Swedes, people who had immigrated to Sweden as children with their Spanish-speaking families, and people who had been adopted by Swedish families from Spanish-speaking countries. Although the adoptees had acquired Spanish before they were brought to Sweden, having arrived between the ages of three and seven, they had rapidly lost it. The immigrants who had come with their families had kept their Spanish, and spoke it from day to day. If first languages interfere with second ones, the adoptees should have performed better than the bilinguals, whose first language would have got in the way. There were no differences between the overseas-born groups, though. Both made more errors than the native-born speakers, implying that the delay in encountering Swedish had impaired their ability to hear the finer distinctions in its set of sounds. Overwriting the first language did not reset the adoptees into a Swedish native condition; missing the early sensitive period had prevented them from becoming altogether native-like.[12]

Whatever the processes at work, childhood is undoubtedly a period of specially privileged opportunity for language. How should parents make the most of this period of opportunity, protracted but varied and in many respects obscure, if they want their children to be able to use more than one language? In some homes, children will be cradle bilinguals, hearing two languages from the day they are born.

In others, parents will have to make choices about when to introduce their children to a second language, so the first question they will face is how soon they should do it.[13]

Within the first year is best, if the child is to take the opportunity to acquire native-grade sound sets for more than one language. For other dimensions of language, though, earlier is not necessarily better. Picking up vocabulary may proceed more quickly if started later, and early starts may not always enhance grammar skills. One study looked at bilingual children, aged five and six, in the Dutch province of Friesland, where the first language of more than half the population is West Frisian (English's closest relative). The ones who had been exposed to Dutch from birth were no better at applying the correct endings to Dutch words than the ones who had not started to learn the national language until the age of four. For a minority language, though, considerations of grammar and vocabulary are secondary. What matters most is becoming established within the protective environment of the home. The earlier the start, the longer the language will have to ensconce itself in the child's networks of knowledge and sense of self, before the blast from school hits it.[14]

Many parents attempt to make learning easier by simplifying the scheme. They divide the household languages between them, each speaking only one to their children. This can be an effective strategy, but it may not necessarily be the optimal one. Annick De Houwer, a linguist working in Flanders, surveyed 1,778 families that had both two parents and two languages. 'One parent, one language' families were much more likely to raise bilingual children than families in which Dutch overshadowed the minority tongue. With two parents speaking Dutch and one also speaking the minority language, only about a third of the children spoke the latter. With each parent speaking one language, three-quarters of the children spoke a minority language – one of seventy-three spoken among the bilingual families surveyed. But in families where both parents spoke both languages,

80 per cent of children spoke both languages too. Although many parents worry that their children will be confused by language-mixing, the children whose parents each spoke Dutch and the minority tongue were more likely to speak the latter than those whose parents segregated the languages.[15]

Even if parents are confident, rightly, that children will not be confused by encountering two languages rather than one, they may worry that the extra workload will delay their children's progress. It might, but not in ways or to degrees that should give grounds for anxiety. Bilingual children may know fewer words than monolinguals of the same age in the language that they share. They hear less of the dominant language than the monolinguals, since what they hear is divided between two tongues, and they may have picked up fewer words of it than the monolinguals, who hear nothing else. But the bilinguals' total vocabulary, spanning both their languages, may be as large as that of the monolingual children. It may also be as large by a different tally, of the things for which a child has words, counting equivalents such as perro and dog as a single item in a child's lexicon. That seems like a truer measure of a child's knowledge.[16]

Vocabularies may be unequal even in the absence of social or economic inequalities. Among a group of well-off children in South Florida, the Spanish–English bilinguals knew fewer English words than the English monolinguals did, though they did know a similar number of words in total. They were also less advanced in putting words together, producing shorter and less complex utterances. The children were first tested around the age of two; there was still a vocabulary gap when they were four. There was also a gap between the bilinguals who had two native Spanish-speaking parents and the others. The ones with two Spanish-speaking parents had larger total vocabularies than those with either one or two native English-speaking parents, and were continuing to add to their Spanish words. When both parents were native Spanish speakers, speaking English in the home did not help children learn English words, but it hindered them from learning Spanish ones. By contrast, having one native English-speaking parent boosted children's English without undermining their Spanish.

According to Erika Hoff and her colleagues, who conducted the studies, the lesson of their work and of other researchers is that learning two languages takes children longer than learning one – but children who learn two languages learn more than children who only learn one. If you only look at one of those two languages, you are likely to see a delay; but if you look at both, you will see a larger whole.[17]

Looking from the outside, however, your exclusive focus is likely to be upon the language that you speak, the one that dominates the larger society. Languages are rarely weighed equally, but instead are weighted according to their economic value, social prestige and political power. Concerns about bilingual children's progress almost always seem to revolve around the child's attainment in English, or whatever the dominant language is. And they play upon parents' anxieties about how their kids are doing in the race, marked out by a series of looming 'milestones', that begins almost as soon as a baby emerges into the light. Bilingual children will reach their milestones in good time, but the question that nags is whether they would reach them quicker with only one language on board.

The one thing that all concerned can be completely confident about is that bilingual children will end up knowing the dominant language just as well as their monolingual peers do. A study of children across Wales, for example, found that by the age of seven the English vocabulary of children from Welsh-speaking homes was indistinguishable from that of children from homes where only English was spoken. Almost everybody in Wales over the age of three can speak English, but only eleven per cent of the population say they speak Welsh fluently. Although the position of the Welsh language appears to have stabilised, after a long history of decline, its future cannot be taken for granted. There can be no such doubt about the future of English in Wales, and its dominance is likely to be even stronger in regions where the minority language is not a national language, like Welsh, that has entrenched itself in the nation's institutions.[18]

Dominant languages will always take care of themselves. Indeed, they seem to take care of themselves whether parents try to support them or not. Hispanic mothers taking their children to Head Start Centers in a Pennsylvania city spoke less Spanish and more English to them as time went on. This had no effect on the children's English vocabularies, which grew steadily as the children went through Head Start and kindergarten, or English literacy, which progressed ever faster, but slowed the rate at which they learned Spanish words. In well-off South Florida and low-income urban Pennsylvania alike, Hispanic parents did not help their children learn English by speaking it to them – except perhaps indirectly, by undermining the children's progress in Spanish. Quality is also a consideration. Children learn best from native speakers. If migrant parents are themselves in the early stages of learning a new language, what they impart to their children is likely to be flawed and limited in scope. They would probably do better to concentrate on giving their children as strong a grounding as possible in the less powerful language.[19]

If your eyes are fixed upon milestones, the landscape will pass you by. Bilingualism is likely to affect many aspects of children's engagement with the world and the people in it, including their beliefs about the nature of things. At the age of five or so, children are strongly inclined to believe in the immutability of characteristics, which makes them right about some things and quite wrong about others. They are confident that a baby born to ducks but raised by cats will have feathers and quack; they also tend to expect that a human baby born to English parents but brought up by Italians will speak English, not Italian. When the beliefs of monolingual and bilingual children living in the Montreal area were compared, the monolinguals and the children who had been bilingual since infancy were similarly inclined to essentialist thinking. Other bilingual children, who had been introduced to a second language after the age of three, saw things differently. Conscious from their own experience with language that initial characteristics can be modified, they were less ready to think that characteristics in general are immutable. Not only were they readier to believe that a baby raised by Italians will speak Italian, but they were also more likely to entertain the idea that a duckling raised by cats would not quack or have feathers. Though their bilingual awareness did not necessarily give them a better understanding of how things are in all instances, it did give them an outlook that was significantly more open to new possibilities.[20]

Openness is a vital quality, but awareness of others is more fundamental still. Psychological experiments test children's awareness of the perspectives of others by placing objects in the child's view and also that of an investigator, who talks to the child. Although the child can see all the objects, some are hidden from the adult. The procedure tests whether the children are aware that what the investigator sees is not the same as what they see, and respond appropriately. There may be two small cars set out, for example, one visible to the adult and the other not: when the adult asks the child to move 'the small car', the correct response requires the child to recognise which one the adult can see. Bilingual children aged three to six have proved better at understanding what others are referring to in such exchanges, as have children who only speak one language but are used to hearing another, and infants as young as fifteen months, who can say no more than a few words in any tongue. This ability may reflect the challenges young children face when they are surrounded by more than one language. Hearing new words all the time, they have to work out which language each novelty belongs to, and which language – or simultaneous combination of languages – a speaker is using. They may be more aware of what other people can see because they look more intently at other people, trying to pick up as many clues as possible to what others are saying.[21]

Their appreciation of the art of conversation may also be heightened, compared to their monolingual peers. The British philosopher of language Paul Grice formulated a set of maxims for the conduct of conversations, covering Quality (tell the truth; avoid statements for which you lack evidence), Quantity (be as informative as is required, but not more so), Relation (be relevant) and Manner (be brief and orderly; avoid being ambiguous and obscure). Researchers tested young children's grasp of these principles by presenting them with conversational exchanges, which were depicted using dolls, and asking them whether remarks conformed to Gricean maxims – or, in the language of the experimental protocol, whether the doll said something silly. As an answer to the question 'What did you get for your birthday?' for example, 'A present' violated the maxim of Quantity by failing to be sufficiently informative, and the maxim of Relation was violated by giving the answer 'I know your name' in response to the question 'What game do you like?'

In several different settings and language combinations – Slovenian and Italian in the Slovenian region of Istria, near the Italian border, German and Italian in the Italian town of Bolzano, near the Austrian border, English and Japanese bilinguals in northern England – bilingual children were better than monolingual ones at identifying maxim violations. Whether or not they knew as many words as the monolinguals in their shared languages, they had more insight into how to communicate with other people.[22]

*　*　*　*

Language loses its priority and privileges once childhood is past. People's efforts to learn new languages have to compete with the ever-expanding range of demands, responsibilities and commitments that constitute maturity. To succeed, learners will need motivation, opportunity and aptitude.[23]

They may also have to contend with aptitude denial. The doctrine of equal potential is a tyrannical thing and its implication is clear and damning: if you fail to make headway in learning a skill, such as learning a musical instrument or a language, it is because you have not applied yourself sufficiently. Extenuating circumstances may be acknowledged, but we live in a world in which you are expected to get over them. Even sympathetic diagnoses, such as a lack of self-confidence, are sugared pills of criticism. It is true, to a reasonable approximation and mindful of the effects of disability or other impairment for some, that everybody is capable of learning a second language. Some people are more capable than others, though, and that inequality must be acknowledged. You do the strugglers no favours by denying that there is such a thing as being good at languages. They stand to gain not only from being spared undeserved guilt, but from insights that might emerge from asking questions about the nature and sources of language aptitude.

In the 1940s and 1950s, the decades of the Second World War, the Korean War and the Cold War, the United States military urgently wanted answers to such questions. More specifically, it wanted to know which of its personnel it should select for training in the foreign languages that its enemies and some of its allies spoke. Giving volunteers one-week courses in Chinese or Japanese and selecting the best performers was an expensive way to go about it. Intelligence tests were not a serviceable alternative, as IQ scores had an erratic relationship with language-learning ability. The call went out for proposals to develop a language aptitude test that would identify talent in an efficient manner. That was the origin of the Modern Language Aptitude Test (MLAT), which dominated its field both in application and in conceptual influence for decades. It remains in use today.[24]

The MLAT was created by John B. Carroll, whose work with languages began at the precocious age of thirteen after he attended a lecture in Hartford, Connecticut, by Benjamin Lee Whorf, the linguist whose name has come to stand for the idea that language influences thought. Carroll was there because it was the town in which he was born and raised; Whorf was there because he was employed as a fire prevention inspector by the Hartford Fire Insurance Company. At the local library Whorf allowed the young Carroll to assist him in tasks such as looking up Aztec words in a Mexican dictionary. He introduced him to linguistics and to his mentor Edward Sapir, with whom Carroll later studied.[25]

Thirty years later, Carroll built his model of language aptitude around phonetics and grammar, concepts that he had first learned about from Whorf at the Hartford library. He identified four factors underlying aptitude. The first was what he called phonetic coding, the ability to retain the words that one hears in a form that allows them to be recalled after their neural echoes have died away. The second was grammatical sensitivity, the awareness of the function of words and their relationships with each other. The third was the ability to memorise associations between words and meanings. The fourth was the ability to infer forms, rules and patterns from foreign speech or text. Though subsequent work has gone beyond these concepts, they are what it is built upon, and they remain compelling as a basis for reflection on what the elements of language aptitude might be. That question is unresolved, as is the theoretical debate in which it is embedded, about whether we owe language abilities to a dedicated system, or whether they derive from general cognitive faculties. Language is unarguably special; the question is just how special.[26]

The most fundamental element of the language complex is memory. You cannot analyse or generate or infer from language if you cannot remember it. As well as faculties of long-term memory, the brain needs a means to form moments. It has to impose a moving frame upon incoming information, holding short sequences together long enough for them to be analysed and retained, if necessary, for storage or further use. A second or two may suffice. Psychologists call this 'working memory'. It may be sustained by a repetition mechanism, or loop, that slows the decay of the information held in the memory store. Science has Alan Baddeley to thank for the concept (and the British public has him to thank for designing postcodes so that they are easy to remember). Baddeley and his colleagues suggested that the working memory loop evolved in order to help children learn new words.[27]

Working memory is often conceived as comprising both a storage system and a control system, the former to store and the latter to co-ordinate information. The utility of a storage element can be seen from the preceding sentence, in which the reader has to keep the verb 'to store' in play until its object, 'information', is reached several words later. Mark Twain highlighted the issue in one of his many jibes at the 'awful' German language: 'I would move the Verb further up to the front. You may load up with ever so good a Verb, but I notice that you never really bring down a subject with it at the present German range – you only cripple it. So I insist that this important part of speech should be brought forward to a position where it may be easily seen with the naked eye.'[28]

People vary in the capacity of their working memory. Those with high capacity may be better able than those with lower capacity to handle 'garden path' sentences, so called because they contain gram-matically ambiguous words that can lead the listener up the garden path. Good working memory helps people get back on track after misdirections of the kind encountered in sentences such as 'The child told the story cried.' It may also help students do well in language classes, and could be a key factor in enabling the highest flyers to achieve near-native proficiency. Those meeting the challenges of German don't need the reform demanded by Twain.[29]

For language learning, as distinct from real-time processing, two different kinds of memory are required. Declarative memory is the remembering of information and events, such as your password, what you did last summer, and linguistic idiosyncrasies such as the fact that, as Mark Twain indignantly reported, the German word for turnip is feminine, but the word for girl is neuter. ('Gretchen: "Wilhelm, where is the turnip?" Wilhelm: "She has gone to the kitchen." Gretchen: "Where is the accomplished and beautiful English maiden?"Wilhelm: "It has gone to the opera."') Procedural memory is the knowledge of how to do things, such as riding a bicycle or typing, without having to consciously think how to do them. It takes experience and practice. In the early stages of learning a language, declarative memory gets the learner started; at more advanced stages, procedural memory plays an increasing part. People vary in their capacities for both kinds. Strong declarative memory helps beginners make progress; strong procedural memory helps advanced learners achieve high levels of proficiency. Unfortunately for ambitious older learners, procedural memory seems to be at its strongest in early childhood, though declarative memory reaches its maximum levels in the teens and early adult years, before going into the inevitable decline.[30]

Perhaps the most demanding challenges for language adepts are the ones simultaneous interpreters have to meet. An interpreter must follow and comprehend incoming speech, while preparing interpretations that respect the different perspectives of the speaker and the addressee. That involves evaluating speech with reference to at least two different sets of rules, norms and associated subtleties, as well as a set that applies specifically to the situation and the interpreter's role in it. The stakes can be high. National interests or people's lives may depend upon interpretations that have to be produced without any time for reflection. High-performance working memory would seem to be an asset for such a task, if not a necessity.

It certainly turned out to be a strong predictor of success for a group of students training to interpret between American Sign Language and English. The ones most likely to succeed were the ones who had high working memory capacity, and who did well when assessed at the start of the course. Noting that only one in ten of those who enter interpreting programmes will end up as interpreters, because they either drop out or graduate without the necessary levels of skill, the researchers suggested that it might be an idea to test performance and working memory before the courses get under way.[31]

So much for effort, then. This does not send the message that you will make it if you only try hard enough. Instead it lends support to suspicions, not always admitted or clearly articulated, that you will have to make do with what you've got. That may include the genetic hand you have been dealt. Evidence bearing upon language skills is still sparse, but a few scouting missions into genomic territory have found signs that certain gene variants may give people advantages in language learning. One followed Chinese students as they went through an English-language immersion programme, finding that the density of nerve fibres increased in the brains of those with certain variants of a gene known as COMT, to the benefit of their grades. Another found that a variant of the FOXP2 gene, the focus of much attention because of its implication in language faculties, helped adult English speakers to learn the tones of Mandarin in an efficient manner. Two-thirds of Spanish–English bilingual students sampled at the University of Houston were found to have a variant of the DRD2 gene that has been associated with cognitive flexibility, whereas only a third of their monolingual peers carried it. Observing that Hispanic people in the United States are generally from poorer backgrounds than the monolinguals in the study, the researchers suggested that this genotype might have helped the bilinguals make the transition from the Spanish they spoke at home to the English they learned at school, and consequently to reach levels of academic attainment high enough to gain them places at the university.[32]

None of these studies are as discouraging as the dogma of equal potential, though. The implicit suggestion that up to 90 per cent of would-be interpreters are no-hopers certainly isn't calculated to encourage people to follow their dreams, but it relates only to the recruitment of a small professional elite. To a reasonable approximation, everybody who wants to learn a language stands to benefit from improvements in the scientific understanding of the cognitive abilities involved, and how those vary between individuals. Looking forward to a more detailed picture of the mechanisms, psychologists Vera Kempe and Patricia Brooks suggest that rather than distinguishing between 'good' and 'bad' learners, we may come to appreciate individuals' abilities in particular aspects of language. One person's strength may lie in grammar, for example; another's in distinguishing sounds. The more they understand about both their weaknesses and their strengths, the better they will be able to learn.[33]

* * * *

After considering how languages are gained, we have to consider how they are kept. For many individuals and communities, it is the loss rather than the learning of languages that determines whether or not they can use more than one.

CHAPTER FOUR

It Must Still Be In There Somewhere

Learning languages may be the easy part: it may be more difficult to avoid losing them.

At the age of eighteen the future Marxist historian Eric Hobsbawm subjected himself, as communists so frequently did, to self-criticism: 'An incorrigible striker of attitudes . . . He is vain and conceited. He is a coward. He loves nature deeply. And he forgets the German language.'[1]

Hobsbawm had been in Britain for three years, having left Berlin in 1933 after the Nazis came to power. A British citizen, he felt no bonds to Germany, and few to Austria, where he had spent his childhood, but German remained his private language, and he made 'enormous efforts' to prevent himself from forgetting it. He wrote his diaries in it not just as a teenager but during the war, while in British uniform. To his chagrin, however, 'my country refused to make any use of my bilinguality in the war against Hitler'.[2]

Although his immediate background was unusual – his mother was from Vienna, his father from London – his affinity with the German language was typical of Jewish people living in German-speaking lands up to the point of his departure. By now Yiddish had been consigned to their history; many had adopted German culture as their own. Then came the Nazis, and the German-speaking majority swiftly turned upon the German-speaking minority. One woman from Düsseldorf, a teenager at the time, recalled how her teacher had made her stand in front of the class, along with two friends, to tell them that 'you Jews' were 'guests' in the country and did not belong there.[3]

That was in 1934; the following year, the Nuremberg laws institutionalised the division of the populace into 'Aryans' and 'non-Aryans', and increased the pressure upon the latter. In Düsseldorf, Jews were banned not just from public swimming pools but also the local hospital. Then, in 1938, came the orchestrated attacks of Kristallnacht and mass incarcerations in concentration camps.

Studying interviews with Jewish people who had once lived in Düsseldorf, but had managed to escape Nazi persecution by leaving the country, the linguist Monika Schmid was struck by how the time of their departure conditioned their use of German six decades later. The ones who left last were the ones whose German had deteriorated the most. Those who emigrated during the first phase, from Hitler's assumption of power to the passing of the Nuremberg laws, spoke the language as though they had never left. Those who left in the middle period, up to Kristallnacht, also spoke German accurately. The third, post-Kristallnacht group stood out from the first two. They made grammatical errors, and many had developed English accents. These speakers no longer sounded native.[4]

In the absence of persecution, the opposite pattern might have been expected: the speakers who left the country of origin most recently, and who had spoken the language longest before their departure, should be the most native-like. The date of departure may not be so significant – after six decades, a few years may be neither here nor there – but the age at departure might count for something. With a mean age of sixteen, the first cohort to leave was adolescent rather than adult, and had several fewer years' experience speaking German than the last cohort, whose average age was close to nineteen. Nor did other plausible factors, such as the degree of continuing contact with German, have any significant effect. It was history that made the difference. The last group to leave experienced the most cruel persecution, and it alienated them from the language spoken by their persecutors. They were far more hostile to it than the earlier cohorts.

Schmid regards this as alienation without dispossession. She believes that the last group of exiles still retained the language of their Düsseldorf childhood intact, but their ability to connect with it was impaired by the emotions it aroused. Their speech was as rich and complex as that of the first group of emigrants: their capacities were greater than they realised. The mistakes they made look like effects of the load their emotions imposed on their language faculties: people make errors when they are stressed because they have too much to process, and so lose contact with their knowledge of how to speak or act. Eric Hobsbawm should not have worried about forgetting German, but only about losing full access to it. His desire to keep it is consistent with the pattern Schmid observed, in which early exiles were less estranged from their native tongue than later ones. More significantly, his British citizenship set him apart from other Jewish native German speakers: in later life he would refute any suggestion that his family were refugees or victims of Nazism. The efforts he made to maintain his German can easily be seen as a struggle against an emotional discord that developed as his private language became an enemy tongue.[5]

Estrangement undermines confidence. One of the Düsseldorf exiles had spoken fluently for forty minutes about her life, but when she received Schmid's letter requesting permission to use the interview, she expressed her relief that Schmid had supplied an English version. She had left Germany in 1939, aged thirteen, on one of the Kindertransport trains that brought Jewish children to England.

After the war, she settled in the United States and rejected her mother tongue, declaring that 'America is my country, and English is my language.' Her German had deteriorated more than that of any other interviewee, yet she made no more mistakes than a younger American woman who had emigrated to Germany and whose command of the language approached native levels. Schmid's analysis of the emigrants' recollections implies that although people may think they have lost a language that was once theirs, it is still in there somewhere. They may, however, prefer to leave it where it is.[6]

Many people lose touch with their first languages under circumstances that are not in the least exceptional. Adults may find themselves at a loss for words after a period abroad. Children who once chatted away happily in their mother tongues become unable to converse in them after a few years of school. People tend to be sceptical that it happens to adults, while taking for granted that it happens to children. They do, however, uphold a pervasive folk belief that first languages are indeed still in there somewhere, waiting to be rekindled. (My evidence regarding the popularity of this belief is anecdotal, but I have accumulated it over a lifetime.)

There appears to be a lot of truth in the idea – but not nearly enough for many of those who might want to recover their first voices. Above all, there is a divide between childhood and adulthood. People who emigrate as adults or adolescents are likely to retain the language they spoke up to the point of their departure, even if they cease to speak it thereafter. Among the Düsseldorf exiles, it didn't matter that one group's exposure to German had been three years longer than another's. What mattered was that all the cohorts were, on average, well past puberty when they left the country. The structure of their German had been completed, and sufficient time had passed for it to have set solid. Children's language structures may be well-developed, but they have not yet set. They may be alarmingly vulnerable to immersion in a new language. One Korean child began to lose touch with her vocabulary only a month into a stay with her mother in the United States, where everybody, including her mother, spoke English to her. After two months her test scores had halved, and before long she was unable to speak Korean with her father on the phone from the home country.[7]

Monika Schmid sees the entrenchment of a language as a process that involves two phases. First, children acquire the basic structures of a language, which will generally be in place by the time they start school. These structures are not yet sufficiently robust to be permanent. They need to be consolidated during the later years of childhood. If that happens, children will enter adolescence with a language system that should last them a lifetime. Any difficulties they may subsequently experience as a result of competition between languages will be problems of access rather than loss. The first language will still be there, but the second gets in its way. As the newer language becomes the main language, it grows too strong to be completely suppressed when the speaker wants to revert to the original one. Second languages can start interfering with first ones as soon as the din starts to rise. After only three months, American students spending a semester in Spain performed worse than fellow students taking a Spanish class back home, when set tasks such as naming as many animals in their native English as they could in thirty seconds.[8]

For Schmid, one compelling reason to believe in the persistence of established languages is that she finds no reason to believe the maxim 'use it or lose it' is any help to people who want to avoid losing their first languages. On her website Language Attrition, she goes so far as to say that '*all* of the available empirical evidence is against it – and, believe me, we have tried'. Although it seems obvious that the more a person uses their first language, the better they will be able to use it, no such clear relationship emerges from research into attrition among adults. Nor do other obvious candidate factors seem to have much effect. The bulk of attrition happens during the first ten years after migrants arrive in their new country and are faced with the demands of the new language; after that, the length of time they have spent there makes little difference. Language aptitude seems to have little effect either. It did not help bilinguals who had lived in Sweden for many years, having come from Spanish-speaking countries as adults, to spot incorrect grammar in Spanish sentences. Those with stronger emotional bonds to their first language had a better command of its grammar, however, echoing the lessons that Schmid drew from the German Jewish exiles.[9]

Schmid did find one group who used their first language in a way that seemed to help keep it polished: those who used it in their working lives. She suggests that this strengthens their ability to suppress interference from the second language, because at work they must maintain a proper separation between languages. At home, the discipline is relaxed: migrants are likely to be in the company of fellow bilinguals who can move without difficulty between the older tongue and the newer.[10]

The prospects are very different for children who become detached from their mother tongues in the middle of childhood. Children can lose languages as easily as they gain them. The structures have not yet set, and can be wiped. Often, part of the problem is that the system has not yet been fully installed: children may start losing touch with their languages before they have finished learning them. Those exposed to two languages from birth may be at a particular disadvantage, compared to those who have a chance to concentrate on the subordinate language for two or three years before the dominant one moves in. Even if a discontinued first language is still in there, it will only be a kindergarten version, frozen and then fossilized.[11]

There may be nothing there at all – or at any rate nothing that can be detected, even with the use of brain scanners. A French research team assembled a group of adults who had come to France from Korea as children – a handful of the 200,000 Koreans, mostly born to single mothers, who have been adopted by Western families since the end of the Korean War. Their ages at adoption ranged from three to eight, so at least some of them were old enough to have memories of their previous lives in Korea, but all claimed that they had no recollection of their first language. Their brain activity was scanned by magnetic resonance imaging while they heard speech in various languages: they responded no differently to Korean than they did to tongues with which they had no connection whatsoever, such as Polish or Japanese. When presented with samples of speech, the Korean adoptees in France were at a loss to say whether a sentence was in Korean or some other tongue. There were no signs of the germ of nativeness, the knowledge of the phonemes that distinguish the words of a language from each other. They were no better than native French speakers at recognising consonants that are found in Korean but not in French.[12]

Contrasting results emerged from studies of children who were born in China and grew up in Montreal. Their exposure to Chinese had ceased when they were adopted, on average at the age of one, and they spoke only French. Nevertheless, their brain activity showed a response to the tones that are used in spoken Chinese, and which cause particular problems for speakers of languages that do not use pitch contrasts to determine meaning. Chinese adoptees' neural responses to French sounds were also different to those of French speakers who had never been exposed to Chinese, but similar to those of Chinese–French bilinguals who had grown up with both languages from an early age. The Montreal researchers took these findings as evidence that language templates created very early in life were not overwritten, and became involved in the processing of sounds encountered later in life.[13]

Among the Korean adoptees in France, the only one who had recently taken a Korean language class did better than the group as a whole, and the effects of relearning have been apparent in a range of studies that have suggested there may be something still in there after all. An ability to discriminate phonemes can be evoked and amplified by training in later life. On a language course at a Minnesota university, students who had been brought to Minnesota from Korea as adoptees in the first year of life proved better at identifying Korean phonemes than classmates who lacked any previous exposure to them. Bringing buried knowledge to light may take time: fifteen to twenty sessions over thirty days were needed for Britons living in the United Kingdom to relearn sound contrasts in Hindi or Zulu that they had encountered living abroad as children. Or it may only take a matter of minutes. Five to nearly fifteen years after coming to America, a group of girls adopted from India were unable to discriminate between contrasts present in Indian languages but not in English. Their performance improved after a few moments' worth of training, while that of their non-adopted peers remained flat.[14]

You have to ask what the value of this ability might be. It is confined, after all, to the very simplest elements of language; it does not help with the formation, modification and combination of words into strings of meaning. If your sole legacy from early experience with a language is a sharpened ear for its sounds, there is no reason to expect that you will be any better at constructing statements and conveying meaning than learners who have come fresh to the language. Heritage speakers tend to be better than ordinary learners at pronunciation, but their ability to put words together will likely be about the same.[15]

The real value will lie in a different kind of communication. It may bring people closer together. If the ability to tune into a language's defining sounds helps in pronouncing them, speakers taking up their lost first languages will sound more native-like than learners without roots. Authentic timbres in their speech may resonate with native speakers, who may be encouraged to welcome the returners back to the speech community. More broadly, native-like traces will serve the same vital function as any other accent, sending reliable signals about where the speaker is from.

* * * *

Two generations and then the graveyard: few things about language seem as inevitable as the shift undergone by migrant communities, from the tongues they brought with them to the one that dominates the territory in which they have settled. The first arrivals speak their native language at home; their children go to school and become fluent in the dominant language, speaking it to each other as well as with their peers. Second-generation children continue to speak the minority language with their parents, but even that dialogue declines as the parents themselves become more used to speaking the dominant language, and as time takes its toll on the first generation. The children of the second generation speak the dominant language to their own children, who grow up monolingual and, in some cases, unable to talk to their grandparents.

That is the classic immigrant story in the United States, which has become notorious as a 'graveyard of languages'. Bilingualism is no more than a transitional phase in the passage from one monolingualism to another. Languages persist for a time, then collapse catastrophically. Between 1980 and 2010, the number of homes in which Italian is spoken fell by more than half, and of German-speaking homes by a third. The drop between the second and third generations is often the most precipitous. Half of second-generation Hispanics in the United States are bilingual, but the level falls to less than a quarter in the next generation. Surveys in Southern California, home to more than five million Mexicans, produced a 'life expectancy' for Spanish of between two and three generations, measured by the ability to speak the language. The likelihood that a great-grandchild of a Mexican immigrant would speak Spanish was only 3 per cent. Nor is the mass abandonment of migrant languages an exclusively American phenomenon. Although the Bangladeshi population of Tower Hamlets, the borough just to the east of London's financial district, has often been regarded as a closed and unintegrated community, its second generation has shifted decisively from Bengali to English.[16]

Leaving their home languages at home, individuals undertaking language shift find themselves in varying states of detachment or semi-detachment. Unlike international adoptees, they have recollections of their heritage languages, and some ability to use them. At one end of the spectrum, speakers may be as at home in the heritage language as they would have been if they had grown up in its country of origin. At the other, so-called 'overhearers' may be limited to understanding what others are saying, without being able to reply. Many people are content to let their heritage languages go; others hang on to them as best they can, and some return to them after years of exile. Heritage learners are tricky to teach because unlike complete novices they know something, but they vary wildly in what they know, and a lot of what they know is wrong. Mutual help is awkward for similar reasons. They are likely to compound each other's errors, and they are divided from each other by differing levels of competence and confidence. The first unspoken question is 'does this person speak our first language better or worse than I do?' Either answer will be unsatisfactory, though for different reasons.

Heritage speakers have to ask themselves questions all the time. In most cases, they turned away from their heritage language when they went to school. By that time they might have grasped the basics of the language, but they would probably not have finished learning it, and their knowledge may subsequently have degraded or become inaccessible. They are faced with a stream of problems – what word to choose, what ending a word should have, what relationship one word has with another – that they must solve using a meagre and inadequate knowledge base. They have to improvise a version of their heritage.

The result is a language of their own. Maria Polinsky, a linguist from Russia who works in the United States, analysed the Russian spoken by adults who had emigrated to America as children. For them, Russian was now a language for conversation with parents or grandparents, but not with siblings. Although their proficiencies varied, their speech had sufficient characteristics in common for Polinsky to identify it as a distinct variety of the language, which she called American Russian.[17]

She could have called it a number of other things: Bodged Russian, for example, or Fools' Russian, or Dumbed-Down Russian. As she has noted, speakers of standard Russian often have harsh words to say about heritage speakers 'murdering the language of Pushkin'. Her documentation of American Russian is a comprehensive indictment of the shame of the heritage speaker. And shaming, she observes, is a Russian national sport.[18]

American Russian is reduced, simplified and slow. Full Russian has six cases; American Russian has two. A Full Russian speaker will say ten words in the time it takes an American Russian speaker to say six, and the American Russian speaker will leave long pauses between them. Heritage speakers struggle with aspects of grammar such as gender, relative clauses (of the kind that begin with pronouns such as 'who' or 'that' in English) and agreement between subject and verb. Their speech is marked by hesitation, deviation and repetition.[19]

Nevertheless, American Russian is a real language with its own internal coherence. It is not, Polinsky underlines, just a heap of random fragments from the ruins of the lost tongue. Lacking a complete language system, heritage speakers have to develop a systematic approach based on the elements that they do have in place. Russian nouns fall into several different declension classes, representing different patterns of case-endings, and knowledge of these classes is necessary to identify the grammatical gender of some words. Having never got as far as that chapter in the implicit textbook, heritage speakers apply a simplified set of rules based on the endings of nouns in their default nominative forms. They often turn neuter nouns into feminine ones, but never turn feminines into neuters. This is a sensible use of probabilities. Feminine nouns occur much frequently than neuter ones, so the feminine gender is more likely to be the correct choice. Some heritage speakers dispense with the neuter gender altogether.[20]

Although heritage Russian speakers vary among themselves, the correspondences in their strategies extend far beyond America. They take a similar approach to gender in Germany and Israel, as they do to the case-ending pronounced roughly like the German exclamation 'ach'. It is easy to hear, and more common than other endings, so heritage speakers in these different countries all overuse it. Resemblances are also detectable between heritage Russian and heritage varieties of other languages, such as Greek or Chinese. Impoverished speakers find similar ways to make up for the knowledge they lack, and organise what they do know into a functional system.[21]

These heritage forms differ from other language varieties, such as local dialects, in that nobody is very fond of them, or cares about their inevitable decline. Plenty of heritage Russian speakers, Polinsky observes, have no use for American Russian beyond saying 'I love you, Grandma, and I need twenty dollars.' For speakers who care about their Russian affinities it may be important, but also a constant reminder that the relationship with the heritage community is both undeveloped and in a state of disrepair. It can be spoken better or worse – using three genders rather than two, for example – but it can never be a language about which a speaker can feel proud. Ambitious heritage speakers aspire to speak a full, and usually standard, form of the language.[22]

Whether they are better equipped to do so than learners with no background in the language is unclear. Casual learners, says Polinsky, often turn to their heritage when presented with language course options at university, because they think it will be an easy A grade.

They soon find out that it isn't. Although there is evidence to suggest that heritage speakers have an edge over novice students in learning the sounds of the language, the advantage does not appear to extend further than that. On the other hand, heritage learners who go on immersion courses in the language's country of origin show more marked improvement over a semester than students for whom it is entirely foreign. Their advantage may be that it is more important to them.[23]

One way they can help themselves is by reading, which improves their speech. Their relatives, friends and acquaintances who speak a full form of the language can help them by being patient, despite the long pauses and frequent repetitions, and by refraining from correcting every little mistake, which undermines their confidence. Strangers can help by not switching to English, a shift that implies the speaker has failed a test. Members of the heritage language community may have to set aside passionately held beliefs about the duty to maintain the quality and beauty of the language far from its homeland. Hearing one's language spoken badly can be disagreeable, jarring and even offensive, but if full members of the language community don't put up with it, aspiring members will be unable to learn from them. And if they do put up with it, heritage learners should be genuinely grateful.

Putting up with it means putting individuals' needs above community demands, though not above the community's needs. Insisting that nothing but perfection is good enough dismisses the benefits that even a shaky grasp on the language gives heritage speakers, and the efforts they have made to attain it. The effect is likely to be that heritage speakers are discouraged from sustaining their efforts, which will weaken their ties with the community. That in turn is likely to weaken the community itself. Although purists may embrace the idea of fewer but better speakers, it is a guaranteed formula for decline.

Where decline is far advanced and potential speakers have deep inhibitions about using a language, it will need a lot more than just tolerance and gentle encouragement. A survey by the First Peoples' Cultural Council (FPCC) of British Columbia classifies only 3 per cent of the First Nations population as 'fluent speakers' of any of the province's thirty-four indigenous languages, though 10 per cent are learning one. It also highlights the existence of 'silent speakers', who understand but do not speak their First Nations language, because they overheard it as children without speaking it themselves, or because they have been persuaded of its inferiority. Some of the older ones were persuaded forcibly, by the punishments meted out to them for speaking their own languages in the residential schools to which Aboriginal children were consigned for assimilation. The FPCC's Silent Speaker Project uses cognitive behaviour therapy to overcome these internalised barriers, following a model developed by Sami people in Norway and Sweden.[24]

Languages mean different things to different minorities. Some groups consider them fundamental to identity: the group is defined by its language, and an individual who cannot speak it does not really belong. Others maintain a rich and vigorous sense of themselves without a defining language that they speak well enough to meet their everyday needs. Irish-Americans, for example, have managed fine without the Irish language. Jewish communities in the United States, Britain and elsewhere share such a wealth of understandings through which to know who they are, that a private language for day-to-day sharing scarcely seems necessary. Hebrew retains its constitutive place from week to week and across the calendar, of course, even for those who do not themselves observe the cycles.

The fortunes of a language may also depend on the degree to which its speakers maintain a boundary between themselves and the wider society around them. Among Israel's ultra-Orthodox Haredim (meaning fearful of the Lord) some of the most hardcore and insular groups speak mainly in Yiddish, preferring to reserve Hebrew for religious use. According to a Hasidic rabbi in Jerusalem, 'Yiddish is a way of preserving our traditions. It helps to keep us apart and safe-guard our children from Western values.'Thus safeguarded, the chil-dren will grow up, marry and remain within the community. The language and the values will sustain each other.[25]

When values are shared with the wider society, the opposite is liable to occur. Languages may succumb to love, or at any rate to intermar-riage. Among third-generation Hispanics in the United States, two-thirds of those who are married have spouses who are not Hispanic. And by the third generation, a quarter of Americans with Hispanic ancestry no longer identify as Hispanic anyway. Of those who do still identify as Hispanic, only a quarter say that their parents encouraged them to speak Spanish, and only a quarter still can. Under prevailing conditions, the remaining Spanish speakers will struggle to carry on.[26]

Although nearly 90 per cent of self-identified Hispanics say it is important that future generations should speak Spanish, the ideal is evidently not important enough on its own. It is certainly hard to see how bilingualism can survive not only a shift to the dominant language within a minority group, but also the assimilation of the group into the population at large. The flags will cease to fly; patriotism will no longer stir hearts or consciences. Language will become entirely a matter of individual choice.

Even when a group remains manifest, and is regarded by its members as a community, individual choices will determine the future of its language. It will depend on the incentives. People will commit to a language if they experience sufficient rewards from using it, or if they expect that it will deliver worthwhile benefits in the future. They may indeed feel rewarded by fulfilling a perceived duty to the community – especially if it is a requirement for belonging – but more narrowly indi-vidual interests are likely to be decisive. A language will feel worth cultivating to the extent that it strengthens people's ties to family and friends, or offers the prospect of better economic opportunities for its speakers and, in time, their children.

The strength of these incentives will vary according to the relationships within the group, and the environment in which the group finds itself. A heritage speaker's most basic requirement is people to talk to, which means people with shared outlooks and interests. American Russians who want Pushkin to be part of their culture will have something in common with Full Russian speakers, even if the latter have mixed feelings about what the former do to Pushkin's language. Many heritage speakers have diverged considerably in outlook and culture from their core community, though. New migrants from the old country may offer an alternative source of new friends and conversation partners, but their availability will depend upon the economic and political forces governing migration.

Heritage speakers' economic incentives will depend upon the value of the language, which in turn will depend on its prestige, its prevalence, and how many people speak it. The sociologist Pierre Bourdieu once observed that 'a language is worth what the people who speak it are worth'. He made a rhetorical point that should be well taken, but English is actually worth far more than its speakers, because much of its value arises from the economic, technological and political domains in which it enjoys widespread dominance, if not monopoly. Historically, prestige has been hard to attain for languages other than English in the United States, which is one of the reasons that so many of their speakers have abandoned them. Prejudice is less of a factor than it was, and ethnic pride may be a more powerful force than it used to be, but the economic might of English remains unchallenged. Up to now, switching to English has seemed the rational course, economically speaking, for most heritage speakers to follow.[27]

In the future, however, the balance between costs and benefits may alter. Although English will remain the surest bet, cultural and technological developments may make the incentives for maintaining heritage languages appear more attractive. Bilingualism itself may acquire cachet, as widespread enthusiasm for bilingual schools among upwardly mobile English-speaking families illustrates. The idea that languages are a valuable resource in a globalised world might make the climate a little more comfortable for people trying to use such resources within a single country, or to reach beyond it.[28]

Technology is the new factor here. If it increases access to markets where a language is spoken – especially in major economies such as that of Mexico – it could significantly increase the language's value. In the United States, the most obvious potential beneficiaries would be Spanish-speaking American business people and professionals, for whom even a fractional increase in access to the Spanish-speaking Americas could open up a host of opportunities. Less obviously, there could be indirect benefits for small domestic businesses that revolve around conversation, such as restaurants and hairdressers. If the high-flyers raised the prestige of the language, more voices would be heard speaking it.

There might also be benefits beyond the marketplace. In the past, a migrant might send a letter to the family back home across the ocean and wait a month before receiving a reply. With such restricted channels of communication, it was pretty well impossible for migrants and the families they left behind to operate as collective entities. The migrants were autonomous by necessity. They had to make their own decisions. Now, however, communication technologies enable family members to be present to each other no matter how many thousands of miles separate them. You can phone your parents back home when-ever you're free, as long as time zones overlap sufficiently, and wher-ever you like – as long as fellow bus passengers don't take exception to your use of your native tongue. Ever-expanding channels and falling costs will make it increasingly easy for transnationally extended fami-lies to discuss matters and make decisions as if round a kitchen table. Conversation between separated relatives – grandparents and grand-children, for example – will become more appealing and feel more natural as video quality improves. Migrants' children will have new incentives, personal rather than economic, to speak their heritage languages.

Communication technologies also make it easier to make contact across distance with unrelated others who speak the same language, for any degree of relationship from casual online chat to intimate partnership and marriage. They increase the bandwidth for popular culture, streaming music, films and telenovelas with a sublime disregard for national borders. If the value of a heritage language grows, economic, cultural and personal incentives will increasingly blend into each other. That will encourage people to believe two languages are better for them than one.

* * * *

In the face of obstacles, objections and resistance, strong incentives may be needed to encourage the use of more than one language. Compelling incentives are promised by the argument that bilingualism is good for the brain, improving cognitive performance and holding back the onset of dementia, but the findings are mixed and the claims disputed.

CHAPTER FIVE

Two Languages In One Head

Bilingualism became a health issue when researchers claimed that it could improve mental fitness and delay dementia – and then became the theatre of a controversy that reflects wider uncertainties about the status of scientific knowledge.

The possibility that using more than one language might strengthen cognitive performance has been taken up enthusiastically by the media. One online commenter was having none of it, though. 'The human brain can only contain a finite amount of information and as English speakers we are fortunate not to need a secondary language,' wrote Falcom, of Cambridge. 'That space is much better utilised for science, history and our rich culture.'[1]

English speakers who do not wish to learn any other languages find it easy to offer reasons why they should not. In contrast, English speakers who would like to speak another language often struggle to imagine how they could. They also lack faith in the brain's capacity. The comedian Eddie Izzard gave satirical voice to the boggled Anglophone mind: 'Two languages in one head? No one can live at that speed!'[2]

They can, of course, and countless millions of human beings do, many of them without giving it a thought. But there are serious scientific questions to ask about their abilities. How does a brain manage two languages or more, each offering different ways to express a thought or convey a message? It must prevent them from interfering with each other, and select the one that is appropriate at any moment – of which there may be several in a single sentence, when bilinguals hop from one of their languages to the other and back again.

Ellen Bialystok of York University in Toronto argues that the answer lies in what is known as the executive control system, which directs attention to where it should be focused and suppresses impulses when it would be better not to act on them. When a brain contains two languages, the executive system must select the appropriate one, and prevent the other from intruding upon it. The effect of this exercise is to strengthen executive functions, producing performance enhancements in activities that have nothing to do with language. People benefit from efficiency improvements in basic cognitive operations such as switching attention, staying on task and sidelining distractions. Bilingualism is a source of cognitive advantages.

This argument offers a mechanism for the suggestion made in a landmark study, published in 1962, that a child might gain 'mental flexibility' from experience with two languages. It ran counter to decades of expert opinion, which took the view that bilingualism impaired children's intelligence and held them back in education. Elizabeth Peal and Wallace Lambert reported instead that bilingual Montreal schoolchildren outperformed their monolingual peers in cognitive tests, including those that involve flexibility of thought. To Peal and Lambert, it appeared that 'our bilinguals, instead of suffering from "mental confusion" or a "language handicap", are profiting from a "language asset"'. The paper marked the beginning of a shift towards more positive views of bilingualism, from language handicap to bilingual advantage. Bialystok's theory, the engine of the most high-profile and high-tension debate in bilingualism research, has powerfully rephrased the bilingual question. It is no longer about whether having more than one language is a burden for children, but about whether it is good for people's brains at all stages of their lives.[3]

Psychologists have a number of simple tests with which to measure executive functions. One is the Stroop test, devised in the 1930s, which plays on the difference between the meaning of a word for a colour and the colour of the letters that form the word. People take longer to respond correctly to the word 'blue', for example, if the letters are red. The task of the executive is to resolve the conflict between the two stimuli, the colour that is perceived and the colour that is understood. Another is the Simon test, introduced in the 1960s, which is based on the observation that responses benefit from proximity to their stimuli. If the task involves pressing a key on the left of a keyboard when a red square appears on the screen, responses will be faster and more accurate when the shape appears on the left side of the screen than when it appears on the other side from the key. Part of the executive system's task is to suppress the impulse to press the left-hand key when any shape appears on the left, regardless of whether it is the target colour or not. Similar demands are made by the flanker test, which presents an arrow flanked on each side by other arrows, sometimes pointing in the same direction and sometimes in a different one. The task requires the test-taker to focus attention upon the central arrow and disregard the others.[4]

Running through all of these tests is a theme of conflict and its control. The bilingual advantage hypothesis is premised on the idea that languages will conflict with each other if they are not controlled by the executive system. Where there is no conflict, or little, the executive will have a correspondingly modest workload, and so is unlikely to have its performance boosted by the demands of bilingualism. Such a situation might obtain when a person has two languages, one of which is spoken and the other is signed. A speaker of two languages can only utter one word at a time, so the languages are competing for a single channel. It has to be either 'dog' or 'perro', but not both. Signer-speakers can sign at the same time as they are speaking, though – and they frequently do, even when talking to non-signers. As Bialystok predicted, when people who were bilingual in American Sign Language and English took flanker tests, they showed no advantage over monolinguals.[5]

The executive control hypothesis is premised on the idea that a bilingual's languages are both activated all the time, requiring the control system to be unceasingly engaged in managing them. One finding in support of this premise emerged from an experiment in which Chinese–English bilinguals were asked whether pairs of English words were related in meaning. The Chinese equivalents of some of the pairs were related in form: the translations of 'train' and 'ham', for example, are 'huo che' and 'huo tui'. Although the bilinguals responded just as quickly and accurately to such pairs as they did to pairs whose Chinese equivalents did not have characters in common, a difference in the way they processed the two kinds of pairs could be detected from the electrical potentials that passed across their scalps. When monolingual Chinese speakers read the words with shared characters, a certain characteristic electrical fluctuation was measured. The same fluctuation appeared when the bilinguals read the equivalent English pairs, implying that their native language was being automatically and unconsciously activated.[6]

An alternative interpretation is that the potentials are a legacy of learning English as a second language, in the process of which the associations between the words were carried over from the first language and became part of the English lexicon. Part of the problem with the hypothesis of bilingual advantage based on executive control is that despite its coherence, it rests on data that are open to other readings. A more serious problem is that they are inconsistent. The advantage is capricious: sometimes it appears, sometimes it doesn't. There are even differences between the results of Stroop tests, Simon tests and flanker tests, despite the similarities in concept and design. And although the experiments may be similar, the subjects vary enormously. Bilingualism takes many different forms: people differ in their proficiencies, patterns of use, histories of language learning, and stages of life. We should not necessarily expect any effects it has on cognition to be universal. Some people might gain advantages, others not. Enhancements might only appear for certain cognitive functions and under certain conditions.[7]

Whether those conditions are to be found outside the laboratory is another question. Research into the bilingual advantage may end up providing considerable new insights into how the brain works, but it may not be possible to confirm that using more than one language provides system-wide benefits in the same sort of way that exercise produces general improvements in fitness. Even if bilingualism can boost test scores in a lab, that doesn't necessarily mean it makes a cognitive difference in real life. One place worth checking for an effect is the school mathematics classroom, maths being a subject in which executive function may have a particularly significant effect on performance. A survey of several thousand American children, aged from four to seven, found that bilingualism did indeed seem to promote their mathematical reasoning and problem-solving skills.[8]

Advantages are much harder to detect once children have grown up and gone to university, though. That could be because young adults are at their cognitive peak, mature but yet to begin their decline, and so their performance cannot be lifted any higher. Enhanced control might stand to make a real difference not at their time of life, the so-called second age, but in the first and above all the third ages. The implications would be much more compelling later in life than earlier. Children might gain enhancements to cognitive faculties they are in no danger of losing, but older adults might stand a better chance of retaining their faculties and holding off dementia, death's mocking revenge on longevity. For societies and governments, a protective effect against dementia would harness bilingualism to a major public health issue. As one research team declared, in their conclusion to a report that the lifelong use of two languages offers protection against the degeneration of brain tissue, delaying the onset of dementia 'is a top priority of modern societies'. They called for government action to support bilingual education.[9]

Ellen Bialystok and her colleagues took the first step towards making bilingualism a health matter in 2007, by reporting that bilinguals seen at a memory clinic in Toronto showed symptoms of dementia four years later than monolingual patients. Scientists had already begun to wonder whether some people were better equipped than others to withstand the pathologies that degrade mental function. A survey in the United Kingdom found that about 30 per cent of people revealed by autopsy to have mild or severe damage of the kind associated with Alzheimer's disease had nonetheless avoided its symptoms. In the United States, Sister Mary was described as the 'gold standard for successful cognitive ageing' in the 'Nun Study', which followed 678 nuns through their later years and examined their brains after they died. She lived to the age of 101, having spent her last years in the same Baltimore convent she had entered at the age of fourteen. By that time she had grown frail, and the autopsy revealed extensive Alzheimer's lesions in a small brain, yet she had appeared cognitively intact.[10]

Scientists started to talk about 'brain reserve' and 'cognitive reserve' as they considered findings like these. Brain reserve was seen as a benefit of having a large brain or a higher than typical number of neurons, providing extra neural capacity that could compensate for lost tissue. Cognitive reserve was conceived as a more active phenomenon, in which the brain countered incipient deterioration by making effective use of its systems or developing workarounds in its circuitry. This might result from mental exercise, developing cognitive fitness in the same sort of way that physical exercise develops physiological fitness. The distinctions between these phenomena are not clear-cut. Physical exercise in early adulthood appears to promote cognitive fitness later in life, for example. Cognitive stimulation may promote the growth of brain tissue in childhood, and reduce the death rate of neurons in adults. Whatever the mechanism, however, cognitive reserve can only provide one line of defence against dementia. It can delay its onset, but cannot slow its progress thereafter. Indeed, once the disease has broken through, people with higher levels of cognitive reserve are likely to deteriorate more rapidly than those with lower levels. Their brains have sustained more damage by the time its effects become manifest, and they are closer to the stage where it becomes overwhelming.[11]

If bilingualism turned out to develop cognitive reserve, that would be evidence for the power of exercise, since most people who learn more than one language do so because their lives oblige them to, rather than because they enjoy some cognitive endowment that monolinguals do not possess. All the bilinguals in the Toronto study had spoken more than one language for most of their lives. According to Bialystok's model of executive control, that would have required the continuous operation of a system to select one language and suppress the other. A practising bilingual would approach old age with well-tuned neural circuitry that might provide the resilience necessary to delay the onset of symptoms. Many people would die of other causes before the delay came to an end, so it would in effect amount to prevention. Four years, the Toronto researchers calculated, would reduce the prevalence of dementia by half.[12]

Brain scans in a Toronto hospital subsequently provided support for the reserve hypothesis, showing that bilingual Alzheimer's patients had lost more brain tissue in regions associated with the disease than monolingual patients who showed similar levels of cognitive function. The bilinguals were better able to cope with brain atrophy. Among healthy older people, lifelong bilinguals had kept their white matter, the brain's connective fibre, in better condition than their monolingual peers had. Elsewhere, neuroscientists reported that ageing bilinguals have more grey matter in certain regions of the brain than their monolingual counterparts. Similar enhancement of grey and white matter was also seen in younger bilinguals, providing anatomical evidence to support the narrative of lifelong brain upgrade through the use of more than a single language.[13]

Across the Atlantic, the theme of cognitive reserve was taken up by Thomas Bak and his fellow researchers at the University of Edinburgh. They had a remarkable local dataset that gave them a handle on the question of whether bilingualism is a cause or a consequence of good cognitive condition. The Lothian Birth Cohort 1936 study followed up 1,091 people from Edinburgh and the surrounding region who had taken an intelligence test at the age of eleven, on 4 June 1947, as part of the Scottish Mental Survey. They took the same test again at the age of seventy. None of them were migrants, and only nineteen of them had learned a second language by the time they took the first test; 243 had learned at least one subsequently, and 90 were continuing to use theirs. With the data from 1947 providing a measure of the cohort's childhood intelligence, the researchers found that learning an extra language seemed to confer some protection against cognitive decline and indeed stood out in this respect. Survey participants who engaged in other mentally stimulating activities, such as reading books, gained no cognitive protection from them.[14]

This was an advertisement for bilingualism in its broad sense: using more than one language, without necessarily achieving high proficiency in more than one, or spending equal time in each. It suggested that choosing to learn a language in adolescence or adulthood might have cognitive benefits in old age – ones that might not be attainable through other forms of mental exercise. Bak and his student Madeleine Long also conducted a study with a complementary message about the possible short-term benefits of language learning at any time of life.

They tested people taking an intensive one-week Scottish Gaelic course on the Isle of Skye, at Sabhal Mòr Ostaig, a college devoted to Gaelic language and culture. At the end of the week, the students' ability to switch their attention had improved. Control individuals who had done courses of similar intensity in other kinds of subjects, such as art or film, showed a more modest improvement. Nine months after the summer course, improvements persisted among those students who were still practising their Gaelic for five hours or more a week. They were attained by students of all ages, from 18 to 78, and all levels of previous familiarity with Gaelic. In the words of Bilingualism Matters, an international network founded by Antonella Sorace, one of Thomas Bak's Edinburgh colleagues and a co-author of the Skye study, 'everyone can enjoy the benefits of having more than one language'.[15]

The bilingual-advantage researchers had woven a compelling collective narrative, beginning in childhood and ending in old age, proposing languages as a means to support the vulnerable, young and old, asserting the value of languages in education and health, connecting science simultaneously with the public sphere and with the intimate domain of the family. It offered a way to popularise science and to popularise bilingualism in the process. Importantly but discreetly, the narrative could help people maintain their bonds with their cultures without drawing attention to those cultures, by talking instead about the educational and cognitive benefits that using more than one language might confer. But as it geared up to move bilingualism away from political controversy, the project found itself embroiled in scientific controversy.

For sceptics, the story was just too good to be true. As with the quest for the advantage in earlier life, findings were inconsistent and contradictory, for reasons that were hard to discern and even harder to agree upon. Toronto found a bilingual advantage in protection against dementia; Montreal found one for bilinguals whose first language was French but not for those whose first language was English – and also that English-speaking monolinguals were diagnosed with Alzheimer's disease five years earlier than monolinguals whose language was French. Dissonances like those between the two Canadian cities appeared all across the field of bilingual advantage research – although other findings were never quite as baffling.[16]

Much of the controversy revolves around claims that investigations fail to isolate bilingualism from other factors that might affect cognitive performance, such as education. Studies of bilingualism in the West are often vulnerable to the criticism that their bilinguals are immigrants who differ from their monolinguals in other respects than language. One suggestion is that immigrants remain cognitively healthy for longer because they are healthier overall, people in poor health being less ready or able to undertake migration. Be that as it may, studies don't have to be conducted in the West. In India it is easy to sample from populations that are both long-established and multilingual. Suvarna Alladi and her collaborators (mostly local, but also including Thomas Bak) examined the records of 648 patients who had attended the memory clinic at the Nizam's Institute of Medical Sciences in Hyderabad. Sixty per cent of them spoke more than one language, the most common combination being Telugu, Hindi and English. As a group they were better educated than the monolinguals, having twice the number of years of schooling. All but 5 per cent of them were literate, while more than 30 per cent of the monolinguals were illiterate. Speaking more than one language appeared to delay dementia by four and a half years.[17]

That result was striking not only in itself, but in its similarity to the delay of four years originally reported from Toronto. The difference between the cities was visible, however, in the patients' ages. In Toronto, the average age of the bilinguals at the time of the appearance of their dementia was seventy-five. In Hyderabad they were ten years younger.[18]

The mixture of dementias was somewhat different to those found in the West, where Alzheimer's disease typically makes up 50 to 80 per cent of cases. At the Hyderabad clinic, 37 per cent of the patients had Alzheimer's disease; vascular dementia accounted for 25 per cent of the cases, and frontotemporal dementia nearly 19 per cent. This reflects the high incidence of vascular disease in India, and lifespans that are shorter than in the West. The mean age of onset of Alzheimer's disease is around eighty; life expectancy at birth in India is around sixty-eight years. Frontotemporal dementia, by contrast, is a disease of middle age. People speaking more than one language were spared it for six years, on average. For vascular dementia the delay was 3.7 years, and for Alzheimer's 3.2 years.[19]

Hyderabad also afforded an opportunity to address another issue that besets Western studies, that of education. Bilinguals may know extra languages because they have spent longer at school than monolinguals. Any cognitive advantages might be the product of education in general, rather than of language skills in particular. Indeed, the bilinguals in the Hyderabad study had on average spent more than twice as many years in school as the monolinguals, yet the bilingual advantage remained after that was taken into account. Moreover, even illiterate bilinguals enjoyed an advantage. There were ninety-eight illiterate patients in the study, eighteen of them bilingual and eighty monolingual. More than half of them were women, and more than half were from rural areas; most had worked in crafts, such as weaving and tailoring, or skilled farming occupations. The advantage associated with being able to speak more than one language was greater than the one associated with being able to read and write. Bilingualism was associated with a delay in the onset of dementia of six years, literacy with a delay of four years.[20]

Alladi and her colleagues also found an impressive difference between the effects of bilingualism and of education in a subsequent study, which this time looked at the onset of mild cognitive impairment. They found that monolinguals began to experience it seven years earlier than bilinguals. There were no significant differences in age of onset, however, between the patients who had less than ten years of schooling and those who had more. Bilingualism appeared to delay the emergence of cognitive difficulties, but education did not. The contrast may reflect the roles that bilingualism and education play in Indian society. Bilingualism has extensive opportunities for influencing cognition, being acquired early in life and practised throughout it. Education may have less influence than in Western countries, for a lack of it is not always the same barrier to social inclusion and cognitively complex occupations that it is in the West.[21]

The implications of a bilingual advantage for poor people were highlighted by another research team, reporting their study of executive function in villagers on the other side of India. Languages tend to overlap along Indian state borders, including the one that separates Kerala from its northern neighbour, Karnataka. Speakers of Malayalam, the main language of Kerala, live closely together with speakers of Tulu, a language used mainly on the northern side of the border. The villagers in the study lived on the southern side and their native tongue was Malayalam, but the bilinguals among them had picked up Tulu in their early years. People learn it from friends, neighbours and, thanks to intermarriage between the communities, family members.

The participants were poor, middle-aged and illiterate. When they took the Simon and the flanker tests, the bilinguals among them responded faster than the monolinguals. This was a rejoinder (and by no means the only one) to suggestions that bilingualism only afforded an advantage to the already advantaged, or that what appeared to be a bilingual advantage was actually an advantage of income and status. As the researchers pointed out, speaking a second language might be one of the few sources of cognitive enhancement for these villagers, who lacked money, education and the cultural stimuli of city life. Fortunately for them, their communities encouraged it.[22]

* * * *

The doubts about bilingual advantage were a detail of a much bigger picture. Questions were mounting about the validity of data in many domains of science. They turned on the issue of replication, the practice in which researchers repeat their peers' studies to see if they get the same results. Surveys of the literature showed that they often did not. A consortium of researchers called the Open Science Collaboration replicated a hundred psychological studies. Only 36 per cent of the replications produced statistically significant results, compared to 97 per cent of the original studies, and the effects indicated by the results were mostly smaller in the replications than in the originals. Investigators raised concerns about replicability in a range of other fields, including neuroscience, genetics, medicine and economics. In the eyes of many scientists, science is undergoing a 'reproducibility crisis'.[23]

The problem, the critics agree, is a systematic bias towards the positive. Most insidiously, researchers may be tempted to select the results they want to see, and to manipulate insignificant data into apparently meaningful patterns. They may, for example, analyse it mid-way through a planned experiment and halt the study early, either because it doesn't look like producing positive results, or because the data so far support the hypothesis and the researchers decide to quit while they're ahead. Or they might subject the data to one statistical process after another until they hit on a treatment that makes the figures look significant.[24]

Another source of bias is the understandable preference of scientific journals for what journalists call stories. An article reporting something new is more of a story than an article reporting a failure to find anything. Editors are more inclined to publish reports of positive results, and researchers may not bother to submit articles reporting negative ones. Scientists regretfully bury those in their files, producing a form of publication bias known as the 'file drawer effect'. The lines of inquiry that didn't work out form a kind of anti-curriculum vitae in a scientist's archives. 'I have cabinets full of research that will never see the light of day,' Ellen Bialystok once told the Toronto *Globe And Mail*. 'You have to be flexible. You have to recognize when a path isn't yielding what you thought.'[25]

The bias towards the positive may also favour findings that are conspicuously so, especially when they are novel. Initial reports need to be eye-catching in order to get over the editorial threshold, but they are likely to be based on exploratory studies that are small in scale and so have what scientists call low statistical power. Subsequent studies, sampling larger and therefore more representative pools of data, will tend to obtain more modest results. The reported phenomena thus tend to become less impressive the more they are studied. This is known as the 'decline effect'. Once it has set in, conditions are favourable for studies challenging the hypothesis, which has lost the glow of novelty. The new story is that the now-familiar idea is wrong.[26]

Publication bias is not easy to measure, surveyors being unable to see into scientists' file drawers. They can, however, look at early public presentations of research, such as the abstracts presented at conferences, and see how much of it eventually gets published in scientific journals. Three bilingualism researchers followed up the fortunes of conference abstracts in their field that addressed questions about executive control. They found that studies unequivocally supporting the idea of bilingual advantage were more likely to enter the scientific literature than equivocal ones, which in turn were more likely to be published than ones that challenged the idea. Their paper (which itself appeared in a leading journal) also provided them with an opportunity to confess that they themselves were 'guilty' of selection bias, having 'contributed to the creation of the accepted wisdom of a cognitive advantage in bilinguals' by selecting for publication the only one of four tests that had shown such an advantage. Now that the media were publishing stories with headlines like 'Bilingual Brains Are More Healthy' and 'Why Bilinguals Are Smarter', scientific bias was affecting the public understanding of science.[27]

By that stage, however, the sceptics had got into their stride. A decline effect had settled upon the field. Leading critics counted the score and announced that more than 80 per cent of studies in the past several years had failed to find any bilingual advantage for executive functioning. The advantage did not exist, or if it did, only manifested itself in certain obscure circumstances. Looking directly at the brain was not much help either, as the images observed were similarly inconsistent and open to varying interpretations. One former enthusiast issued a critique in the form of a recantation, inviting the remaining 'true believers' to consider whether they might be mistaken.[28]

The dementia question became a secondary theatre of contest. A difference emerged between prospective studies, which follow people as they age and see what happens to them, and retrospective studies, which look at people who have already become patients. Prospective studies tend not to find that bilingualism delays dementia; retrospective studies tend to find that it does. Critics consider that prospective studies are more rigorous than retrospective ones. The people who attend clinics may not be representative of the population at large. It is better to sample a community as a whole, rather than to rely on a subset that has been selected by its own members or their relatives, through the act of seeking help from health services. Another issue is the quality of the data. People's cognitive condition can be assessed professionally at all stages of a prospective survey, identifying the onset of dementia at the time it occurs, whereas a retrospective study has already missed the event it has set out to investigate. Retrospective studies have to infer the onset of decline from when a person first visits a clinic, or from what a relative says about when they first noticed signs of impaired function. Those data don't look as smart and authoritative as the prospective ones, which are under the control of the doctors rather than the patients. That does not mean the retrospective data are spurious, however, and on such a major question of health, the findings of a four- to five-year delay in the onset of dementia for bilinguals are too remarkable and consistent to dismiss.[29]

With its headline finding, a delay of four and a half years, the Hyderabad study is right in the middle of the range, and is a show-piece of retrospective research. Even the leading critics of the bilingual advantage hypothesis acknowledge its importance. The researchers did have to obtain their information from a 'reliable family member', but they did that for monolingual and bilingual patients alike. The two groups were broadly similar in socioeconomic profile – though 20 per cent of the bilinguals were classed as professional, while just one monolingual made that grade – and largely shared a Hindu back-ground, judging by the predominance of Telugu speakers. Neither group were migrants. There seems little reason to suppose that they would have differed in the way they reported signs of cognitive impair-ment. As well as avoiding the confound of migration and accounting for the effects of education, the study underlined its point with the finding that the onset of dementia was delayed even among those bilinguals who could not read or write.[30]

In a subsequent study, Suvarna Alladi and her colleagues added the finding that bilinguals were twice as likely as monolinguals to retain their cognition undamaged after suffering strokes. They were no more likely to retain their ability to speak, however. Although it might seem surprising that the only faculty bilingualism failed to protect was one of language, that was just what the bilingual advan-tage camp would expect. It was what they had been saying for years: the advantage comes from exercising the brain's powers of control over languages, not from the languages themselves.[31]

Suvarna Alladi is a neurologist, as is Thomas Bak who collabo-rated with her on the Hyderabad studies. Bak feels that as a clinician, he has a different outlook on scientific knowledge from the sceptics. He is less concerned with methodological precision and more with the patterns he can detect in the data. In clinics, information is human and untidy. Clinicians have to accept real-world conditions. It is not possible to conduct the flawlessly designed experiments to which theoretically-minded psychologists aspire. The differences in their environments create a cultural difference between the two research communities. Ideally, the different perspectives brought to the field by researchers from different disciplines would complement each other, but against a background of epistemological crisis affecting large swathes of science, polarisation into adversarial camps seems inevitable. The frustrations of the debate are apparent in Bak's tart observation that 'some authors seem to have made their living out of inventing 100 ways of saying "no"'.[32]

Bak notes that research tends to be positive about bilingualism in countries that are positive about it, such as Canada, and negative in countries that have an ambivalent attitude towards it, the United States in particular. The prevailing climate of opinion might influence the attitudes researchers bring to their studies, the answers they expect to find, the way they interpret their data, and what kind of research proposals are likely to find favour with funding bodies. It could also affect how bilinguals perform in tests. If the dominant view surrounding them is that their bilingualism is a disadvantage, it might stifle advantages that would be visible in more sympathetic conditions.[33]

The contrast with attitudes to education is telling, Bak suggests. Everybody agrees that education is a good thing – and nowhere more so than in academia. 'After all,' he points out, 'education is our profession, our mission and, to a large extent, our raison d'être.' Everybody welcomed reports that education may counter dementia. Some studies qualified that message, finding that the benefits only manifested in certain circumstances, or varied from country to country. Yet those qualifications did not shake the belief in education as a protector of the brain. In striking contrast, Bak claims, 'any study not showing a "bilingualism effect" was readily taken as a proof that the whole idea is a "myth"'. If a study showed a possible benefit from bilingualism, and a link between bilingualism and education, it was assumed that the credit for the benefit was really due to education. 'In other words: if a study did not find an effect of bilingualism, the problem was with bilingualism. If a study did not find an education effect, the problem was with the study.'[34]

Bak asks whether the benefit of education upon cognition in later life is 'just a myth that we like to believe because it provides us with one more argument for the importance of schools and universities?' That, as he affirms, is not his message. But if we are talking about what we like to believe, we should ask the equivalent question about bilingualism. Although everybody agrees that education is a good thing, a lot of that agreement is lip service, and there is widespread suspicion of people who are felt to have too much of it. Health, on the other hand, is unequivocally and unarguably a good thing. It is certainly the best possible good thing as far as bilingualism is concerned. If you argue that the use of more than one language binds communities closer together, or supports people's senses of identity, you are likely to provoke resistance, resentment and even rage in some quarters. But if you can establish that bilingualism is good for the brain, especially when that organ is at its most vulnerable in the later stages of life, nobody will be able to say a word against you.

When Kenneth Paap, Hunter Johnson and Oliver Sawi declared in the journal *Cortex* that the bilingual advantage in executive functioning probably does not exist, they began by stating their belief in the advantages that bilingualism confers 'across a host of personal, economic, social, and cultural dimensions'. Their article was accompanied by a series of responses from other researchers in the field. Commenting on these, Paap and his colleagues noted that only one, Virginia Gathercole, had mentioned the sociopolitical overtones of the debate. She recalled how political ideology and scientific opinion had converged in the United States during the early decades of the twentieth century, with nationalist sentiment insisting that immigrants renounce their native languages for English, and psychologists inferring from immigrants' results in intelligence tests that bilingualism interfered with mental activity. 'One unspoken issue' in the debate, Gathercole observed, was concern that the 'positive press' enjoyed by bilingualism thanks to the advantage claims might be sent into reverse.[35]

In other words, researchers believed that bilingualism was valuable for reasons other than the possibility that it confers cognitive advantages. Only the most trenchant critics of the advantage hypothesis seemed to feel obliged to say so, in this session of the debate at least. Supporters of the hypothesis might feel less able to affirm such beliefs in public, because it could lay them open to suggestions that their values had biased their science.

If the data had been more obliging, and the idea of a lifelong bilingual cognitive advantage had won a consensus among researchers, advocates of plural language use would have felt they had been dealt a trump card. They would be able to insist that obstructing bilingualism threatened children's cognitive development and denied the elderly respite from the onset of dementia. With the high ground captured, there would be no need to continue the trench warfare over community and identity. Except, as we know from the issue of climate change, public debate doesn't work like that. No matter how overwhelming a scientific consensus is, it will be furiously denied by those who feel threatened by its social and political implications. Language simply cannot be separated from people's ideas about who they are, who others are, and how relations between them should be organised.

A case in point is Falcom, the online commenter, who described the idea of learning a second language to counter the effects of ageing as 'this science twaddle'. The climate is becoming increasingly conducive for such reactions. Science's 'reproducibility crisis' can only fuel the kind of scepticism that encourages lay people to think that their opinions, however inexpert or uninformed, enable them to dismiss scientists' claims as twaddle. The scientific process is supposed to purify knowledge, raising it to a plane above human biases, ambitions and weaknesses. If that process doesn't work, and subjective bias is part of the fabric of scientific knowledge, then science's claims to epistemological superiority are gravely compromised. Scientists are no better than the rest of us, the sceptics will gloat.

Falcom's premise was that the brain can only hold so much information; the proposition was that English speakers are better off filling their limited neural storage space with 'our rich culture' (as represented by Shakespeare, Dickens, Keats and Wordsworth). A second language is 'a luxury we certainly don't need and [we] can put that space to better uses'. In form this is a folk neuroscience argument, framed in utilitarian terms; in content it is a claim about exceptionalism and cultural superiority. It is based on confidence that English speakers don't need another language as an instrument of communication, and that other cultures don't contain anything valuable enough to make allocating them brain capacity worthwhile. The first belief may be true enough, given modest ambitions and shrouded horizons. The second resembles the rhetorical question 'Why go abroad, when there's so much to see in this country?' Once commonplace, it is not heard so frequently now that, from many parts of Britain, going to Prague is quicker and cheaper than going to Penzance.[36]

Belief in monolingual advantage, based on sentiments of belonging and assumptions of sufficiency, will always defy any empirical evidence science may offer. Scientists can certainly assure people that there is ample room in their heads for extra languages as well as whatever fragmentary souvenirs remain from their school English literature lessons. But the true monolingual believers will not waver in their conviction that when it comes down to it, the language they speak is the best one.

* * * *

Executive control is not the only kind of brain activity that could be affected by the use of more than one language. Differences between languages may lead to differences in how their respective speakers apprehend the world. People who know more than one language may perceive things differently in each. Although the effects may be subtle, they may be consequential.

CHAPTER SIX

Speakers In Search Of An Endpoint

> *Different languages may affect thought differently, and they certainly shape the relationships among their speakers in different ways.*

ASPECT

One day a native German speaker and a native Spanish speaker went for a walk in the English countryside, in the north-western county of Cheshire. Suddenly, to their surprise, they were addressed by a disembodied voice, which turned out to be issuing from a loudspeaker. It informed them that they had trespassed onto the Duke of Westminster's estate, and should leave it by walking across the field diagonally. This baffled the German, so the Spanish walker pointed to a path across a field, at the far side of which a church was just about visible. After studying the scene for a few moments, the German realised what was intended: 'You mean walk towards the church?'

Two language researchers, Panos Athanasopoulos of Lancaster University and Manne Bylund of Stockholm University, happened to be with them. Curious about why one walker had understood the instruction but the other had not, the two professors launched an investigation into whether the reason lay in differences between the walkers' native languages.

They obtained the walkers' permission to use the incident in their research, but undertook to protect their identities. When Professor Athanasopoulos related the anecdote in a talk about 'learning to think in another language', he adhered to his undertaking scrupulously. His story caught my imagination, but gave me scant details with which to visualise the scene. In their absence, the past – or rather, an imagined storybook past – came irresistibly to mind. Scholars from different corners of Europe, peregrinating through English countryside, their discourse suddenly interrupted by a command to get off a nobleman's land: the scene seemed to belong to days of yore.

And who else should be right there in the middle of it, but the Elizabethan occultist John Dee? The disembodied voice: that was just the kind of trick he would pull. As a student at Trinity College, Cambridge, he created a special effect for his production of Aristophanes's play *Peace*, in which the central character appeared to fly up to the Palace of Zeus, located below the roof of Trinity College's hall, upon a giant scarab, or dung, beetle. Dee travelled widely across Europe, conversing with scholars from Leuven to Kraków in Latin, their lingua franca. It was in Kraków that he and his medium Edward Kelley conducted the 'scrying' sessions, seeking contact with angels, that yielded much of the data on which his descriptions of the Adamic or divine language was based. Earlier in his career, before he took up his magic crystal in search of revelation, he saw potential in the analysis of earthly sources. He was persuaded by the arguments of the scholar Guillaume Postel that human languages were the corrupted descendants of the language of divine creation, and that the secrets of the sacred language could be revealed through the study of the forms of Hebrew letters. Postel reasoned that Hebrew was the least corrupted language, being ancient and therefore closest to the original. If Spanish and German were to be ordered according to this line of argument, Spanish might be considered purer, being closer to its ancestor Latin, a language of antiquity.[1]

Being modern scientists, Athanasopoulos and Bylund did not consider that as a possible explanation for why the Spanish speaker understood the instruction but the German speaker did not. Instead they surmised that the native German speaker's confusion might have arisen from differences in the ways in which languages represent the unfolding of events in time. These differences turn on the distinction between events that are bounded, by beginnings or ends, and ones that do not have bounds placed upon them. Completed events are bounded; ongoing ones are unbounded. This is a distinction in what linguists call aspect. In English, it determines the choice between 'is' and 'has', '-ing' and '-ed'. 'They are walking' is an example of progressive aspect, in which the action has no bounds placed on it; 'They have walked' illustrates perfective aspect, in which the action is completed and therefore bounded by an endpoint in time.

Other languages also mark aspect in their grammar, sometimes going to remarkable lengths to do so. Sesotho, spoken in South Africa and Lesotho, has fifteen aspectual forms. Russian and Polish verbs sort themselves into pairs, one of each being used for unbounded actions and the other for bounded ones. When it comes to motion, Polish divides unbounded actions into ongoing and habitual ones, with entirely different verbs for the two classes. A Polish speaker might use the verb iść to describe a one-off or a particular walk across a field, and the verb chodzić when talking about a walk regularly undertaken. A German speaker, however, does not have any such options. While the Germans' Slavic neighbours appear to have organised more or less their entire inventories of verbs around aspect, German has managed without any grammatical means to mark bounds to events or their absence. It's hard to imagine why two neighbouring language communities, with broadly similar cultures, environments and ways of life, should have taken such different approaches to speaking about time and motion ... unless this is one of those cases in which peoples purposely shape their languages so as to increase the differences between themselves and their neighbours.[2]

As Athanasopoulos, Bylund and other researchers have found, the effect of imbuing a verb with progressive aspect is to draw the listener's attention to the action itself, and away from its beginning or end. It encourages the listener to be in the moment, creating a habit of conceptualising events without bounds in time, and a tendency to zoom in on actions, leaving the beginnings and ends of the actions outside the field of view. These habits are reinforced whenever speakers, listeners and readers are obliged to take account of aspect, which is all the time.[3]

Conversely, languages that do not load their verbs with aspect promote broader attention that takes in the whole scene. Since information about a movement's course through time is not contained within the verb, speakers and listeners will be induced to look around for it. They will take a broader view of the event as a whole, scanning the scene to identify its bounds in time, and thus taking a particular interest in where the movement is likely to end up. A speaker of Spanish, which marks progressive aspect, will find it easier to grasp an instruction that specifies what they should do but not when they should stop doing it – 'leave by going diagonally' – than a German speaker, whose grammar does not include progressive aspect. The German speaker grasped the instruction when the Spanish speaker pointed out the church, which the German speaker could then interpret as a destination.[4]

If they hadn't been able to identify a finishing point, they might have imagined one. Shown movement in video clips that contained possible endpoints but finished before these were reached, and asked to describe the sequences, German speakers were inclined to tell stories with endings that they inferred from what they had seen. Not only did they mention endpoints more than English speakers, but they differed in their whole style of narration. Describing the events of an animated film, English speakers rode the progressive aspect, speaking in the moment – 'he's looking around, he's scratching his head, he's blinking again' – and tending to speak of actions as ongoing rather than complete. German speakers stood back and reviewed the scenes, paying more attention to the outcomes of actions – 'he wonders how he should get back down from there . . . now he has again discovered water'. The English thus gave running commentaries, updated every couple of seconds, whereas the Germans provided summaries at longer intervals, omitting minor details that the English were inclined to report. A similar contrast can be observed between English and German TV football commentaries: English commentators keep the air filled with speech, whereas their German counterparts are under less obligation to say something about every single movement, regardless of its significance.[5]

You might surmise that this has something to do with the German habit of leaving the verb to the end, which might increase the interval before a speaker feels ready to comment on an action, but speakers of Norwegian and Swedish share German speakers' inclination to attend to endpoints, although they introduce their verbs earlier on in their sentences. Norwegian and Swedish also lack aspect, as does Dutch. Speakers of languages in which aspect is more of a feature, including Arabic and Russian as well as Spanish and English, are less likely to refer to endpoints. The Czechs seem to be an exception, speaking an aspect language like Russians but looking for endpoints like Germans. Their language appears to have been influenced by its German neighbour. In the light of aspect, we can see how a single strategic difference in grammar might colour whole streams of speech and place speakers of different languages in different relationships to the events they are describing.[6]

These alternative dispositions can also be found within individuals who have a language of each kind at their disposal. Bilingual speakers of German and English place more weight on endpoints when they are using German to assess scenes of motion than when they use English. Native English speakers learning German place more weight on endpoints as their grasp of German strengthens. The more that speakers of isiXhosa, a non-aspect language, have been exposed to English, the less attention they are likely to pay to endpoints. And Swedes who watch a lot of English-language TV tend to pay attention to the ongoingness of scenes, rather than to the endpoints that their native language favours. Manne Bylund and Panos Athanasopoulos detected the effect by showing students three video clips of things or people in motion, and then asking which of the first two the third most closely resembled. Some of the first two clips depicted endpoints, such as a car driving into a garage, and others showed scenes without endpoints, such as a car driving along a road; in the comparison clips, the presence or absence of an endpoint was not so clear. Swedish students in Stockholm were more inclined to base their judgements on the presence of endpoints than a group of their English counterparts in England. But the more English-language TV they watched, the more English they were in their judgements, giving less weight to the presence of endpoints. Bylund and Athanasopoulos suggest that movies and TV programmes made in English may not only say less about endpoints in their scripts than ones made in languages without aspect, but also show less of them in their scenes. Their visual grammar may reflect the grammar of their language.[7]

Not only do speakers of non-aspect languages pay more attention to endpoints when talking about what they have seen, they spend more time looking around their field of view for them. Perhaps that is only to be expected, though, when people are looking with a view to speaking about what they can see. Anticipating the need to report upon a scene, people may examine it for information that fits the grammatical framework in which it is to be placed. This is known as 'thinking for speaking', an expression coined by the linguist Dan

Slobin. As he observed, 'one fits one's thoughts into available linguistic forms'. Although one can find a way to say anything in one language that can be said in any other, there is rarely good reason to spend time and effort constructing utterances that listeners may not readily understand. Conversely there is often very good reason to evaluate a situation and make an easily grasped statement about it as quickly as possible, particularly when it includes expressions of motion such as 'coming this way', 'falling down', or 'get out'. Even when the message is not itself urgent, thinking for speaking has to be done quickly. Grammar lends itself to rapid thought because it provides ways to communicate that are highly familiar, largely automatic and easier than looking round for words.[8]

To find effects of grammar upon the way people talk about events is to show language having effects upon language. In that respect, language affects thought. But does language affect thought beyond the thoughts that are put into words? Does language create habits, such as attending to endpoints, that spread into other domains of mental activity?

One step towards finding out involves giving people tests that do not require them to describe what they see. When shown video clips of motion and asked to identify screenshots from them, German speakers looked at things that might be endpoints, such as buildings in the distance, more often than Arabic speakers did. Their eyes seemed to be guided by their tongue, even though it was not in use.[9]

The German endpoint preference also showed up in electro-encephalograph recordings made during a study in which speakers of English and speakers of German were shown minimal, schematic images of motion, in which dots moved towards geometrical figures. But although experimenters can detect variations in their volunteers' brain activity, they still cannot know what the people they test are really thinking. Perhaps the subjects are putting their thoughts into words and allowing language to exert a hidden influence on how they make their choices. Although the second-long animations were designed to be difficult to think about in words, and the people shown video clips of real-world scenes were also required to pay attention to loud beeps, hindering them from devising conscious strategies to tackle the task, these experiments did not entirely exclude the possibility that language was at work on the inside.[10]

To frustrate any such occult activity, Panos Athanasopoulos and Manne Bylund ran experiments along similar lines to the ones in which they detected the effect of television on attention to endpoints, showing people video clips of motion scenes and asking them to judge similarities between them. Swedish speakers paid more attention to endpoints than English speakers in one of these experiments, but the difference between the groups vanished when the experimenters asked their subjects to repeat strings of numbers while watching video clips of motion scenes. This verbal load seemed to prevent the subjects from using language to help them remember the scenes while they made their comparisons. When they were unable to draw on language, the Swedish and English speakers appeared to think alike.[11]

Athanasopoulos and Bylund perceived common ways of seeing in their English and Swedish speakers, affected but not overridden by differences between the two languages. The effect of language, they suggested, is to fine-tune, rather than shape, perceptual processes 'that are likely to be universal and unchanging'. But fine-tuning is a process that makes a significant difference. And as the incident that set off their investigations showed, malfunctions of understanding caused by subtle differences in tuning can leave a person baffled about which way to turn. Apparently inconsequential differences may have real consequences in the field – all the more so because they will generally pass unrecognised for what they are. You can't expect a couple of professors of bilingualism to be on hand to witness them.

AGENCY

The writer Ariel Dorfman was born in Buenos Aires, then taken by his parents at the age of two to live in New York. There he swiftly abandoned his native Spanish, spending his childhood in English until he was twelve, when the family returned to the Southern Cone of South America. He spent his adolescence in Chile, speaking Spanish and rejecting English as decisively as he had previously rejected his mother tongue.

Dorfman was sixteen when he first came to feel that he was not just speaking Spanish, but having his habits subtly 'infiltrated' by the language. One day in a carpentry class he struck his bodged wood-work construction with his hammer once too often, and it broke. That's what he told the teacher with a shrug: 'Se rompió.'

This incensed the teacher – not the breakage, but the usage. 'Se, se, se,' he hissed. 'Everything in this country is se, it broke, it just happened, why in the hell don't you say I broke it, I screwed up. Say it, say, Yo lo rompí, yo, yo, yo, take responsibility, boy.' Even in distant retrospect, Dorfman betrays a hint of reluctance to do that. He remarks that 'Spanish was beginning to speak me.'[12]

Later, he would find himself in rooms filled with smoke and endless political discussion, himself filling with frustration aroused in part by the use of passive and impersonal forms, provided and encour-aged by the language, which people would use to talk about what should be done instead of actually doing anything. They evidently didn't share the woodwork teacher's conviction that what was wrong with the country was se, the monosyllable that enabled a national abdication of moral responsibility.

More dispassionate evaluations have suggested that the teacher had a point. Spanish speakers in general seem to be drawn towards se: towards what happens, and away from who or what makes it happen. Se takes the focus off agency. Its use implies that who or what does something is not especially important. The familiar sign 'se habla español', which is reasonably translated as 'Spanish spoken here', assumes that what matters is that Spanish is spoken, not who speaks it. Se is used when the agent is unknown, and also in speaking of involuntary physiological phenomena that are beyond the speaker's control, such as 'se me hace agua la boca', 'my mouth is watering'.

Unsurprisingly, children and foreigners take time to get the hang of all the ways in which this 'multiply ambiguous' item can be employed. The young Ariel Dorfman, re-entering his first language, used the basic construction 'se rompió', 'it broke'. Spanish speakers can also describe such an event in a way that binds them into it but does not necessarily implicate them as the cause of it. They could say 'se me rompió', which can only be rendered nonsensically or awkwardly in English: 'it broke to me', 'to me it happened that it broke'. Anybody who is not an on-duty linguist is just going to translate it as 'it broke'.[13]

Se is not all about me, though. Spanish speakers use it to avoid pointing the finger. In particular, they use it to distinguish accidents from intentional acts. An inclination among Spanish speakers not to ascribe blame for accidents became evident in a study that compared the way Spanish and English speakers described such events. Shown videos of events made to appear either intentional or accidental – such as a man deliberately breaking a pencil and looking pleased, or a man breaking a pencil while writing and looking surprised – the two groups described the intentional acts similarly, noting the agents of the acts equally often. They differed, though, in their descriptions of accidental acts. Spanish speakers noted the agents of accidental actions less often than English ones did (and the overwhelming majority of their agent-free descriptions were constructed using se). They also differed in their memory for accidents. When asked who had performed the actions they had seen in the videos, Spanish and English speakers remembered the agents of intentional acts equally well, but the Spanish speakers' recollection of who had done things accidentally was not as good as that of the English speakers.[14]

Whether through accident or intention, these differences between languages and their speakers could have consequences. The implication of this study – which the researchers replicated with Japanese speakers instead of Spanish ones, and found a similar pattern – is that members of some language communities may recall details of accidents less well than others. These are the kind of findings that need to be rigorously tested by scientists before they get into the hands of lawyers. Accident and intention are not as clearly separated in real-life cases as they were in those experiments. Acts may look accidental but actually be deliberate. Moreover, accidents may be culpable. In cases where establishing the facts could determine whether charges are brought or defendants convicted, lawyers may well be on the lookout for arguments to suggest that some witnesses are less reliable than others.[15]

A much more pervasive risk, and one that is actual rather than conceivable, revolves around the translation of testimony. Police interviews of witnesses or suspects are investigations intended to answer questions about who did what and why, not seminars in comparative linguistics. Interpreters are there to provide instant translations, without commentary or caveats, in forms that the interrogators can understand and use. A real-life example from California illustrates the problem: an English-speaking police officer asks a Spanish-speaking homicide suspect, 'Okay, you said before that she fell or you dropped her on the steps?' The interpreter translates the question, to which the suspect replies 'Sí, sí, se me cayó', in which 'cayó' means 'fell', not 'dropped', and 'se me' means 'it happened to me', not my fault. Yet the interpreter tells the officer that the suspect said 'Yes, I dropped her.'

'Dropped' could be accidental, but it could also be intentional, whereas the suspect's answer represented the event as an accident.

The translation introduced a bias into the course of the interview – and failed to clarify whether the suspect said he dropped the victim accidentally or deliberately, even though the officer asked the question nine times in all. Yet this bias could quite easily have itself been unintentional. Luna Filipović, the researcher who analysed this and some 10,000 other pages of Californian police interview transcripts, observes that 'I dropped her' is the most natural and typical way to describe such an occurrence in English. Under pressure to play an efficient part in the process, the interpreter is likely to reach for the phrasing that comes most readily to hand.[16]

Too much rests on the interpreter in this situation; on their skills, their sensitivity and their good faith. Spanish is spoken in some 30 per cent of Californian homes. The more that law enforcement officers are able to understand what people are saying in such an extensively spoken minority language, and to converse with them in it, the better they will be able to protect and serve the community. They don't all need to sound as if they learned it from their mothers or passed an exam in it at the highest grade. A measure of useful familiarity can go a very long way. The interpreter may still be needed, but if the officer can understand something of the language, they will be able to form their own impressions about the person whose speech is being translated. If the interrogator hears 'se' and has a sense of how it is used, that will help them to understand the stance the suspect is taking. In the interview that laboured over the difference between 'dropped' and 'fell', a grasp of se could have mitigated the interpreter's distortion of the suspect's response. And it might have spared the officer from having to ask the question nine times.[17]

EVIDENCE

It took Sümeyra Tosun a while to work out why she felt there was something wrong when she spoke English. After graduating in psychology, she left her native Turkey to continue her studies in the United States. She got the hang of city vernaculars well enough to understand New York subway conductors, and passed an English proficiency test. But all the same, she felt there was 'something missing'. Something was putting her in an uncomfortable position. It was making her feel that she was being untruthful most of the time.[18]

Eventually she realised what it was. Turkish obliges its speakers to specify whether information is first-hand or not, by attaching suffixes to the ends of verbs: di or variants thereof for first-hand information, miş or variations of it for information that is not first-hand. Tosun had never paid any mind to this grammatical requirement before, but when she ventured into a language that lacked it, she felt its absence as unease.

She availed herself of the options that English offers instead of obligations in respect of information sources, conscientiously applying qualifiers like 'apparently' and 'as far as I know' to her statements. Other Turkish speakers do the same, Dan Slobin observes. 'My Turkish friends and colleagues speak fluent and beautiful English,' he writes, 'but when I listen carefully I note an abundant use of expressions like "apparently" and "it seems". These are perfectly grammatical and contextually appropriate, yet their abundance can sometimes be pragmatically unsettling. I wonder why the speaker is hedging so frequently.' Slobin adds that he finds himself doing the same on returning to English after a spell of speaking Turkish. The obligation is still felt, even in a language where it is merely an option. And its effects can still be unsettling even when, like Tosun and Slobin, one has insight into their cause. Tosun cannot help but miss the Turkish suffixes when speaking English. 'If I use a simple past tense, I feel like I'm lying,' she says.[19]

She does not feel suspicious of native English speakers, however: they are just using their own language, after all, and its grammar does not cast any doubt on their honesty. Nor does she feel that using words like 'apparently' is 'gross and intrusive' compared to modifying verbs, as speakers of Turkish-influenced languages have been reported to do. But it sounds very wrong to her when she hears people using the first-hand form in Turkish to speak about events they could not possibly have witnessed, such as things that happened in their parents' childhoods. Such errors, she explains, are made by people who have learned Turkish as a second or additional language, and have not grown up with its rules concerning what linguists call evidentiality.[20]

Having finally identified the cause of her unease, she made it the subject of her doctoral degree, which she researched at Texas A&M University. She found that while Turkish and English speakers were equally good at recognising first-hand information they had previously been shown, and identifying it as first-hand, Turkish speakers were not so good at recognising second-hand information, or identifying it as second-hand. For Turkish–English bilinguals who had grown up with both languages, it depended on which one they used. They performed like Turkish monolinguals when tested in Turkish, recalling information less well if it was presented as second-hand, and like English monolinguals when tested in English. But the later the Turkish–English speakers had begun to learn English, the worse they were at recalling second-hand information in the second language. Late Turkish–English bilinguals performed like Turkish monolinguals.[21]

Evidential grammar is not a peculiarly Turkish phenomenon. A quarter of the world's languages have it. In the Balkans, languages such as Bulgarian and Macedonian acquired it under Turkish influence during the centuries of Ottoman rule. The Turkish version, with one suffix for directly-witnessed events and another for all other kinds, is at the basic end of the range. Tariana, an endangered language spoken by around a hundred people in the north-western Amazon region of Brazil, distinguishes between events that have been seen, events that have been heard, inferred events, events assumed to have occurred, and ones learned about from somebody else.[22]

The Turkish miş suffix can mean much more than 'not seen or otherwise known for certain'. It is used to express surprise, for example when an adult meets a child whom they haven't seen for some years, and cannot help but exclaim 'You've grown so much!' It is also used when recounting dreams, which are direct and visual experiences but not real, or other narratives of the imagination, such as folktales, jokes and pretend-play games with children. Doubled, mişmiş, it signifies third-hand information, heard from somebody who heard it from somebody else, and also indicates scepticism: 'I'm telling you what I heard, but I don't believe it really happened.' And it can also be used to disclaim culpability, by implying that an action was accidental rather than deliberate, in much the same way as the Spanish se. For Sümeyra Tosun, the various ways of employing miş are all forms of the same basic function, which is to put distance between the speaker and the speech.[23]

That will also put distance between listeners and what they hear. Tosun's Turkish speakers discriminated between first-hand information and information from other sources. They were more inclined to neglect the latter, implying that they treated it as less valuable than the kind that has come straight from the horse's mouth. The grammar of their language seems to have installed a heuristic that tells them to assign priority to first-hand information, and to devote fewer mental resources to other kinds.

She also found that they set more store by inference than by hearsay, which also suggests that first-hand information comes first, even when it is incomplete. Everyday inference is based on what people see for themselves – the grass is wet, so it must have rained last night; the fans are celebrating, so their team must have won; the car is outside, so the neighbours must be at home. It is based on believing one's own eyes.

Her investigations echo the experiments in which Spanish and Japanese speakers recalled the details of accidents less well than English speakers, suggesting that members of different language communities may not be equally reliable witnesses. Tosun's experiments are ambivalent in their implications about whether Turkish speakers might be more accurate in their recollections than English speakers, or vice versa. Court cases revolve around events that may have been directly witnessed by more than one person, or by many people, then talked about by people who didn't witness them. By the time a witness takes the stand, their body of memory about the incident may be largely filled with scenes from news reports, remarks they have heard and tweets they have read. If Turkish speakers tend to forget information that is not first-hand, they may base their testimony more solidly upon their own recollections than English speakers would. On the other hand, if Turkish speakers are not as good as English speakers at remembering whether a piece of information is second-hand, they might be more prone to mistake bits and pieces from the mass of second-hand information for elements of their own experience.

Newsreaders use first-hand markers, Tosun observes, even though they are speaking about events they have not personally witnessed. By doing so they convey certainty, vividness and authority. Certainty has a powerful appeal. It is efficient. If you receive a message you can be sure of, you need spend no additional effort verifying it. But people do not always accept what the authorities tell them. In the Andes, a variety of Spanish has developed under the influence of Quechua and Aymara, pressing one of its past tenses into service to mark evidentiality in imitation of the indigenous languages. Speakers of Andean Spanish sometimes reject texts written in standard Spanish, which in their view neglect attention to sources, and demand to know what sources news reports are based on.[24]

Grammar is only one genus in the complex ecosystem of trust, though. It is easy to conjecture that people high in the Andes, far from the bases of power in their country, distanced from them by way of life, heritage, language variety, and one of the world's most formidable mountain ranges, might take issue with the referencing of sources as a way of articulating a general alienation from authority. Conversely, it is easy to infer that a population largely trusts its broadcasters if they accept that the default mode for news reports is the first-hand form.

Given a sufficient degree of trust, a speaker may not even need the first-hand form to be believed. In July 2016, elements of the Turkish armed forces attempted to overthrow the government of President Recep Tayyip Erdoğan. Watching from abroad, Sümeyra Tosun was surprised to hear the president using mostly second-hand forms in his addresses to the nation, which began with a video call to a mobile phone held by a television presenter and then transferred to more conventional modes after the coup attempt collapsed. She offers several possible reasons for his choice of suffixes. The most straightforward is that a lot of the information he received was indeed second-hand, because the conspirators launched the putsch when he was on holiday. He might also have wanted to convey his surprise about an event that came out of the blue. Or he might have wanted to distance himself from the intelligence failure that left him and his government so surprised by the attack. A person of lesser prestige would not have made much of an impact using miş suffixes, Tosun suggests. But then, she observes, people tend to believe the president whatever he says.

* * * *

Aspect, agency and evidentiality are just three features of language in which hints of an influence on thought can be perceived. They are not even the features most wrangled over during the decades of argument about whether speakers of different languages see the world differently, one of the theatres of the war between those who want to affirm humanity as universal and those who want to affirm humankind's diversity. This is the collection of ideas labelled the Sapir–Whorf hypothesis, after its originators Edward Sapir and Benjamin Lee Whorf. One of its most captivating notions was Whorf's argument that speakers of English and speakers of the Native American language Hopi have deeply different concepts of time. That claim was later subjected to re-examination and criticism – some of it collegial, some of it bordering on caricature – but a new, circumspect and restrained 'neo-Whorfianism' has established itself as a source of questions for empirical research.[25]

In the area of motion, the difference that investigators have found most compelling is between languages whose verbs express the manner of movement and those whose verbs carry information about its path. Whereas an English speaker might say 'the ball rolled out of the box', for example, a Spanish speaker would say 'la pelota salió de la caja rodando', which is roughly equivalent to 'the ball exited the box rolling'. The place of manner seems more secure in the English sentence than the Spanish one, where manner only puts in an appearance at the end, and looks as though it might quite easily drop off. Findings concerning whether speakers of manner languages pay more attention to it than speakers of path languages are, predictably, inconclusive.[26]

What does seem clear by now is that nobody is going to demonstrate any radical differences that nobody else would then dismiss. If they exist, the effects of language upon thought must be subtle and individually small. The psychologist Steven Pinker, vexed by researchers' refusal to stop looking for such effects, dismisses them as 'mundane'. Being subtle and small does not necessarily mean being insignificant, however. Individual pixels don't catch the eye, and the patterns they form may not be noticed, but cohering together they change the picture.[27]

To Pinker, though, language is not a screen but 'a window into human nature, exposing deep and universal features of our thoughts and feelings'. Any feature that alters the view must therefore be a flaw in the glass. And it must be minor, for large alterations would distort language's relationship with thoughts so much that speech would become unusable. His preoccupation is with the universal – and with affirming, against competing relativist claims, that there is indeed a universal human nature. But it doesn't have to be a choice between either and or.[28]

For the past half century and more, the headline topic in these debates has been that of how languages divide the visible light spectrum into colour categories. Its major statement was delivered by Brent Berlin and Paul Kay in their book *Basic Color Terms: Their Universality and Evolution*, which appeared in 1969. Some languages have only two terms, one for black and one for white; others, including English, Japanese and German, have eleven, by Berlin and Kay's count. Russian distinguishes between light and dark blue; many languages lump green and blue into a single 'grue' category. On one side are Berlin, Kay and others who see a common pattern underlying these variations, arising from the neurophysiology of the visual system; on the other are those who find exceptions that prove languages can organise themselves without reference to biology, like so many humanities scholars and social scientists.[29]

In recent years, however, some researchers have begun to put together a story striking a welcome balance between perspectives that should never have been set against each other in the first place. Language can affect the processing of colour signals coming in from the retina: Russian speakers can discriminate between two shades of blue more quickly if they are on different sides of the boundary between 'goluboy', light blue, and 'siniy', dark blue, than if both fall within either of the two categories. The effect depends on language, disappearing if the speakers are required to allocate their language-processing capacities to unrelated verbal tasks. But colour categories are not solely products of language. Babies a few months old distinguish between blue and green. They react more quickly to targets presented against a different coloured background – a green dot on a blue field, for instance – than to targets that differ from the background in hue but not category, such as a lighter green against a darker green.[30]

This happens only when the targets appear in the left visual field, which is processed in the right hemisphere of the brain. In adults, it's the other way round. They react more quickly to images that cross colour category boundaries when these appear in the right visual field, which is handled by the left hemisphere. That is also the half of the brain where, in the large majority of individuals, the bulk of language processing takes place. The shift from the right to the left hemisphere can be observed in toddlers as they learn words for colours. It looks as though language overlays categories already created by neural architecture – in many cases fusing green and blue into grue. As one paper puts it, Whorf was half right: right about half the brain, and half right about where colour names come from. It is not a matter of either universal or local, but of both.[31]

Why should this be so difficult? In many quarters there is a deep resistance to any claim that elements of human thought are the product of a universal human nature. This has been compounded by the model around which the colour debate has turned. Brent Berlin and Paul Kay loaded not one but two trigger words into the subtitle of their book: universality and evolution. They argued that languages followed a particular evolutionary sequence in adding words for basic universal colour categories, up to the maximum of eleven that they identified. That jarred with scholars whose prime anthropological directive forbade any suggestion that some cultures might be superior to others. With its overtones of progress towards increasing levels of sophistication, it seemed like an unsavoury throwback to a discredited way of thinking.

What Berlin and Kay proposed, however, was an account in which the prevalence of colour terms shed light upon the priorities the visual system assigns to different parts of the spectrum. If a language had a term for one other colour besides black and white, for example, that colour was invariably red. There are two issues here: the value of perceiving colours in categories, and the value of having words for those categories. The two are not necessarily linked. Under many conditions of life, being able to see a colour may be a vital ability, but being able to put a name to it may be an irrelevance. It is very easy to make plausible conjectures about why naturally evolved colour categories might be valuable. The assessment of potential food is an obvious example. If fruits look green when unripe and red when ripe, or leaves look green when fresh and yellow when dying, it is a lot easier to identify food that is good to eat than if the differences are merely points on a spectrum. At the same time, it is equally easy to see how people who eat what they gather or grow might have very little need for words to label the colour categories they perceive. Even if they needed to point out the state of food plants to others, what matters is not the colour as such, but whether the fruit is ripe or the leaves are rotting.

Appreciating this becomes easier still if we recognise that we do not have to tell ourselves that 'this fruit is red' or 'these leaves are green'. People can think such thoughts without putting them into words. But we use words to help fix our thoughts in consciousness, and so that is how we tend to remember them. It becomes tempting to think that thought is only thought if it is formulated using language. Our inner commentary is only part of our thought, but many of us take it to be the whole thing. Thoughts that we do not phrase are swirling clouds and fireflies, more than likely to be beyond us as soon as we have thought them. Not only is it hard to recover them, but it is hard to recognise them for sure as thoughts, distinct in character from other mental phenomena such as sensory impressions or images in the mind's eye. Yet thought without language is possible. Some people think in images instead. 'I have no language-based thought,' wrote Temple Grandin, who has been described as a 'rock star in the seemingly divergent fields of animal science and autism education'. 'Language and words are alien ways of thinking for me. All my thoughts are like playing different tapes in the videocassette recorder in my imagination. Before I researched other people's thinking methods, I assumed that everybody thought in pictures.'[32]

The preoccupation with thinking is another reason why the significance of differences between languages seems so difficult to bring into focus. Framing the issue as the relationship between language and thought has two major consequences. One is that it shifts attention away from language as a means of communication and a constitutive property of a community. The second, following from the first, is that the data will be biased towards the stuff of thought, which is the small stuff. Experiments may reveal traces of differences in thought that are measured in milliseconds. These will tend, as Panos Athanasopoulos and Manne Bylund put it, to be fine tuning. We should not discount the possibility that pinpoint differences have pervasive consequences. Pixels dotted across the screen, subtly altering image after image, may transform the picture even if the viewer is unconscious of the difference. The data themselves will be about micro-effects, though, and consequently modest. But when researchers look at communication, such as the re-telling of recollections about who did what, or the distortions of translation, significant and potentially consequential differences quickly come into view.

The most arresting assertions about the true purpose of language have come from Noam Chomsky, who transformed linguistics by claiming it from the scholars who had hitherto dominated the discipline. Their modus operandi was the collection of data about individual languages, but Chomsky dismissed the details as trivial. 'A Martian scientist,' he observed, 'might reasonably conclude that there is a single human language, with differences only at the margins.' The task of terrestrial scientists is therefore to elucidate the universal grammar of language. It is a modernised, secular reinvention of the vision of an interior truth within language, an original core disguised by local deviations, that inspired the occultist John Dee. When Chomsky's book *Syntactic Structures* appeared in 1957, the anthropologist Chris Knight observes, it 'excited and inspired a new generation of linguists because it chimed with the spirit of the times'. Language could now be studied as a cognitive module, a neural machine or computer, rather than by going to live in people's villages and filling notebooks with details of their speech. Detached from traditional anthropology, linguistics 'would at last qualify as a mathematically based science akin to physics'. The 'cognitive revolution', spearheaded by Chomsky and driven by the idea that mental processes can be treated as forms of computation, rapidly spread through psychology and philosophy too.[33]

Chomsky's understanding of science excludes not only social sciences but the entire shared human experience of which language is part. Chris Knight makes a persuasive case that Chomsky performed this radical amputation because of his need to maintain his institutional base at MIT while pursuing his left-wing political commitments. To separate his science from his politics, he separated language from society. One result was his egregious declaration that 'language is not properly regarded as a system of communication. It is a system for expressing thought: something quite different.' Certainly it can be used for communication, he allows, 'as can anything people do – manner of walking or style of clothes or hair, for example'. As far as Chomsky is concerned, observes Knight, language 'exists for talking to just one person – *yourself*'.[34]

Chomsky is out on his own there. Even his fellow MIT universalist Steven Pinker has rejected the claim that language is not a system of communication, along with many other elements of Chomsky's later theorising. As a communicative act, the proposition appears as much as anything to be an assertion of dominance: 'My

intellect is so formidable that I can make such preposterous statements with no fear of provoking rejoinders that might undermine my
status.' It also serves as an auto-caricature of the tendency to look
inward, rather than outward, for effects of language on thought.[35]

There is a range of ways in which different languages might induce
their speakers to see the world differently. At the most immediate
and literal level, they may intervene in the processing of signals from
the eye. With colour categories this may happen in a tenth of a second,
before the viewer is conscious of what they are viewing. In the most
expansive sense of seeing, the metaphorical kind, they might promote
different worldviews. We have tentative data about the literal kind of
seeing, and elusive notions about the metaphorical kind. At the latter
end of the range, the all-embracing term 'worldview' takes us back-
wards rather than forwards, effacing the important distinction
Wilhelm von Humboldt drew between Weltansicht, the organisation
of experience into concepts, and Weltanschauung, which is closer to
'worldview' in the sense of a belief system or ideology. Humboldt's
thought emphasised Weltansicht, everyday world-processing, but
worldview, Whorf's term of choice, encourages grander pretensions.[36]

Worldviews, however, are what this is all about, and what it has been
about all along. 'Every nation speaks . . . according to the way it thinks,
and thinks according to the way it speaks,' declared the eighteenth-
century philosopher Johann Gottfried Herder. He regarded language
as 'the tool, the content, and the form of human thoughts', to the extent
that 'in ordinary life it is indeed apparent that thinking is almost
nothing more than speaking'. Since languages differed from each other,
it followed that their speakers thought in different ways. Isaiah Berlin
identified Herder as the 'father' of the notions of nationalism and the
Volksgeist, the conviction that each people, Volk, has its own unique
spirit, Geist. As Berlin noted, Herder was one of the leaders of the
Romantic revolt against Enlightenment universalism. This revolt
became a permanent revolution: in that respect the eighteenth century

shows little sign of drawing to an end, though science is now providing material that offers a way out of it.[37]

The preoccupation with thought is perhaps easier to understand if we recognise it as a long-standing tradition with origins in philosophy. But there is so much more to the diversity of languages than thinking, or seeing. Language is social or it is nothing. Above all, it is a means of forming, conducting and comprehending relationships. Its effects on thought are disputed. Its effects upon the relations between people are indisputable.

* * * *

A conversation may proceed satisfactorily in various directions, as long as the people having it do not reverse away from each other. After exchanging tokens of positive disposition and respect, they will try to find topics and styles of conversation that tend to reduce the distance between them. They may arrive at a mutually agreeable equilibrium of informality; they may in some cases pursue an ever closer connection; but what they don't want to do is draw closer and then step sharply back.

In Britain and America they are likely to start half way down the road. First-name terms have become the default, honorific titles discarded. We've barely shaken hands and we're already addressing each other with a degree of familiarity that our grandparents, or parents, used to reserve for friendships that had been established for many years. And even they were informal by comparison with large numbers of foreigners, since English does not bother to differentiate between polite and informal modes of address. It used to, but abandoned the distinction several hundred years ago. The English aristocracy copied the French polite plural in the Middle Ages, casting 'you' as the distanced form and 'thou' as the familiar one. By the middle of the seventeenth century, 'you' had driven 'thou' out of standard English altogether – possibly because middle-class people now comprised an increasingly influential section of society, but were unsure where they stood in relation to each other, and so felt safer using the polite form to avoid the risk of giving offence. 'You' now covers the entire second person, singular and plural, close and distant.[38]

This presents me with a difficulty and an immediate source of anxiety when I'm introduced to a Pole in Britain, and in English. If the conversation proceeds agreeably, I will feel increasingly uncomfortable that it is not in Polish. That might be inconsiderate to the person with whom I'm speaking, since switching would oblige them to put up with my sketchy grammar and limitations in vocabulary. The main thing that keeps me speaking English is not considerateness, though, but the Polish default mode of address. Unlike English, other languages have retained alternatives within the second person – tu and vous in French, tú and usted in Spanish. German has du and Sie, the latter distinguished by context from the third person plural. Polish has a close second-person form, the pronoun for which is ty, but for distanced address it reaches beyond the second person. By default one addresses people as if in the third person, using honorific titles, in the manner of a pre-war English butler inquiring whether Sir will be dining tonight.

I can't help but feel that going from first names to the third person is a sharp step back. Not only do I find myself going back the best part of a century for a comparable English usage, but it is hard to imagine such an abrupt change of tone occurring within an English conversation unless triggered by a mortal insult or a grossly offensive remark. I also find it difficult to shake off the feeling that we have stopped looking at each other, and are now looking past each other.

This is not because the usage is foreign to me. I've been using it my entire life. The problem does not arise if I meet a Pole in Poland and in Polish. (The polite form is losing ground there in any case, and it's not unusual to be fast-tracked onto 'ty' terms at the start of a conversation.) It arises when the context does not firmly determine the language, opening up a choice between two languages that place their speakers in markedly different positions relative to each other.

Although the choice carries an unambivalent emotional charge as far as I'm concerned, its implications are not inevitable. Switching to a formal mode may actually assist the process of reducing conversational distance – or rather, establishing the optimal distance – if one of the speakers feels more comfortable using it. Sümeyra Tosun observes that while she is not perturbed by English speakers' lack of obligation to indicate their sources, she does feel that the absence of a polite form of address is an obstacle between her and English-speaking acquaintances. Being fluent in another language is not always the same as being at ease in it.

The speakers are not the only people implicated in the conversation. Choosing a language is a manoeuvre that adjusts one's relationship not just with the person one is talking to, but with the larger speech community of which they are part. It is a claim to enter that community, even if only as a guest. But correct usage may only get you so far, as I realised during a Polish conversation in which I was addressed as 'Pan', 'Sir', by a native English speaker. Her usage was appropriate in Polish terms, but both I and the native Polish speaker in the conversation found it very odd. It didn't feel like a step back, or a cooling of disposition, but there was something inauthentic about it, like pretending we hadn't previously met. As native English speakers, our acquaintance was based on a familiarity that persisted across languages and could not authentically be translated into the terms of the other one. Socially, we were part of the English speech community, whatever language we were speaking.

Languages can shape relationships not just by presenting different modes in which people can speak to each other, but by presenting different categories that people can use to speak about their relationships with each other. English is casual not only in its grammatical indifference to formality, but also in its indifference to degrees of friendship. A friend in English can be anything from an acquaintance to an intimate. People may apply some discrimination at the distant end of the range, often to disclaim friendship – 'She was just an acquaintance'; 'I've met him in the past, but I wouldn't call him a friend.' Within the category of friendship, though, differentiation is optional. Sometimes we will make a point of saying that someone is a close friend, or a good friend, or a dear one, but we are not obliged to – and in many if not most contexts we would risk sounding like we were overdoing it. Russian speakers, by contrast, are obliged to select from three or four degrees of closeness when referring to a friend. 'Drug' signifies deep friendship, with mutual trust, reliance and devotion. The term 'podruga' is often used in describing female friendship that is close but not as deep as the kind signified by 'drug'. An ordinary friend is a 'prijatel', if male, or 'prijatelnica', if female; and then there is an outer orbital band of friendship denoted by 'znakomyj' and 'znakomaja', which translate as acquaintance but are somewhat warmer than that.[39]

As with so much about Russia, these divisions seem impressive but daunting from a British point of view. They imply an emphatic quality to friendship that contrasts with a certain lack of confidence about it in many parts of British society. What if we had such categories? It's bad enough when romantic feelings aren't reciprocated. How awkward it would be if there was a mismatch in friendship classification; if somebody put you in the dearest class, but as far as you were concerned, they were just a friend.

English speakers are not, of course, prevented from forming deep friendships by the absence of a distinct category for such relationships in their lexicon. There is no reason to presume that close Russian friendships are deeper than English ones. But the existence of categories must affect people's understanding of their social networks. As the great psychologist William James observed, having names for things may make those things seem more different than they would if they were not assigned by their labels to different categories. He offered the example of claret and burgundy wine, which may be hard to distinguish the first few times they are encountered, but settle into stable categories as they and their names become more familiar: 'The names differ far more than the flavors, and help to stretch these latter further apart.' James went on to recall that he had recently been struck by an odd-looking kind of snow, which he dubbed 'micaceous', perceiving a resemblance to the mineral mica, 'and it seemed to me as if, the moment I did so, the difference grew more distinct and fixed than it was before'. Assigning our friends and acquaintances to categories of closeness – 'drug', 'podruga', 'those who are to be addressed using an honorific form' – must inevitably sharpen the distinctions we perceive between them, drawing the close closer and pushing the distant further away.[40]

As well as defining relationships between self and others, categories provide valuable detail about relationships between other people. In an English conversation, A may only learn that B knows C, D and E. In Russian, A becomes aware as soon as they are mentioned that B is merely acquainted with C, is a midrange friend of D's, is very close to E, and so on. With friendship categories, people's mental maps of their networks are more informative and less ambiguous than they would be if friendship were not routinely sub-classified. They will know more about what people are to each other, with a greater degree of confidence. Or at the very least, they will know more about what people say they are to each other.

'Drug' is also a term of address, allowing a person to affirm their closeness not just to third parties but to the individual concerned. The act of affirming the deepness of a friendship may have the effect of deepening it further. English, by contrast, is woefully short of equivalents. In Britain and Australia, males have instead the all-purpose 'mate', which is protean enough to signify affection, fellowship or merely a non-threatening disposition towards strangers construed as approximate social equals. As the linguist Anna Wierzbicka points out, you're unlikely to call somebody 'my friend' in English if they really are your friend. It tends to make the hackles rise. English is liberally stocked with terms of endearment, but they are ambiguous through and through. 'Dear' and 'darling' can be sincere or insincere, or camp expressions that are sincere while pretending that they aren't, or the reverse. One can be addressed as 'love' by an intimate, a close relative, or a complete stranger.[41]

This is not to suggest that anybody addressed as 'love' in a shop will mistake it for an expression of affection. People don't have to rely solely on labels to understand where they stand in relation to each other. But it is to illustrate that differences in the representation of relationships pervade languages at a range of levels and degrees of forcefulness. Modes of address are not determined by grammar, but norms of distance are powerful and can be intimidating. (Although they are usually described as 'formal' or 'polite' modes, those terms are not always apt. Poles, for example, may use the 'polite' form when insulting each other – 'Pan jest idiotą'; 'Sir is an idiot'.) As well as imposing internal order, they may present a daunting obstacle to outsiders – especially ones learning Korean, who are faced with seven levels of formality, though they may not encounter all of them in practice. Informal terms of address set traps of their own for unwary speakers who are not as attuned to the unwritten rules of conversation as they think they are.

* * * *

There are countless points of possibly consequential difference between languages. People may be oblivious to them, or peripherally aware of them, or all too painfully conscious of them. Pinning down the details of whatever effects they may have, and evaluating the impact of those effects, is one of those projects that will probably always be in search of a consensus. But in one respect, as the Cuban-American writer Gustavo Pérez Firmat points out, 'the ultimate validity of the Sapir–Whorf Hypothesis is not relevant'. Bilinguals themselves often believe that they think differently in each of their languages, or feel differently, or behave differently with other people, or see the world differently. 'What may not be true for Spanish and English in any objectively demonstrable way may be true for an individual's apprehension of Spanish and English,' Firmat observes. 'Although the notion that Spanish is more "passionate" or "baroque" than English may not stand any sort of rigorous test, individual writers or speakers, believing this to be so, may use the two languages in ways that make it true for them.' If you believe that you think differently in different languages, then you do.[42]

∗   ∗   ∗   ∗

The search for objective evidence about the possible effects of languages upon thought leads to the question of subjective experience. What does it feel like to be bilingual?

CHAPTER SEVEN

Being Somebody Else

Being bilingual often seems strange to bilinguals themselves.

People with more than one language at their disposal often feel that they have extra selves to explore as a consequence. In the largest survey of its kind, more than a thousand of them were asked 'Do you feel like a different person sometimes when you use your different languages?' Two-thirds answered 'Yes'.[1]

This was nothing like a representative sample of the world's multilinguals. It was recruited through the internet, and distinguished by strikingly high levels of education. A third of the respondents had doctorates. Most worked in professions closely bound up with language, such as teaching and translation. The results revealed little or nothing about how, say, transcontinental lorry drivers or migrants in domestic service feel when they use their different languages. But they were intriguing and suggestive precisely because the respondents were so strongly attuned to language. The most sensitive souls are the most sensitive instruments.

For some of those who answered the questionnaire, feeling different was a natural consequence of a change in culture and manners. Speaking a language entailed adopting the style of behaviour that went with it, in dimensions such as attitude, tone of voice, gesture, posture and direction of gaze. Each verbal language has its corresponding body language. It also has a characteristic set of associated norms, assumptions and conversational preferences, arising from the culture with which it is intertwined. 'Language and culture are a package,' observed one respondent, Louise, a speaker of English, German, French, American Sign Language and Lakota. Anna, whose languages are Greek, German, English and French, commented that if she spoke English in the 'very lively and very expressive' manner in which Greek people speak, it would lead (and often had led) to misunderstandings.

With his characteristically breezy scepticism, the linguist John McWhorter has suggested that the whole phenomenon is simply an effect of inadequate knowledge. People feel like different people not because bilingualism has magical powers of transformation, but because they have learned a second language as adults and are not as adept in it as they are in their mother tongue. They feel like people who are less witty or more blunt than their usual selves because their command of the subtleties of the language they are speaking is limited. It is easy to imagine that a person clocked speaking English at 145 words per minute felt different when he switched to American Russian and slowed down to 59 words per minute.[2]

Jean-Marc Dewaele, one of the authors of the questionnaire, checked this proposition against the survey data. He found no relationship between the age at which a person acquired a language and the likelihood that they would say they felt different in it. Some did say that their limitations in speaking a language made them feel different, but statistically the association between levels of proficiency and feelings of difference was insignificant. Those who remained monolingual until after they reached the age of three were not significantly more likely to report feeling different than those who had acquired more than one language in their first two years of life. So far from being merely a side-effect of limited fluency, the feeling of being a different person is as likely to cast its spell over people whose entire experience of personhood has been in more than one language as it is to affect those who do not enter a second language until they are long since out of the cradle. That is a measure of the power, and strangeness, of the phenomenon.[3]

The sensation of feeling different in another language may arise because people experience different feelings in it: the emotions evoked by words may not be the same in degree or quality. A mother tongue is likely to be more steeped in emotion than a language learned in a classroom many years later. Mother-tongue taboo words, such as swear words, have more force than their equivalents in second or subsequent languages. So do other words that induce alarm, fear and shame in childhood. The enduring power of reproof was demonstrated upon Turks living in the United States, most of them in their twenties, who had learned English after the age of twelve. Reprimands such as 'Don't do that!', 'Go to your room!' or 'Shame on you!' were delivered in Turkish and English, on screen and by a native speaker in a 'lightly admonishing tone'. In Turkish they induced a jolt to the nervous system (as measured by a momentary increase in the electrical conductivity of the skin) but had little effect in English. After the tests, several of the participants mentioned that the reprimands had evoked memories of family members uttering those words – presumably in anger.[4]

A language that fails to arouse emotion may seem inauthentic to the person speaking it, who may feel inauthentic in turn. 'I don't feel quite real in German sometimes,' commented George, whose first language is English. Federica, an Italian woman living in England, feels 'as if my voice is not coming from me'. Another Italian in

England speaks of using emotions 'as an actor would do'. People sometimes think that they take on a different persona when they move from their first language to a later-learned one. 'I feel I'm acting a part,' said George.[5]

One or two feel more strongly than that. They talk not about feeling like a different person, or adopting a persona, or playing a part, but about being somebody else. 'Speaking a different language means being a different person belonging to a different community character type emotional type,' declared Marina, who speaks Russian, English, Hebrew and Ukrainian. 'I am a different person, I have different emotions, I also use a different name when speaking English,' says an Italian woman living in the United States. 'It's like someone else is speaking this language . . . as if I have a different "self" co-habiting my mind.'[6]

The ways in which people describe the sensation of differentness vary according to the quality of the experience, its intensity, and the frameworks, often precarious, that they construct to analyse it. Marina reaches for the categorical certainties of a traditional Herderian model, sorting humankind into peoples, assigning to each an essential spirit that is intimately bound up with its defining language. This rigid order does not admit identities that cross boundaries, and therefore implies that speaking different languages means being different people. George and Federica retain the sense that they have a single self, but whereas George also retains a sense of agency, feeling that he is acting a part, Federica experiences a paradoxical alienation from her own voice. People who live in more than one language often struggle to describe and explain the sensations that arise from moving between them. They welcome being asked if they feel different in different languages, though, because they have asked themselves the same question. In this sense it is undoubtedly a real phenomenon. But is it more than a subjective one? Can observers detect any signs that languages activate changes in behaviour or personality, or alterations of the self?

If a later-learned language is less deeply embedded in a person's emotions than their cradle language, it might induce them to think more dispassionately than they otherwise would, and tone down the emotional colour of their decisions. The psychologist Daniel Kahneman speaks of 'thinking, fast and slow': either in a fast, emotionally accelerated mode, essential for when rapid assessments and decisions are needed, or in a more reflective, detached mode, which may be necessary to address complex problems or to avoid bad consequences from impulsive choices. Choosing to think things through, rather than reacting instinctively or acting upon feelings, is a key responsibility of the brain's executive control system. It might have an easier job in the environment of a late-learned language, where the atmosphere is thinner and clearer. An alternative explanation is that the extra cognitive load imposed by a foreign language might put the brain into the slow-thinking mode, which it would also apply to the other matters it had to address. These possibilities are not exclusive, and may be complementary.[7]

Psychologists expect people to be loss-averse, even when rational calculation indicates that they are likely to end up better off by taking a risk. They mostly prefer to be sure of keeping a dollar than to take a fifty-fifty gamble in which they will either lose it or win two dollars. This bias against loss can be revealed by the way in which problems are framed. Daniel Kahneman and his collaborator Amos Tversky asked subjects to imagine a scenario in which 600 people faced death from a new disease, and to choose between two alternative programmes for countering the epidemic. The subjects' choices were steered by how the consequences were presented. If they were told that one of the options would save 200 people, they were much more likely to favour it than if they were told 400 people would die despite it, although the two accounts describe the same outcome. When Tversky presented the problem to a group of public health professionals – the kind of people who make decisions about how to respond to real epidemics – he found that they were also prone to the bias against loss. So were American, Korean and Arabic-speaking students tested more recently by bilingualism researchers, when presented with versions of the scenario in their native languages. Their biases disappeared, however, when they were tested in other languages of which they had knowledge: Japanese or French for the Americans, English for the Koreans, Hebrew for the Arabic speakers. Foreign languages enabled them to evaluate the problem more objectively.[8]

Using an alternative language can give you a clearer idea of where your own interests lie, too. American students were readier to gamble their own money on a toss of a coin when the game was played in Spanish – 'cara' instead of 'heads', 'cruz' instead of 'tails'. With their aversion to losses diminished, it was easier for them to calculate dispassionately that they were likely to end up better off than they started. Foreign languages can also help gamblers avoid their most fatal bias, that of excessive optimism, when they hit a lucky streak. If you toss a coin, the odds on it coming up heads are fifty-fifty. If it comes up heads six times in a row, the odds on it coming up heads on the next throw are still fifty-fifty. One toss of a coin can have no influence upon the next, so the probabilities for each throw are the same. Nevertheless, people are intuitively reluctant to admit that six heads in a row are merely a succession of coincidences. When we see a pattern, especially an improbable one, our intuition whispers that it must be the work of an invisible hand – the kind of player you would be a fool not to bet on. People are not so vulnerable to the illusion of the lucky streak if they are distanced from their emotions by a foreign language, though. When told in English that they had won an even-odds gamble, Chinese speakers were less ready to bet in the next round than when they were told in their native language.[9]

The belief that luck is more than just luck extends far beyond gambling and forms the basis of many diverting superstitions: good luck to find a four-leaved clover, or to encounter a black cat in Britain;

bad luck to walk under a ladder, to break a mirror, or to have a brush with a black cat in mainland Europe. Asked how they would feel about superstition-triggering experiences such as walking under a ladder on the way to an exam, Italian students were less troubled when the scenarios were presented in English or German than when they read them in their native language. As with the Chinese gamblers, the foreign languages seemed to disconnect them from their emotions, and hence their susceptibility to superstitions. A broken mirror made a less vivid image when evoked by a foreign language than by a native tongue. Imagination may be dimmed by foreign languages, which do not connect to the memories people use to create new mental images; feelings and choices may be less coloured by emotion in consequence.[10]

Using a foreign language may affect how people perceive uncertainties in the public sphere as well as the personal one. Asked to rate features of modern life such as air travel, pesticides and nano-technology in terms of their risks and benefits for Italian society, Italians assessed risks as lower and benefits higher when tested in English than when they used their native language. Language choice may also have an influence upon moral dilemmas. In the 'trolley problem', philosophy's most popular thought experiment, a runaway trolley is hurtling down a track towards five people, who will die if it strikes them. You can save them by pulling a lever to divert the trolley (or tramcar, as it would be called in Britain) onto another track, where it will hit one person. People generally agree that this is the morally correct choice, since one person will die but five will be saved. Told that the only way to stop the trolley is to push somebody from a bridge onto the track in front of it, however, they are less sure. Actually pushing someone would feel like killing them in a way that pulling a lever would not, although the effect is equally fatal in each case – and what an act feels like may carry more weight than what its result is.[11]

Choosing in a foreign language, without the emotional embedding of a native tongue, people are readier to take the utilitarian view.

Presented with the lever option, a group of more than 700 Spanish and English speakers were equally likely to make the utilitarian decision, to pull the lever, whether they were speaking their native language or the one foreign to them. Asked about the footbridge option in their own language, four-fifths of them declined to push the man off, but nearly half were prepared to do so when asked in the foreign language. Emotion seemed to be implicated in the difference. Further investigation suggested that people make more utilitarian choices not because using a less familiar tongue induces them to deliberate more slowly and carefully, but because it muffles their emotional reactions to breaches of categorical rules such as 'killing people is wrong'.[12]

Rules and social norms are embedded in native languages. If people are disconnected from their mother tongues, they may be disconnected from channels to personal memories that are the source of powerful sentiments about right and wrong, such as those Turkish speakers' uncomfortable childhood recollections that were triggered by hearing reprimands such as 'Shame on you'. Another study presented Italians with scenarios involving acts that people recoil from, but find it difficult to say why. They felt it was wrong for a man to eat his dog after it had been run over and killed, but they felt it was less wrong when they were told about it in German than when the example was given in Italian. The investigators observed that the responses were those of people 'guided by a muted intuition', rather than of people transformed into cold-eyed utilitarian calculators by the use of a foreign language.[13]

These researchers also remarked upon the possible importance of the 'foreign language effect' in international bodies such as the United Nations and the European Union. Discussions within such organisations are generally conducted in a lingua franca, usually English. Most participants will therefore be speaking a language foreign to them, and so may be less strongly in touch with their moral sentiments than they otherwise would. They will also be professionally skilled in rational calculation. The result may be to make international co-operation somewhat more utilitarian than national endeavours. This hypothesis offers a compelling explanation (though far from the only one) for a phenomenon subsequently observed as the United Kingdom negotiated its exit from the European Union. Britain, speaking English and only English, based its decisions on emotions and found itself in disarray. The twenty-seven countries on the other side, speaking English among themselves, achieved a remarkable degree of coherence, based on a clear understanding of their collective interests.

* * * *

Regarding personality, psychologists are confident of two things. One is that it is basically stable. However long we live, we end our lives with more or less the same personalities that have taken shape by the time we enter adulthood. Our behaviour may change profoundly between different stages of our lives, but the temperament that under-lies it will remain recognisable as what it always was. Anxious people will always tend towards anxiety, though they may become calmer as time goes by, or circumstances change; calm people will tend to stay calm, though their composure is unlikely always to remain unruffled. A glass-half-full person is unlikely to turn into a glass-half-empty person, or vice versa. The other is that personality can be resolved into five dimensions, known as the Big Five, or by the acronym OCEAN – Openness, Conscientiousness, Extraversion, Agreeableness and Neuroticism. Psychologists have conducted extensive statistical anal-yses in order to demonstrate that ratings on these dimensions are objective measures, as distinct from judgements of character.

A person is more than their personality, but if that broad constant appears to alter, then it is tempting to say that they seem like a some-what different person. In a study of Mexicans and Mexican Americans in Texas, California and Mexico itself, people scored more highly on Extraversion, Agreeableness and Conscientiousness when responding in English than when they were tested in Spanish. Conversely, they scored lower on Neuroticism in English than in Spanish. At first glance, it looked like a clean sweep for prejudices about friendly, hardworking Americans and lazy, temperamental Mexicans. But bilingualism itself appeared to promote Extraversion, Agreeableness and Conscientiousness, since the bilinguals' scores on those scales were consistently higher than those of monolingual English speakers in the United States and monolingual Spanish speakers in Mexico. The Mexican bilinguals were more American, stereotypically speaking, than the Americans themselves. Bilingualism also appeared to inhibit Neuroticism, which was lower in bilinguals than in monolinguals. People presented different personalities when using different languages – and possibly had personalities different from those they would have had if they only knew a single language.[14]

Many of the people who took part in the study had immigrated to the United States, or were the children of immigrants. They had probably acquired a considerable understanding of how America expects the self to be presented, and responded to those expectations when placed in a linguistically American environment. Some of them might just have been putting on an American face, but living in America is likely to have had a deeper effect on most of them. Culture helps to shape personality; living in two cultures may create a personality with a shape more complex than one formed within a single culture. If the two cultures have different languages, each one may leave different parts of the shape in shadow.

Languages encountered in childhood make a deeper impression than ones learned later in life, but even late encounters can influence the expression of personality. A study of late learners in Berlin – native German speakers who had learned Spanish as adults or in adolescence, and native Spanish speakers who had learned German at similar ages – found that personality scores aligned with the language of the test, rather than the subjects' native tongues. When the tests were given in German, both native German and native Spanish speakers scored more highly on Agreeability; when the tests were in Spanish, scores on Extraversion and Neuroticism were higher for both groups. As in the American study, Spanish appeared to encourage neurotic and disagreeable responses, while German appeared to discourage them. German contrasted with its transatlantic English cousin, however, in that it seemed to make people less extravert than they were in Spanish.[15]

These results offer only limited support for lurking stereotypes of orderly Germans and volatile Latins. Native German and native Spanish speakers did not differ in Conscientiousness or Openness. And it was not as though they were on neutral ground, either. In Berlin, German is the public language, and Spanish a foreign one. For native speakers of both languages, German was the language of work, bureaucracy and study (almost all the native Spanish speakers were students). That may have inclined them to give more co-operative, agreeable responses when using it.

People may not always show themselves in what, to others, is their best light. Even though they may be capable of expressing their personalities fluently, their styles may be cramped by their cultures. The researchers who compared the expression of personality in Spanish and American English were disconcerted to find that Spanish was associated with lower levels of Agreeableness than English. After all, the quality known as simpatía is valued as a characteristic of Hispanic, Latin American and especially Mexican social life. It involves being friendly, likeable, easy-going, polite, and of course sympathetic. As the researchers remarked, 'Simpatía can be thought as the Spanish term for Agreeableness.'

They came up with an explanation for the 'paradox': simpatía requires modesty, so 'for Hispanics to present themselves as agreeable would itself be disagreeable because it would denote arrogance'. In Spanish, they would talk themselves down – but they would tend to behave more agreeably than their words would suggest. To test this explanation, Nairán Ramírez-Esparza and her colleagues showed video recordings of Mexicans speaking either in Spanish or English and asked observers to rate how agreeable the speakers seemed. The sound on the recordings was muted, and none of the observers even realised that two different languages were being spoken. Going solely on what they saw, they judged the speakers as more agreeable when the language was Spanish. Without knowing it, they affirmed the Mexicans' simpatía.[16]

All the people who took part in the Berlin study were multilingual, with some knowledge of at least two European languages besides their native tongues. They therefore met the European Union's target for language capacities, as did about a quarter of the EU's citizens at that time. That raises the question of how they differed from the other three quarters, and in particular the 46 per cent who were unable to hold a conversation in any language but their own. Income levels and social class are obvious candidate factors. But if we are wondering whether languages can have effects on personality, we should also ask whether personality can affect the likelihood that somebody will use more than one language.[17]

In the American study, bilinguals were more agreeable, more conscientious, more extravert and less neurotic than monolinguals. It is certainly possible that bilingualism made them so, but it is also possible that their personalities helped them to become bilingual. Agreeableness, conscientiousness and extraversion are just the kind of traits that would help a person to learn a language and then to speak it. Neuroticism is a measure of anxiety, depression and hostility, a combination of qualities that would tend to have just the opposite effect.

Personality traits might also influence whether people feel that languages are affecting their personalities – though so far we have few clues as to which traits might influence people's feelings, or in which direction they might influence them. Among a collection of adult English speakers learning French, it was the introverts who were more likely to feel different when speaking the new language. With a sample of Poles living in Ireland and England it was the other way round: the more extravert, agreeable, open and emotionally fluent of them were somewhat more likely to say that they felt different when speaking English. The investigator in this latter study speculated that people with high levels of emotional and social skill may notice subtle alterations in their own personalities and behaviour that occur when they switch to a second language, whereas people who are less sensitive to feelings, their own and those of others, may remain unaware of such changes in themselves.[18]

However subtle the alterations may be, they are significant to the bilinguals who experience them. Observers can confirm their experience by detecting changes in behaviour accompanying changes of language. On both the inside and the outside, though, the causes of feeling different remain elusive.

✳ ✳ ✳ ✳

Even if moving from one language to another does not make you feel like a different person, it may make you feel as though you are in a different place. According to Elen, a Welsh–English bilingual, speaking the mother tongue is 'like being at home with all the familiar worn and comfortable clutter around you. Speaking the second language is like being you but in someone else's house.'[19]

Coming from a Welsh speaker, the metaphor of a house is ambivalent. In what is after all supposed to be the United Kingdom, one would hope that she felt English also belonged to her, even if only as a second home. On the other hand, if a person is in someone else's house, they are usually welcome there. The image is basically reassuring. It keeps the person within a comfort zone.

In that respect, it understates languages' powers of transport. Passing into another language may be more like entering a great city than visiting a single house within it. The experience may be comparable in magnitude to becoming a different person, even though the individual is under no illusion that they have turned into somebody else. It may be especially dramatic if the person is immersed in a sea of the language – if, for example, they actually have entered a great city where it is spoken. A conversation with a single person may have just as profound an effect, though. For human beings, language is a major and defining part of their environment. Moving from one language to another entails a change of habitat that may be like crossing from one continent to another. As with intercontinental travel, there will be those who take it in their stride, but others will feel it throughout their being.

That may be because they are imperfectly adapted to the environment they have entered. Uncertainty intensifies attention, which expands perception. If you don't speak a language very well, you have to concentrate. Precisely because you are not fully inside it, your awareness is heightened. You attend to details that you would overlook in your dominant language. You turn expressions this way and that, in order to gauge their tone and meaning. You keep what you hear and say under continuous surveillance. Unfamiliar terms and usages create a constant stream of novel stimuli, which are what keeps the nervous system lit up. When reading, you are forced closer to the text, peering at it and searching for handholds. An hour spent in an uncertain language is like a day spent in one's dominant tongue. Immersion is imperious and exhausting. For an undertrained executive control system, it's just too much. Three days in Poland, speaking only Polish, and when I see one of eastern Europe's signature birds in a field through the train window on the way back to the airport, I find myself thinking 'bocian' rather than 'stork'; three days later, I find Polish replies coming to mind in English conversation.

More proficient bilinguals will not have to work so hard or pay such close attention. Their consciousness will not be heightened by uncertainty. On the other hand, they will be able to experience the alternative language environment in higher definition. They will perceive the forms and the details more clearly than those for whom the scenes around them are partly blurred, scrambled or invisible. The differences in tone, texture, style and significance will be readily legible to them, in the same way that the textures, contrasts and details of an urban quarter will be richly appreciated by a visitor who has lived there in the past, knows its history, has a decent understanding of architecture, and has no need of glasses.

Either way, whether a person's degree of fluency is entry-level or near-native, it opens up the possibility of transformative experience. The ability to toggle between two languages is about as near as one can get to being in two places at once. And above all, a knowledge of more than one language – even a highly unbalanced knowledge – creates an awareness that in different languages, a myriad details of the world are different. Sometimes conscious, sometimes tacit, sometimes hovering discreetly in the background, this sense of alternatives can be a powerful stimulus to look at the world from different perspectives, and to appreciate that others do too.

Not that bilingualism is unalloyed enlightenment, though. For many people, the experience is not one of fluid cosmopolitanism, but of intrusive contradiction that can never be properly resolved. Introducing an anthology of essays by bilingual writers about their languages and their selves, Isabelle de Courtivron highlighted remarks strikingly similar in imagery and sentiment to those collected by Jean-Marc Dewaele and Aneta Pavlenko in their internet survey of bilingualism and emotion. As among the survey respondents, a sense of inauthenticity was apparent. Vassilis Alexakis felt like an actor watching himself in a dubbed version of a film. Ilan Stavans compared his experience to borrowing another person's suit. Nancy Huston opened her chapter in de Courtivron's anthology with the dramatic declaration that anybody who chooses to leave their native land for one with an unfamiliar language and culture will for the rest of their life 'be involved in *theatre, imitation, make-believe*'. Some writers take the trope further, making inauthenticity a matter of bad faith. Ariel Dorfman calls migrants like himself 'wandering bigamists of language'. The French-Argentinian novelist Héctor Bianciotti says that bilingualism compels us to lie.[20]

As if from higher and clearer air, the critic George Steiner claims to 'experience my first three tongues as perfectly equivalent centres of myself'. He speaks and writes English, French and German with 'indistinguishable ease'; he dreams with 'equal verbal density and linguistic-symbolic provocation in all three'. Gustavo Pérez Firmat finds the equivalence of the centres a little too much to swallow. 'I'm impressed,' he admits, 'but I do not quite believe him.' Firmat questions how the centres could have remained in perfect balance under the pull of the forces in Steiner's early life. As a child, Steiner migrated from the old world to the new; from Paris, where he was born, to New York. If his parents had not taken the family across the Atlantic when they did, ahead of the German invasion of France in 1940, he would almost certainly have been dead by the end of the war. He was thus relocated from the country of one of his centre-languages, French, to that of another, English, because of conquest by the nation of the third language, German. Many other Jewish children who escaped to safe territory underwent a profound transformation in their relationship with the German language, as Monika Schmid's work has illustrated. That it should have remained entirely undisturbed in Steiner's case is indeed hard to quite believe. Perhaps the assertion of equivalence, embedded as it is in a catalogue of his mental powers and erudition, may be understood as a claim to an achievement of intellect and will, maintaining an inner equilibrium while skies fell and oceans churned.[21]

Firmat, born in Havana and raised in Miami, is sensitive above all to imbalances of power between languages. Steiner, whose heritage travelled with the family from the kaiserlich und königlich, imperial and royal, dually monarchical and irreducibly multilingual Habsburg Empire, is aware not just of the balance but also the diversity of his linguistic constitution: 'Strong particles of Czech and Austrian-Yiddish continued active in my father's idiom. And beyond these, like a familiar echo of a voice just out of hearing, lay Hebrew.' He attributes the shaping of his identity not to one influence or another, but to all of them together, integrated in a 'polyglot matrix' that organised and imprinted within him the complexities of Central European and Judaic humanism. The integration of his languages provided the basis for the richness of his culture.[22]

It is also significant that his family belonged to the educated classes of central and eastern Europe, among whom the use of multiple languages was standard practice. Joseph Conrad, the son of Polish aristocrats, born in a Ukrainian town under Russian rule, is another pertinent example. His reputation in the English-speaking world is backlit by awe at his ability to achieve literary acclaim in a language he did not learn until well into adulthood – an awe surely heightened by the feeling that to learn a language in adulthood is quite an achievement in itself. But where Conrad came from, socially and geographically, there was nothing remarkable about picking up extra languages. It would have been surprising if he had grown up unable to speak in several tongues. He contrasts with Steiner, however, in his attitude to the language of what he regarded as a hostile nation. His parents were active in the Polish national cause, and in consequence the family was sent into internal exile, during which his mother died. Russian was not part of his birthright in the way German was part of Steiner's; he learned it but rejected it.[23]

Conrad's language biography thus highlights the disruptive effects of power, which can be seen throughout much writing about bilingualism. Often the reason that people speak more than one language is that they have travelled, actually rather than metaphorically, from one city or country to another. Often, given the kind of pressures that frequently induce migration or exile, there is an imbalance of power between the new country and the old. The resulting tensions create a miniature theatre of struggle in the bilingual speaker's mind. One effect of this may be that writing about bilingualism is not representative of bilingual experience as a whole, because much of it is by existentially unsettled migrants seeking a resolution to their interior drama. Steiner is a prodigious exception here. By and large, writers whose experience of bilingualism is untroubled may be inclined to write about other matters instead.

The importance of power emerges compellingly from the work of many authors who do write about what it is like to live in different languages. To understand it better, we must consider how political power is brought to bear on people's use of language, especially in public space, and what responses it provokes. To counterbalance the examples of conflict, competition and coercion this entails, we may bear in mind that George Steiner's polyglot matrix, a coalition of languages sustaining a deep and awesomely fertile humanistic culture, was not a fantasy, a fluke or an experience confined in its general form as well as its particular details to a single individual, but a real, historical and wide-scale collective achievement. It is an existence proof that co-operation among languages can help enrich people's understanding of the world and how to live well in it.

✳ ✳ ✳ ✳

At this point, it's time to shift the gaze from how languages are managed in individual brains and minds to how they are managed by states and societies. People may know how to speak a language, but be inhibited or prevented from doing so by laws, policies and hostile attitudes. Laws and public attitudes may also support the use of more than one language – though they are likely to support some more than others.

CHAPTER EIGHT

One Nation, One Language

States seek to impose order upon the languages their citizens use, to different degrees and with differing aims. Citizens themselves often have strong views about the languages people around them should speak.

'MY TRAIN, MY LINGO'

A Friday night in London, an Underground train heading east. A woman breaks the social contract of British public transport and begins to address the carriage at large. She complains about the state of her neighbourhood, and starts on about immigrants. When she hears two men near her speaking a language she doesn't understand, she becomes abusive. At this point a passenger called Jay, on his way home from watching the England football team beat Lithuania at Wembley Stadium, raises his phone and captures her tirade on video. 'Don't fucking sit on my train and speak about me behind my back in your lingo,' she rants. 'You know English when you want a job. You know English when you want a flat. You know English when you want fucking anything. But when you want to try and talk about us on the train you talk in your own lingo.'[1]

The tropes are familiar, around the globe. Those New Guinean villagers who avoided speaking their language in front of strangers, for fear they would be suspected of practising witchcraft on them, would have recognised the sentiment. Though the specific accusations are contemporary – the woman's parting shot is about her targets 'sponging' welfare benefits – the mistrust of strangers speaking strange tongues is timeless. They will be damned when they do, and damned when they don't.

Yet on this occasion they were not damned out of hand. The woman did not tell them to go back to where they came from. She did not tell them they should not be in her country. A year and a few months later, after the referendum that produced a majority for leaving the European Union, she might have done. Quite a number of people did, in the outbreaks of triumphalist spite that followed the vote. People from continental European Union countries became nervous about speaking their own languages in public. Don't speak too loudly if you're out with your children, one German woman warned her compatriots. Better not phone home to your mother while you're on the bus. A student, Bartosz Milewski, was stabbed in the neck with a broken bottle and hit over the head with a piece of wood after being ordered to leave a park, and the country, by men who objected to him conversing with his friends in their native tongue. One of these language vigilantes declared that he had a daughter living round the corner and he didn't want her to hear them speaking Polish. With their crude but potentially lethal weapons, the Englishmen protected the child from the mere sound of foreign words, drifting through the air on a warm summer's evening.[2]

At the time of the woman's outburst, though, the election that led to the calling of the referendum had yet to take place. The political context of an Underground train journey was different. A person with xenophobic sentiments was not yet able to imagine that they had some kind of democratic mandate for their hostility.

What the woman said was thus subject to a modicum of restraint, and the more interesting for it. 'My train', she called it, asserting that the train and by extension everything else that is British belongs to her. She also called it a 'public train', defining it as public territory in which only the indigenous language may be spoken. Foreigners may ride in it, but their discourse must always be available for inspection. This demand breaches the British convention, generally accepted if not generally observed, that other people's conversations are nobody else's business.

The peculiar tensions of train, bus or tram travel arise because public transport accommodates passengers but not their personal space, confounding the distinction between the public and the personal. This may help to explain why the woman claimed it was 'my' train, rather than 'our' train. At the same time public transport is conspicuously rule-bound, with spoken, written and symbolised injunctions from ceiling to floor. The woman was taking her cue from the rules all around her, and pronouncing a new one that she made up herself on the spur of the moment.

In doing so, she proposed a particular, pre-Brexit settlement for one aspect of the relationship between natives and foreigners in Britain: if you are here, you have to speak English when you are in our presence. Despite its intemperate expression, it was more modest than the proposal advanced earlier the same month by the then Mayor of London, Boris Johnson, who argued that the city's immigrants should speak 'the language of Shakespeare' not just in public but at home too, so that they are properly assimilated into British society. The nationalist politician Nigel Farage also had something to say about the speaking of foreign languages on trains in London. He recounted how he had caught a train from Charing Cross, stopping at London Bridge, New Cross and Hither Green – suburban commuters often count off their lives by stations in this way – but it wasn't until they got past Grove Park that he heard a word of English.

That made him feel 'awkward', though he hastened to add that he wasn't saying people on trains should be forced to speak his language. The reason for his discomfort, he indicated, was that the foreign voices reminded him of the large number of homes in which languages other than English are mainly spoken.[3]

When politicians try to bring home languages into the political arena, it is liable to be taken as an affront to the idea that everyday family life is none of the state's business. In 2014 the Christian Social Union, the right-wing Bavarian party allied with Angela Merkel's Christian Democratic Union (CDU), proposed that immigrants seeking to settle permanently in Germany should be encouraged to speak German within their families. Merkel and the CDU laconically distanced themselves from the suggestion. The CDU's general secretary, who is from Hesse, gave Twitter to understand that politics should have nothing to say about whether he spoke Latin, Klingon or Hessian at home. Amateur and professional satirists made merry with jibes about the Bavarian dialect, the general theme being that the Bavarians should speak German themselves.[4]

Farther east, however, the sound of the German language on a Warsaw tram resulted in a blow to the head for Jerzy Kochanowski, a professor of history at Warsaw University, and subsequently a ten-month prison sentence for his attacker. Kochanowski was riding the number 22 tram through the city, chatting with a colleague from the University of Jena, when another passenger told them not to speak in German. Kochanowski explained that his companion could not speak Polish, whereupon the man jumped up and punched him. In protest against this outburst of xenophobic violence against two European scholars engaged in collegial conversation, demonstrators rode number 22 trams speaking foreign languages and reading aloud from books in German and Russian.

When the case came to court, the judge rejected the prosecution's argument that this was a crime motivated by hatred of another nationality. Her grounds were that the attacker knew his victim was not a foreigner, because the professor had replied to him in Polish. This reveals an intriguing legal nicety: hatred of another nationality can only be an aggravating factor in a crime if that nationality is embodied in an individual victim. The law, or at any rate the judge, did not recognise hatred as a factor in the case of a victim who was attacked for entering into another nation's culture by speaking its language.[5]

As the German scholar Wilhelm von Humboldt said, every language draws a circle about the people that possess it; and everywhere people are constantly adjusting that simple geometry. Living in Paris, and wrestling with the question of whether to write in Greek or French, the novelist Vassilis Alexakis observed how his Vietnamese neighbours drew the line. They spoke to each other in Vietnamese, but they spoke French to the stray cat they had adopted. It was, after all, a native.[6]

States can be equally idiosyncratic in the laws they devise to order the relationships between populations and languages. Communities evolve or assert norms to govern what languages should be spoken where, when, and by whom. Each nation strikes its own balances and draws its own lines. Each is different, but each sheds light on the others – and sometimes the ones that are the most singular are the most illuminating.

'BOTH MY NATIVE LANGUAGES'

Stalls await, a perimeter of grills, pointed canopies, an encampment. One sign advertises 'Caucasian Shashlik', in Russian. On the asphalt path in front of it, someone has stencilled 'RUNĀ LATVISKI!' – 'Speak Latvian!'

Two policemen loiter in an inflatable motor boat on the pool beside the Victory Monument, a seventy-nine metre obelisk guarded by a statue of two rugged Red Army heroes, one brandishing a subma-chine gun. The Latvian flag flies from the array of poles behind them, and hangs at the stern of the small dinghy too. Old newsreels play on a video screen: Stuka dive-bombers loom and Red Army T-34 tanks roll. It is the morning of 9 May, Victory Day, and the stage is set.

First there is the laying of wreaths, led by Nils Ušakovs, Mayor of Rīga, a procession of dignitaries from ex-Soviet republics following him. Afterwards, ordinary citizens take their turn to lay flowers, and they will continue throughout the day. Even at dusk, as people watch bands and dance, a constant stream of tribute-payers hand over their flowers to cheerful teenagers in red and white commemorative t-shirts. By then the bouquets are piled up at the wall and laid out in a sweeping spiral on the grass; white, yellow and red, but it's the red that stands out.

There's less red than there once was, though. Latvia banned the display of Soviet symbols in 2013, a measure that has gone only some of the way to temper the resentment provoked in many ethnic Latvians by the annual Victory Day gatherings, which they see as a celebration of the army that occupied their country in 1940 and did not finally leave until 1994. Victory Day is indeed an exclusively Russian affair. It takes place the day after the West's VE Day, a symbolic separation enabled by the chance circumstance that at the hour of Nazi Germany's surrender late on 8 May, 1945, it was already 9 May in Moscow. The victory it commemorates is not that of the Allies, but of the Soviet Union; the conflict is not the Second World War, but the Great Patriotic War. In Latvia it is a minority history, speaking principally to the quarter of the population that is ethnically Russian, and alienating to the majority.[7]

Here in Rīga the symbols have been carefully nuanced. The stage backdrop is a star, but it is formed with circumspect diplomacy from the words for victory in Latvian, Russian and English. Period uniforms are popular for adults and children alike, but are worn without badges. The roles people play in these costumes are at the mildest end of militarism. A young girl in forage cap and tunic sings solo in front of a women's choir in magenta gowns and lace headdresses; afterwards a couple of her backing singers are among the people served soup by two fellows dressed as soldiers, manning a replica field kitchen. A troupe of six teenagers, boys and girls in vintage army and navy uniforms, sing jaunty songs to a merry crowd. One young woman, attracting attention from photographers, has enhanced her cap and tunic with sunglasses, a narrowly cinched belt, and stiletto heels that add at least six inches to her height. A small boy, three or four years old, is the centre of attention for a group of adults who stand him on a wall in his miniature uniform and try to coach him in a song.

He probably won't remember the moment when he is older, but he might well be able to teach his own children the words. Beneath the dressing up and the singing along there are depths of affinity more profound than most Westerners can fathom. Not all the flowers are laid on the ground. A few surviving veterans are present, weighed down with their medals. People approach them to pay respect to the still living. Young parents, born decades after the war, gently push their children forward to give a carnation or a posy to an aged veteran. It is a moving and humbling sight, this moment of communion across the generations, among the people.

A tributary procession, the march of the 'Immortals Regiment' to the Victory Monument, makes ancestors into icons. People carry placards bearing photographs of deceased family members who took part in the war, to the accompaniment of wartime music. The ritual originated three years previously in the Siberian city of Tomsk, and was then taken up by the Russian government, attracting scepticism in consequence: Meduza, a website run by independent Russian journalists who have relocated to Rīga, reports that Russia's culture ministry shared a photo on its Facebook page showing somebody, presumably not a family member, bearing the image of the wartime Soviet secret police chief Lavrenty Beria. But here in Rīga there seems no reason at all to doubt the authenticity of the people holding placards, some produced on the spot from photographs they have brought.[8]

As evening approaches, the tone changes. Balalaikas and choirs give way to guitars – though the master of ceremonies continues to intone poems, giving Russian verse an outdoor airing rare in this city. Crowds press towards the monument along the avenue leading to Victory Park from the Daugava river bridge, past the ramparts of the new National Library where European Union heads of government will gather a fortnight later, the Ukraine crisis at the top of their agenda. Russian flags appear with increasing frequency, making the approaching droves look like an advancing column. A few men are wearing Putin t-shirts. A few more are swaying drunk. It's turning into a music festival with overtones.

When the maverick film director Emir Kusturica takes the stage with his No Smoking Orchestra, one flag-draped man cries 'Serbiya – Rossiya'. (Kusturica is a self-made Serb, his parents Bosnian Muslims from Sarajevo.) Two policemen attempt to persuade another man to take his flag off its pole: inside the park people are permitted to drape themselves in the Russian flag, but not to fly it. A few metres away, a man swathed in a Belarusian flag and a woman in a Russian one pose for photos. As the Slavs unite, Kusturica makes a language choice that possibly only he could get away with. He has retained his sense of mischief while becoming ever more stridently anti-Western, and tonight exercises it by singing in German: a No Smoking Orchestra live favourite called 'Drang Nach Osten', Drive To The East, a catchphrase for German expansion into Slavic lands.[9]

The band omits the studio version's lyric about Drang nach Osten in a Volkswagen, but the theme is playing out on the roads round the park. German-built vehicles seem to be favourites for a kind of drag travesty in which they are labelled 'T-34' and covered with the slogans that Red Army soldiers painted on their tanks. One car even has a mock turret on its roof. The direction is reversed, of course – 'To Berlin!', proclaims a VW minibus. A BMW flying a Russian flag and sporting an illegal red star is labelled 'Trophy'.

A car with a Latvia ice hockey shirt draped over the rear wind-screen offers a riposte, but nobody rises to the bait. Despite the symbols and the numbers – tens of thousands over the course of the day, certainly, though perhaps not the 220,000 the organisers claim – and despite the US State Department's warning to Americans in Rīga that they should avoid the Victory Park area, the prevailing mood remains calm and civil. This is not an incipient revolutionary mob, and Latvia's Russian speakers show little inclination to follow the catastrophic course set by the Russian-speaking separatists in eastern Ukraine. As residents of a European Union country, free to travel and work anywhere in the Union, they have more attractive options. And many of them see themselves as somewhat different from the Russians across the south-eastern border in Russia. According to stereotype, they are calmer in temperament: more like Latvians. The term 'Russian speakers' is widely used because it covers not just ethnic Russians but also other Slavic minorities – Ukrainians, Belarusians and Poles – who mostly speak Russian at home. It now serves as a label for what looks like an emerging ethnic group, a population with its own distinctive outlook and identity, defined by language preference. All together, the Russian speakers add up to more than a third of Latvia's population.[10]

A key element of this identity is that Russian speakers are also Latvian speakers. Almost all now have some facility in Latvian, thanks to a combination of what former education minister Ina Druviete calls 'sticks and carrots'. The younger ones are normally fluent by the time they finish school, thanks in part to an increase in the proportion of classroom Latvian implemented during Druviete's tenure. Few if any people at Victory Park would have had trouble reading the food stall menus in Latvian – a legal requirement for anything classed as public information – though few if any will have chosen to speak the 'state language' there that day. (When a woman drops a flyer and I hand it back to her without speaking, she mutters 'Thanks' in English.)

Attitude surveys offer plenty of reassurance that Russian speakers agree that they should be able to speak Latvian. What unsettles Ina Druviete and everybody else concerned with social integration, whatever form they think it should take, is that for many Russian speakers Latvian is no more than a tool for use in everyday transactions and dealings with officialdom. Russian speakers accept it as a requirement of life in the Republic of Latvia, but they do not live in it themselves. They prefer Russian pop music to the choirs that Latvians continue to enjoy. They watch Russian TV and bookmark Russian websites. Latvia does offer its own Russian-language TV programmes, but it can't compete with the Russian channels' ample budgets. The result is that the Russian speakers within Latvia's borders live inside the Russian 'information space'.

On 9 May that space becomes a theatre of war, centred on the immense display of weaponry in Red Square. Two days later, the Rossiya channel is still broadcasting a seemingly endless military parade, the newsreel Stukas and T-34s segueing into scenes from the Moscow display, with captions detailing each modern weapon system as it passes. The Topol-M nuclear missile launcher is on heavy rotation, a long fat cylinder with a rounded end: this symbol of Russian hard power isn't exactly subtle. For variety there are clips from a heavily armed parade in the Donetsk People's Republic, one of the breakaway Russian-backed statelets in eastern Ukraine. I watch for an hour and barely see a soul who is not in uniform.

The orange and black stripes of the St George ribbon feature in identical emblems on the sides of tanks in Moscow and Donetsk; the ribbons themselves adorn the jackets and blouses of thousands of people at the Victory Monument in Rīga. This military symbol dates back to the eighteenth century, but owes its current prevalence initially to its revival by the Russian RIA Novosti news agency for the sixtieth 9 May anniversary in 2005, and latterly to its adoption as a cockade by the pro-Russian fighters who erupted into action across Ukraine's eastern provinces in 2014. Like Ukrainians, Latvians who feel threatened by the ribbons' association with violent separatism call them 'colorados', alluding to the stripes of the Colorado beetle, scourge of potato crops. Whatever the ribbons mean to the Russian speakers who wear them in Victory Park, they affirm that 9 May in Latvia is part of the Russian symbolic sphere, even if the only 'tanks' are fashioned from cardboard and sticky-backed plastic.[11]

That's certainly Olga Dragiļeva's problem with it. She spent 9 May in Moscow filming a report for the Latvian current affairs programme *De Facto*, delivering her piece to camera as the armour rumbled past behind her, and returned to Rīga appalled by the monstrous illusion of war that the state has cast like a spell over its people. Although she reports in Latvian, her native tongue is Russian. 'I feel really comfortable in Moscow; I love it,' she says. 'It's liberating to speak your own language, and see the signs in your language; it's nice. I feel like I come from there, in a way. But I can't say it publicly, because Putin has hijacked all of that. He has hijacked Russian language. It's now a language of war, of propaganda.'[12]

Although her own public language is good enough for Latvian television, her Russian accent isn't acceptable to some of her audience. 'I constantly get comments on Twitter that "she is crippling the Latvian language",' she says. Off air, when she is on a bus or tram speaking Russian on her phone, she sometimes catches herself wondering whether she is annoying somebody with her choice of language. 'I'm sure sometimes I do,' she says. 'And it doesn't feel good.'

Ina Druviete also acknowledges that Latvia has 'tram conflicts'. But Latvian trams ply their routes through urban space upon which a unique Latvian political settlement has been established. There is no need for language vigilantes, angrily trying to enforce rules that they're making up as they go along. Instead the state maintains an elaborate bureaucracy of regulations and inspectors to uphold a minutely defined linguistic order, the most striking effect of which is the absence in public space of words written in the language that Olga Dragiļeva and more than a third of the republic's population speak when they have the choice.

* * * *

The day after 9 May is a Sunday, a day for a spring excursion. Ina Druviete and her husband Jānis drive me out of Rīga to a region known as the Latvian Switzerland – a tongue-in-cheek term, since at its highest point Latvia reaches just 312 metres above sea level. We won't talk about that 'insult' yesterday in Victory Park, Ina declares as we set off. Instead we stop to look for mushrooms in pine woods and for beavers by a stream, unsuccessfully in each case. There are, however, storks in the fields and on nests atop telephone poles. This is one small tract of the vast eastern European whole.

Though devoid of mountains, the landscape is folded enough to contain a high-vaulted cave in the sandstone side of a valley. It has a kind of lobby at its entrance, the walls of which are inscribed with names. Many of them are set within hearts. Most are Latvian or Russian though some of the older ones are German, reminders of the Baltic Germans who dominated the region for hundreds of years until Latvia became independent after the First World War.

All have been drawn here by a legend. It tells how a baby girl was found alive among the piled corpses after a battle for the nearby castle of Turaida, part of the struggles between Poland and Sweden that tormented swathes of eastern Europe for the first three decades of the seventeenth century. The girl was named Maija; later, as her beauty unfolded, she became known as the Rose of Turaida. She fell in love with a young man who worked as a gardener at another castle nearby; but as their wedding approached, a Polish soldier lured her to the cave with a forged note and entrapped her. Choosing death over rape, she told the Pole that her scarf had magical powers to protect its wearer from injury. She invited him to prove its magic by striking her, and thus he killed her with a blow from an axe. He hanged himself in remorse; her true love stood trial for her murder but was acquitted after the attacker's accomplice confessed the plot.

The cave, and Maija's grave up by the castle, have become sites of pilgrimage for newly-weds seeking to infuse their unions with the spirit of devotion and fidelity she epitomised. The stream that flows out of the cave in a channel around its wall is supposed to be Maija's blood, Ina tells me. Those who drink from it and wash themselves with it may be blessed with the beauty the Rose embodied. Jānis avails himself of the opportunity.

At the castle it turns out that today is also a symbolically significant one. It is Maija's nameday, which must of course fall in May. Her grave has a marble stone and above it a linden tree, now collapsed upon itself, that is said to have been planted by her beloved before he left these parts forever.

The castle itself is largely a modern reconstruction, guarded only by a young woman in folk costume. Inside, the images of predatory knights, faceless in their tank-like helms, echo the theme of suffering wrought by cruel invaders that underlies the legend of the Rose of Turaida. These were crusaders, the Brothers of the Sword, sent to convert the pagan Livs whose wooden fort they replaced with their red Teutonic brick.

Modern Latvia honours its Liv, or Livonian, roots. Its Language Law affirms that Liv is the only language besides Latvian itself that shall not be regarded as foreign, committing the state to the maintenance and development of Liv as the language of the 'indigenous' Livonian population. The tongue was already on the verge of extinction when the law was passed in 1998, and now only exists in reanimated form: fewer than 200 people in Latvia identify themselves as Livonians, and none of them are native Liv speakers. The last of those died in Canada in 2013, at the age of 103. Meanwhile the Language

Law does not even mention the 'foreign' language spoken as a native tongue by around 700,000 people in Latvia, out of a population numbering fewer than two million in all. It does however affirm the rights of ethnic minorities to use their native languages.

Down the hill, near the gate, stands a large notice board summarising the significance of language in the Latvian Republic. This text is the Preamble to the Constitution. It mentions the Latvian language three times in its six paragraphs, identifying loyalty to it as the sole state language as one of the foundations of a cohesive society. Ina, who has taken a keen interest in constitutional references to language around the world, observes approvingly that three mentions is a lot by international standards.

The Preamble is a recent addition to the Constitution, the core elements of which date back to Latvia's original period of independence between the world wars. It was passed in 2014, in part as a response to a referendum held in 2012 on a proposal to make Russian a second official language. Three-quarters of those who voted were against the measure – and so, it seems, were quite a few of those who voted for it. Among them was Elizabete Krivcova, one of the organisers of the Immortals Regiment march. When I meet her a couple of days later she tells me that a majority of the Russian-speaking minority does not want the language to become official, but does want respect for it as a minority tongue.[13]

The view that the referendum was a way of claiming respect is widespread, in part because of remarks to that effect by Nils Ušakovs, the Mayor of Rīga. A popular and adept political communicator, he leads the social democratic party Saskaņa (Concord), the main element of a wing of Latvian politics that wins around a quarter of the votes in parliamentary elections but has never entered government. Those votes come mainly from the Russian quarter of the population, and other Latvian parties have been unwilling to co-operate with a political group that entered into a formal co-operation agreement with

Vladimir Putin's United Russia party. Its rivals cannot complain about its line on language law, though. Saskaņa's programme echoes the Preamble to the Constitution, affirming the importance of recognising Latvian as the only official language, and the need to create mutual respect between the people of Latvia.[14]

Over lunch, before we head back to Rīga, we stray onto the subject of the Victory Day event after all. Ina is dismayed by Emir Kusturica's involvement. We love his films, she sighs ruefully, and goes on to bring up the topic of respect herself. Ina and Jānis Druviete grew up in a society where Russian dominance licensed open contempt for their language. Latvian was called a 'dog's language', Ina recalls. Jānis says that Russians would tell Latvians to 'speak human'.

Across eastern Europe the collapse of the Soviet order gave a new generation of intellectuals the chance to put what they had studied at university into political practice. Mostly it was economics, but in Ina Druviete's case it was philology, the historical study of language. Her first doctoral dissertation was about a pioneer linguist who installed the basic infrastructure for a national language by compiling a Latvian dictionary and helping to devise the Latvian alphabet, introduced in 1908. She entered politics in a polity where knowledge of this kind was regarded as existentially important, and continued her academic career alongside her parliamentary one. During her first term as Latvia's education minister she faced protests from Russian speakers against proposals to reduce the proportion of school classes taught in minority languages, and during her second term she faced renewed protests at proposals to reduce the proportion further still.

Since regaining its independence, the Latvian republic has been profoundly conscious of its language's defining idiosyncrasies, and has relied heavily on the law to maintain them. In 2006 the Latvian cabinet refused to comply with the European Union rule that the name of the EU currency, the euro, should be the same in all the countries of the Union. In Latvia, it would be the eiro. Druviete, the minister of education at the time, declared that the 'eu' diphthong was 'alien to the Latvian language', and added that Latvia might take its case to the European Court of Justice if necessary. Years later, as it prepared to adopt the currency, Latvia agreed to call it the euro ... but only in formal documents, and in italics to underline that the word is foreign.[15]

This was one instance of the awkward contradiction that faced a number of nations as they reasserted themselves after the collapse of Soviet power. Independence was their most treasured possession, but to secure it they had to surrender some of it to a new set of higher powers. To become part of the European institutions on which their stability and hopes for prosperity depended, they had to conform to European norms. In Latvia, bodies such as the Council of Europe and the Organization for Security and Co-operation in Europe (OSCE) found themselves drawn into the defence of Russian speakers' rights. Their expressions of concern helped to moderate the national-ising zeal of the newly revived state.[16]

At the heart of the matter was the premise that this was not a second Latvian republic but the continuation of the original one after a seventy-year hiatus. Its citizens were those who were citizens on 17 June, 1940, and their descendants. This excluded the great majority of Russian speakers, most of whom are descended from people who came to Latvia after it became a Soviet Socialist Republic on 21 July, 1940. In 1991 many of them voted to restore Latvia's independence; independent Latvia then took away their right to vote.[17]

Latvia's population now includes a special category of 'non-citizens', with their own special passports, indigo instead of European Union burgundy. Their numbers have diminished over the years through death, emigration and naturalisation, but at the beginning of 2015 there were still over a quarter of a million of them – about 13 per cent of the popu-lation, and about a third of the Russian-speaking minority. They can become citizens if they demonstrate that they are fluent in the Latvian language, and meet other conditions such as knowing the national anthem. Some non-citizens, especially elderly ones, may feel daunted by the language exam – nearly half fail the first time. Some may refuse on principle, like Alexander Gaponenko, an instigator of the 2012 language referendum, who is able to articulate his pro-Russian views in excellent Latvian. Others may regard the inability to vote as a price worth paying for the mobility benefits of non-citizenship. Their non-citizen passports allow them not only to travel freely throughout the open-border Schengen Area of the European Union, just as Latvian citizens can, but also to enter Russia without visas, which Latvian citizens cannot.[18]

For its part, the Latvian state regards Russia's 'compatriot policy', which seeks to cultivate connections with ethnic Russians beyond Russia's borders in the 'post-Soviet space', as a threat to its national security. The Ministry of the Interior's annual Security Police report for 2013 includes a section on the Non-Citizens' Congress, an activist group, illustrated with a photo of its founder Elizabete Krivcova. It describes the Congress as one of the most significant vehicles for the implementation of compatriot policy. Among the activities noted are approaches to international bodies such as the United Nations, setting up an English-language website, and organising a debate on the Preamble to the Constitution.[19]

In his preface to the report the head of the Security Police remarks that they are often asked what they are doing about threats to national security. As the English version puts it, 'Why aren't the persons, also the ones mentioned in this report, tarnishing the image and discrediting Latvia, putting the statehood and national fundamental principles in doubt, imprisoned or extradited? The answer is as simple as that – Latvia is a democratic country where the principles of rule of law persist.' Nevertheless, the Security Police report devotes much of its attention to legal political activities.

What Latvia fears from Russia is the old familiar threat, the treatment of small nations as pawns or land ripe for grabbing, that is the motor of European history and the stuff of legend: the Brothers of the Sword, the Rose of Turaida, the Drang nach Osten. At the same time it perceives a new threat to its language from globalisation. The Republic of Latvia regards itself as the protector of a tongue that has no other territory and belongs to a branch of the Indo-European language family, the Baltic, with only one other surviving member, Lithuanian. The guidelines for the state language policy warn that Latvian faces competition from two languages, Russian and English, that have very high economic value. State language policy is intended to ensure the competitiveness of Latvian, while at the same time imposing a system of measures to protect it from its competitors.

In Rīga, the most remarkable effect of this system is that Russian is heard but not seen: the city is bilingual in speech, monolingual in writing. Although half the capital's 700,000 residents speak Russian as their native language, Latvian enjoys a monopoly in public text, from street signs to movie posters. Actually, the cobbled Old Rīga quarter is one zone where Latvian would enjoy an advantage in a free language market, its Latin-based alphabet being much easier for Western tourists to puzzle out than the Cyrillic characters of Russian.[20]

* * * *

The State Language Centre occupies a freshly laminated suite of offices in a gloomy building whose age, dilapidation and peripheral site on a small, tree-screened square of limited character would make it an ideal setting for a spies' lair in a Cold War thriller. This is the source of pronouncements intended to improve the competitiveness of the Latvian language by providing a vocabulary for modern life, such as Protocol No. 39 § 1, of 14 January 2015, which confirms Latvian names for baked confectionery items including the brownie (brūnītis), the muffin (mafins) and the cupcake (glazūrkēkss). Five months later they were working on a word for the wrap, as in the rolled alternative to a sandwich, considering two possibilities: the sound-alike reps, or tītenis, which alludes to a traditional dish wrapped in cabbage leaves. In due course the centre announced, not even slightly ironically, that the Latvian for hipster is hipsteris.[21]

Ina Druviete talked of using sticks and carrots to support the Latvian language: the State Language Centre is where the sticks are kept. An asset of the Ministry of Justice, its mission is not just to enlarge the language, but to enforce its use as the law requires. As far as dissidents like Elizabete Krivcova are concerned, this is the head-quarters of the 'language police'. When work resumed after the 9 May weekend, a complaint from a member of the public landed on the desk of Viesturs Razumovskis, one of the Centre's regional Heads of Language Control, alleging that a councillor in another city made a speech in Russian at a 9 May event. That is not illegal in itself, Razumovskis and his colleagues explained to me. The question to be investigated was whether the man spoke as a private citizen or as a public official. If it was the latter, the organisers might be liable to an administrative fine for not providing a translation in the state language.

Subsequently it was announced that 9May.lv, the organisers of the Rīga event, could likewise be fined for failing to subtitle Mayor Ušakovs's speech, in which he recalled his family's war experiences. Ušakovs replied on Facebook, suggesting a complaint to the centre about the town hall cat's failure to communicate with members of the public in Latvian. But, the mayor continued, although Kuzja is a council cat he does not receive a salary, so perhaps the language laws do not apply to him. It seems that even Latvians struggle to grasp the subtleties of their language legislation.[22]

Much of the State Language Centre's enforcement activities are directed towards the use of the state language in public settings such as shops and businesses that receive clients. It sends out inspectors, like the public health officials who check hygiene standards in restaurant kitchens. In 2014, Language Control Department officials carried out 5,100 checks, leading to 769 administrative punishments.[23]

The centre staff assured me that exceptions can be made for the sake of public safety. It has been criticised in the past for overstepping that mark, though. In 2009 it blocked the distribution of leaflets in Russian inviting women to have check-ups for breast and cervical cancer. As breast cancer screening is most effective among women over fifty, and Latvian language skills are weaker among older Russian speakers, this decision obstructed the delivery of potentially life-saving health messages to many of the women who might benefit from them most. Three years later the State Language Centre brought a case against the State Police for displaying booklets in Russian about road safety, drug abuse and avoiding robbery. And in 2013 the centre objected to the display of bilingual posters produced by the Corruption Prevention and Combating Bureau, urging patients not to bribe doctors. It accepted that the posters could be put up in locations that were not publicly accessible – such as the doctors' own offices. One thing the Language Control Department cannot be accused of is a reluctance to ruffle the feathers of their colleagues in other branches of public service.[24]

The common theme in all these examples is the priority given to language over other public goods, including the health of individuals and the integrity of institutions. I left the State Language Centre with copies of its regulations translated into English. A disclaimer above the Regulations regarding the Ensuring of Interpreting at Events, the ones the 9 May organisers appeared to have breached, notes that while the English translations use gender-neutral language, the authentic Latvian texts use the masculine singular pronoun and gender-specific nouns instead of terms like chairperson. Latvian happens to be particularly gender-conscious. To make it gender-neutral would require rewriting its rules, and in Latvia, linguistic correctness trumps political correctness – or rather, linguistic correctness is the highest-ranking form of political correctness. The perceived needs of the language stand in the way of change that other societies have decided is necessary to promote fairness and equality. Society serves the language, not the other way around.

The rules extend to people's names. A foreign man will find an 's' tacked onto both his forename and surname, even if either already ends in 's'. This form of nationalisation is a particularly sore point, I was told at the Latvian Language Agency, which conducts research into society's relationship with its languages. It's not the Westerners who complain, they say. Indeed, I'm quite amused to find myself rendered as Mareks Kohns. Likewise Toms Hārdijs and Šarlīze Terona would probably not object to their billing on the posters for the Mad Max, or Makss, film that was showing in cinemas during my visit. But they continue to be Tom Hardy and Charlize Theron in their own countries, while I can leave my gender-conforming 's's at the airport. It's different for people who are obliged to live with a name that has been rewritten for them.

One man took his to the United Nations, where the Human Rights Committee ruled that 'the forceful addition of a declinable ending to a surname . . . is an intrusive measure, which is not proportionate to the aim of protecting the official State language'. The Latvian state disagrees. Name standards oblige individuals to defer to the requirements of the language and the state that guards it down to the last suffix. This is necessary, the Language Agency's director Jānis Valdmanis and his colleagues explained to me, because gender-specific endings are part of the language's structure, and if you fail to maintain standards in one part of it, you degrade the structure as a whole. Such views are not unique to Latvia. The Académie française, France's language authority since 1635, is alarmed by the proliferation of usages adopted in efforts to promote fairness and gender equality. In 2017 it warned that inclusive language is an 'aberration' that creates a disunited tongue and has put French in mortal danger. According to the 'immortels' of the Académie, unity and inclusion are not compatible. The Minister of Education, preoccupied not just with the integrity of the language but of the Republic itself, evidently felt the same way. 'Il y a une seule langue française, une seule grammaire, une seule République,' he tweeted.[25]

Older Latvians remember what it is like to be on the receiving end of a nationalising language policy. Among the documents from the Soviet period compiled by the Language Agency is a letter sent in 1959 to a Rīga newspaper from a Mr Reiznieks, who relates how he heard a man on a tram complaining that in russifying his name, officials had turned him from a 'noble animal' – his surname in English would be Deer – to a 'nightmare', which was what his identity card now labelled him in Russian. Mr Reiznieks recalled his own protests at the 'liquidation' – that most ubiquitous and chilling of Soviet terms – of the 's' in his surname. But the Agency presents this as an example of resistance to russification, not as a vignette illustrating how people feel about officials issuing them with new names.[26]

Like the State Language Centre, the agency is concealed in a dark old building with a cavernous stairwell. Blocks of similar vintage are abundant in the city, giving it a handsome bone structure under weathered features. A good number – enough to win Old Rīga UNESCO World Heritage Site status – stand refreshed and proud in the state of decorative abundance their Art Nouveau architects intended. Across the street from some notably fine specimens of fantasy harmonised with geometry, stands a cafe furnished from parquet to cornices in wood that seems have been lacquered with bourgeois elegance. Over tea in superior china, Maria Golubeva takes the long view of linguistic correctness. Now an analyst at Providus, a public policy think-tank, she grew up speaking Russian and spent much of the 1990s at universities abroad. When she returned, she found that her attitude to learning had changed, and she could no longer face a course of formal study to reach the standards of Latvian fluency now required of her.

Having studied history, she consoled herself with the thought that the 'anal approach' to language, the preoccupation with correctness, was a nineteenth-century phenomenon that would yield to the age of globalisation. The Latvian republic's nationalism is nineteenth-century through and through, being a Romantic vision populated with choral singers, tragic maidens and the bear-slaying hero who gives his name to Lāčplēsis Day, the public holiday on which the soldiers who fought for Latvian independence are remembered. Behind its officious pedantry – which seems to bespeak a systemic lack of confidence on the part of the state – the language bureaucracy has a Romantic soul. But that doesn't mean its time has passed. With globalisation losing its aura of inevitability, Romantic bureaucracy might turn out to be a surprisingly resilient combination in the febrile age the world now seems to be entering.

Though Romantic nationalism reached its full flower, in poetry and bloodshed, during the nineteenth century, its seeds began to germinate in the eighteenth. One of its most vigorous shoots arose in the middle of Rīga, where Johann Gottfried Herder preached as a minister and taught at the cathedral school between 1764 and 1769. At the age of twenty, in the months before he came to the city from Königsberg, he wrote an essay with a title that reads wryly in today's Latvia: 'On Diligence In The Study Of Several Learned Languages'. This was the text in which he introduced his grand theme of national character, and the national character of each language. The essay strives to reconcile the specialness of a person's mother tongue with the need to understand other languages so as not to be sealed off from the world's knowledge. Here they are, intertwined from the moment they emerge into the light, the two great contradictory impulses of language use: on the one hand, the urge to draw inward and to draw a circle around one's own; on the other, the awareness that one cannot really flourish without entering into other languages. Latvia's idiosyncratic language policies are inspired by the former, and haunted by the latter.[27]

Herder himself engaged with the Latvian language – though part of the reason for his departure from Rīga was a rival minister's sermon questioning his ability to preach in it. Later in life he included Latvian folk songs – he coined the term, as Volkslieder – in the collection of lyrics from around Europe which he used to affirm his belief in the common people as the bearers of national spirit; 'an affirmation', in the words of the ethnomusicologist Philip Bohlman, 'of the selfness of each nation and its songs'. He listed them among peoples of the Baltic coast, such as Old Prussians, Lithuanians and Estonians, whose 'history is the true source of their language and way of thinking'. A Herderian conception of national selfness, contained in an indivisible soul combining language, history and thought, is the wellspring of the Latvian republic's preoccupation with grammar and vocabulary. To allow the language to degrade, or to be infiltrated or supplanted by foreign influences, would be to allow the nation's character to deteriorate.[28]

A square by Rīga's cathedral is named after its one-time teacher and preacher. In it stands his statue, a bust correctly captioned 'Johans Gotfrīds Herders'.

* * * *

Rīga Secondary School Number 74 is a warm, welcoming and homely place, if the principal's office is anything to go by. On a grey Monday morning I speak with Irina Frolova, via her colleague Luda who interprets for us, over a large and open box of chocolates. Ms Frolova began teaching here in 1981 and has been head for the past thirteen years. She presides over 650 students, all of whom are Russian speakers, and sixty teachers.[29]

The picture that emerges is as calm and reassuring as the hospitality. Exam results are good; students graduate with equal grammatical competence in Latvian and Russian; the ministry of education is supportive. There were serious problems when the percentage of lessons taught in Latvian was increased, with parents unhappy and teachers unprepared, but those are all in the past. I'm shown the paperwork: tables recording how many hours per week are taught in each language at each year grade in each subject.

Maria Golubeva feels that this goes for the school system as a whole. 'The compromise is working,' she says. 'It produces people who are proficient in their mother tongue and Latvian. Students in bilingual schools are not lagging behind.' And educational equity, she observes, is at the core of social cohesion.

'The one respect in which it's not working is that it keeps people apart socially,' she adds. Here, Secondary School 74 is possibly a special case. I ask the teachers whether the students speak Latvian outside class with friends. The answer is yes: at lunchtimes they go out the back and talk to the students of Secondary School 64, their Latvian neighbour. If the two schools were any closer together, they would be integrated.

Instead, policy proposals envisage keeping the minority schools separate, but increasing the proportion of classes they teach in Latvian still further. Irina Frolova thinks these plans are nonsensical, and would provoke protests. But she doubts they will be implemented, as does Maria Golubeva. The mass protests against the earlier school language reforms brought Russian speakers together as a political force. Ten years later, the smaller demonstrations against the new proposals coincided with the outbreak of conflict in Ukraine – a crisis in which moves to alter Ukraine's language law played their part, as Vladimir Putin noted in his speech hailing Russia's annexation of Crimea. 'Politicians understand this is not the moment to make the Russian-speaking population unhappy,' Golubeva says. In 2018, however, the politicians evidently judge the moment to have passed. They proceed with plans to make Latvian the sole language of secondary education, apart from lessons for minority students who want to learn about their language and culture in their mother tongue.[30]

The 2014 protests against the education proposals revived the slogans of ten years before. Māra Laizāne, who was in her early teens during the first wave of protests, now found herself surprised that she didn't know what her minority neighbours were feeling. 'Some topics we don't publicly discuss, and that's not OK,' she says. She led a project to find out, exploring attitudes among Russian-speaking school students aged fifteen to nineteen years old.[31]

Her findings were of a piece with other research into how Russian speakers see their place in Latvian society. The students feel they belong to Latvia – the land and its nature as well the state. They do not feel themselves to be Latvian, though, because they are not of Latvian descent. As they don't have a strong sense of what elements constitute their own identity, they rely upon their home language as their defining characteristic. At the same time they are relaxed about language choice, switching easily between Russian and Latvian.

For Ina Druviete – who played a key role in the development of Russian speakers' sense of identity by provoking their protests against her school language reforms – it is the Latvians who are too relaxed about switching between Russian and their own language. She is frustrated by the readiness of native Latvian speakers to switch to Russian when they find they are talking to Russian speakers. Her complaint is echoed in a Latvian Language Agency report that criticises Latvians for being 'too tolerant in the choice of communication language'. But the default language for strangers initiating exchanges tends to be Latvian, and the compromises are working throughout Latvian public life. By its efforts to advance and embed Latvian while recognising the minority's rights to use its own language, the Latvian republic has created a society in which nearly every member of each language community has a useful knowledge of the other community's language. As a nation its bilingualism is very asymmetrical, and highly idiosyncratic, but enjoys broad public assent. Russian speakers accept not just in practice but in principle that they should be able to speak the official language, and that the official language of the Latvian republic should be Latvian.[32]

They also appreciate that speaking both languages is in their economic interest. It has not escaped the Language Agency's notice that the historic shift from Russian to Latvian might actually work to the disadvantage of ethnic Latvians in the labour market. While young Russian speakers' command of Latvian has steadily improved, there are signs that young Latvian speakers' Russian skills are declining. If this trend continues and Latvians lose touch with Russian, Russian speakers will enjoy a bilingual competitive advantage.

Within their own families and their own lives, people work out their own compromises. Many work them out in mixed marriages: about a third of marriages in Latvia are between partners with different native tongues. Irina Frolova tells me that her daughter Katya is about to marry a Latvian. Katya is an actress at Rīga's Russian Theatre, named after the Russian-turned-American actor Mikhail, or Michael, Chekhov.[33]

By a coincidence that leads me to suspect Rīga may be a smaller place than its area and population figures suggest, I have an appointment at the Theatre the next day. In the darkened main auditorium, a woman stands centre stage smoking a cigarette and speaking Russian, a large rhomboidal frame forming the set behind her. Her fellow actors are arranged around it, dressed in 1960s-style costumes. This is in fact a rehearsal for a production of the British writer J.B. Priestley's 1932 play *Dangerous Corner*. In the theatre's smaller auditorium they are performing *The Dover Road*, written in the early 1920s by A.A. Milne, creator of Winnie the Pooh.

Much of the theatre's repertoire is Russian in origin, however, and all of it is performed in Russian. Indeed Elmars Senkovs, a Latvian director who works with the company, says that Russian is the only language in which Russian plays can be performed. Meanwhile all the theatre's signs are in Latvian, as the law requires.

As his surname suggests, Senkovs has Russian roots: his father watched Russian TV and read Russian papers, which helped Elmars pick up the language. He spent his childhood in Latgale, the south-eastern province where the majority of the population speaks Russian and many people speak Latgalian, which is recognised by the Latvian Language Law, but only as a variety of Latvian rather than as a language in its own right.

Olga Procevska, who runs a multilingual copywriting agency in Rīga, grew up there too. Her family is Russian but, like so many other Russian families in Latvia, pragmatic about language. Her parents sent her to a Latvian school because it was the best in the area and the language would be useful to learn. She also speaks English, Spanish and French. Yet she is most awed by her native tongue: so vast and so complicated, she says, too big to ever know fully. It is so difficult that in her agency they assign two proofreaders to each Russian translation. (The linguist John McWhorter is similarly impressed: he finds the language 'so horrifically complex that part of me always wonders whether it is an elaborate hoax'.)[34]

Procevska casts herself as a borderland person in the sense that borderlands are understood across the indistinct terrain between Russia and the West, marginal zones of variety and mixture. 'I dislike too much certainty,' she says. She thinks that questions of language and identity may have been less acute in Latgale because of its distance from the ideological disputes of the capital. When she was twelve, however, she suffered from continuous headaches which doctors suggested she might have brought on herself by using two languages.

It's not just in Latgale that individual experiences and family histories reveal a mosaic of diversity underlying Latvian society's division into two language communities. The Latvian Language Agency boasts staff with Estonian, Finnish, Lithuanian, Belarusian and Russian heritage, among them a native Russian speaker. Elizabete Krivcova tells me that on her Immortals Regiment march she carried a picture of her grandfather, a Cossack from Krasnodar, east of the Black Sea, who met his Polish wife when the Red Army fought its way through Poland. He took her back to Krasnodar, but they lost a child in the famine that descended over the region more than a year after the war ended. They went to Latvia where there was food, and which she preferred because it was more European. Krivcova's other grandmother was from an Estonian-German family, but was interned in a Nazi concentration camp despite her German roots.

There are intricate language backstories at the Russian Theatre too. Svetlana Voronetskaya, a stage manager, is from the Karelian region of Russia and is married to a Russian speaker. His mother is Latvian and his father Belarusian; her own mother is one of around 35,000 people whose native tongue is Karelian: Svetlana didn't learn it from her mother, but does speak Finnish, which belongs to the same language family. Svetlana and her husband have a six-year-old daughter whom they gave a Latvian name, Aija, at his insistence – 'We are living in Latvia,' he pointed out. It pays off when Svetlana takes Aija to the polyclinic: she has observed that the staff become friendlier when they hear the child's name. In Edinburgh, the bilingualism researcher Thomas Bak thought along similar lines when his daughter was born. He is Polish-German; his partner is Spanish; they named their baby Alba, which means sunrise in Spanish, and Scotland in Scottish Gaelic.

Svetlana's colleague, actor Alexander Malikov, is the son of a Russian fighter pilot. Having grown up in all the different corners of Soviet and then Russian territory to which his father was posted, he did his own military service in a performing troupe that visited several western European countries, before being recruited to the theatre in Rīga. His girlfriend Līga Sudare was born in an entirely Latvian village. According to Līga, her father says that the only reason to know Russian is to know the enemy's language – but he watches Russian TV because the shows are funnier. Alexander and Līga have had political arguments, they tell me, based on what they have read on the same internet portal: he takes his information from the Russian-language side and she takes hers from the Latvian. Alexander feels himself to be caught between intolerance on both sides. He isn't sure about his 'place', meaning where he belongs. This is his place, he says at first, but later he says that this isn't his place, and his old place is no longer his either.

One sphere that offers speakers of both languages a rough and ready unity is sport. Nora Krevneva is an official photographer for the Latvian football association, and travels with the national team. It is largely Russian and so are its supporters, but Nora confirms that the fans chant in Latvian. So do fans of ice hockey, a more popular sport in Latvia. Nora's friend Olga Dragiļeva, the Latvian TV reporter, recalls seeing two Dinamo Rīga supporters drunkenly discussing a win; one in Latvian, the other in Russian: 'They said it doesn't matter what language they speak, Dinamo won.' Olga goes to Dinamo home matches herself sometimes. 'It's the only place where you can feel a united nation,' she says.

Olga Procevska wonders drily how the country might change if people came to regard language as assets rather than identities. That may be easy if you can speak five of them, as she does. But the country would also change if people embraced the identities that inhabit its languages as well as acquiring their syntax and vocabularies. Igor Nazarenko, a young actor at the Russian Theatre whose education was in Russian and whose father is Ukrainian, offers a simple formula for integration. 'I was born in Latvia,' he says. 'Russian and Latvian: they are both my native languages.'

MOTHER TONGUE LAH

Singapore, formerly a Far Eastern outpost of the British Empire, crowds well over five million people into a city state of well under a thousand square kilometres: a population larger than Scotland's in less than a hundredth of Scotland's area. Being an island nation, it has natural boundaries, and at the same time is fundamentally multi-ethnic, its population accumulated in migrations from various directions since the colony began to develop in the early nineteenth century. Like Latvia, it is a small nation with a strong sense of purpose and a preoccupation with language; but unlike the Republic of Latvia, the Republic of Singapore has embraced multilingualism, and regards the two superpower languages, English and Mandarin, as assets rather than threats.

Crucially, Singapore did not so much achieve independence as have independence thrust upon it. In 1959 it became self-governing – which is to say, governed by the People's Action Party, as it has been ever since. Its first prime minister and founding father Lee Kuan Yew declared independence in 1963, an overture to the city's merger with Malaya, two weeks later, to form Malaysia. The new federation was vulnerable to ethnic tensions from the start, with the Chinese a majority in Singapore but a minority across Malaysia as a whole. Within a year, clashes between Chinese and Malays in Singapore left dozens dead. The year after that, Lee Kuan Yew later recalled, Malaysia's prime minister 'kicked us out'.[35]

The leaders of the newly independent island-city-state realised that it needed above all to be internally cohesive, to integrate its different ethnic communities, and externally connected, to achieve prosperity that could not be generated within its borders. This paternalistic and illiberal government became an early adopter of what came to be known as multiculturalism and globalisation. Internally and externally, languages were key to its strategies.

Singapore's government regards languages as both assets and identities – or rather, it regards English as an asset and Asian languages as vessels of identity. The country has four official languages: Mandarin, Malay, Tamil and English. Malay is also the sole 'national language', the Malays being recognised as the nation's indigenous people, and the language of the national anthem. That is pretty much the extent of Malay's official role, however. English, the 'first language', is the language of administration, work and learning. It is the means by which Singapore has become a city of the world, economically speaking.

Singapore's governing party began promoting English at the expense of Chinese languages as soon as it began to govern, but it could never fully embrace the Western language. While it was convinced that Singaporeans had to be fluent in English in order to be at the forefront of technological and economic development, it was equally certain that they had to remain anchored to their traditional values in order to avoid contamination by the undesirable elements of Western society, the loose morals and disorderly lifestyles, to which they were unavoidably exposed in the English-language information space.

The solution was to treat English as a purely functional language, for making a living and getting things done. It could also serve as a neutral lingua franca among Singapore's ethnic groups, not being a native tongue for any of them. But it would not, in Lee Kuan Yew's words, 'be emotionally acceptable as our mother tongue'. It was not from where Singapore's people were from, historically or psychologically. 'Becoming monolingual in English would have been a setback,' he observed in his memoirs. 'We would have lost our cultural identity, that quiet confidence about ourselves and our place in the world.'[36]

Singaporeans thus require English as their 'first language' and the appropriate Asian language as their 'mother tongue'. For Chinese Singaporeans, who make up three quarters of the population, their mother tongue may well be their mother's tongue, but it may well not be their grandmother's. When the People's Action Party came to power in the late 1950s, only about 3 per cent of Chinese Singaporeans spoke Mandarin at home. The vast majority spoke Southern Chinese varieties such as Hokkien, Teochew and Cantonese, lumped together by the government as 'dialects'. Today nearly half speak Mandarin at home, and the so-called dialects are spoken by less than 15 per cent. This must in large measure be due to the government's efforts to standardise Mandarin as the mother tongue of the ethnic Chinese. In 1980, the year after Lee Kuan Yew launched the Speak Mandarin Campaign, 60 per cent of Singapore's total population were dialect speakers. Only 10 per cent spoke Mandarin: the proportion trebled over the following thirty years.[37]

The campaign's ultimate goal is to make Chinese Singaporeans 'a single people, speaking the same primary language, possessing a distinct culture and a shared past'. Singapore likes a simple, tidy set of ethnic categories – these are used in another key harmonisation policy, the setting of quotas in housing to prevent the development of ethnic enclaves – and the Mandarin campaign has successfully reduced the diversity hidden within the 'Chinese' category.[38]

In the process, a policy with the stated aim of improving communication and understanding among Chinese Singaporeans has also had the effect of obstructing communication and understanding among different generations within Chinese families. 'Parents want their children to retain traditional Chinese values in filial piety, loyalty, benevolence, and love,' observed Lee Kuan Yew, proposing Mandarin as a means though which those children could emotionally identify themselves with an ancient civilisation and its values. Yet school-taught Mandarin can divide children from their older relatives, who are likely to be the most deeply immersed in those values. 'When I talk to my grandfather there's a deafening silence that falls between us,' says student Risa Tan, in an English-language talk, 'when

I don't know how to describe how I'm feeling, he doesn't know how to describe what he's feeling because his mode of fluency is Hokkien and my mode of fluency is Chinese B at Standard Level.'[39]

Singapore stands out as a nation that prides itself on getting its people to use more than one language. 'Bilingualism will give Singapore a competitive edge over any other Asian city for years to come,' said Senior Minister S. Iswaran in 2009. 'It gives us our distinctive identity as a people – while we share a common cultural heritage with many of our neighbours in the region, we are unique in the cohesion and vibrancy of our multicultural society.' All things being equal, a nation that bases its identity on bilingualism is likely to sustain its languages far longer than nations that would ideally prefer to have just the one. But when the policy is that one of the two languages has to be English, all things are not equal. English is advancing rapidly as speakers of Malay, Tamil and non-Mandarin varieties of Chinese convert to it. In 2000, less than a quarter of Chinese Singaporeans spoke English more than any other language at home; by 2010, the proportion had risen to almost a third. These trends seem to suggest that in the long run the country could end up with an effective English-Mandarin duopoly. There are obvious incentives to adopt the languages of the world's largest economies: as China's trading power has grown, Singapore has increasingly seen material as well as moral value in Mandarin.[40]

What such figures don't reveal, however, is the vitality of a kind of English that is a source of mortification for the regularising, aspiring Singapore government. As far as the elite is concerned, there is only one right way to speak English, and since 2000 it has urged Singaporeans to support the Speak Good English Movement. The target of the campaign is Singlish, described in 1999 by the then prime minister Goh Chok Tong as 'broken, ungrammatical English sprinkled with words and phrases from local dialects and Malay'. For Singaporeans like Risa Tan, it is the language of 'emotion and experience', of everyday life, which enables them to express thoughts and feelings in an idiom evolved by the communities of Singapore, not prescribed by the government. For some of them it is the basis of a shared distinctive identity – 'it may be the ONLY thing that makes us uniquely Singaporean,' says one supporter.[41]

The Speak Good English Movement was launched to counter the threat posed by Singlish, in the government's view, to the national goal of becoming a first-class world economy. Singlish was to be discouraged because it inevitably undermined the quality of standard English spoken by Singaporeans, making it harder for foreigners to understand them. Proper standards are urged even when there are no foreigners present: the list of 'Singaporean Blunders' on the Speak Good English Movement website begins 'At Home'. It would be safe to say that with slogans like 'Grammar Rules Matter', the Speak Good English campaign is aimed at minds rather than hearts.[42]

Singlish offers a popular, organic alternative to the carefully planned multiculturalism engineered by the nation's leadership and implemented from the top down. All Singapore's ethnic groups are represented in its vocabulary, which is rich in words from languages and dialects that are declining in the face of policy pressure and competition from more prestigious tongues. 'It's as if we took teaspoons of local dialects, of Tamil, of Malay, of Mandarin, and we stirred them into a tea of our colonial past,' says Risa Tan. 'We poured in a heavy Singaporean accent, and Singlish was what we got.'[43]

Although Singlish is indeed a variety of English, its Chinese influences are apparent in its grammar, sounds and rhythms, as well as in the multi-purpose particles, most notably 'lah', without which no utterance seems complete. Jock Wong, who speaks Singapore English as well as studying it, distinguishes three different forms of lah. Spoken in a low tone, it serves to impose an idea on the hearer; in a rising tone, it is used to persuade them of it; and in a falling tone, it suggests that the idea is obvious. In other varieties of English, and other languages, such tags commonly take the form of questions: isn't it?, n'est-ce pas?, nicht wahr?. They are formally uncertain, even though they may actually be intended to affirm certainty. Wong suggests that Singlish tags do not entertain any such doubts, even formally, because Singaporeans like to get to the point. 'A Singapore English speaker will not hesitate to attempt to change the addressee's way of thinking,' he observes, '... while an Anglo English speaker is more likely to acknowledge another individual's point of view.' Yet while an English speaker from Britain might find Singlish directness rude, a Singaporean who does not use particles in everyday exchanges with other Singaporeans 'may be seen as impersonal or even pretentious'.[44]

The government does have a point: this product of grass-roots openness and exchange can be baffling to outsiders. But when mixed with standard English, as it typically is, its appeal is readily apparent. Asking someone to 'off' the light, omitting 'turn', is both economical and comprehensible (although it is at the top of the list of 'Singaporean Blunders'). So is the Singlish riposte to the Speak Good English Movement's prescriptions: 'Go and die lah!'

Official attitudes may be softening, though. Lah featured as an 'icon of SG' on the website of a Minister-led body celebrating the fiftieth anniversary of Singapore's independence. The government has acknowledged the voice of the people.[45]

Commenting online from Australia, Singaporean emigrant Ahmad Nazhar welcomes the acceptance of Singlish, though it presents him with a domestic challenge. He and his wife speak 'impeccable English' but use Singlish as a 'secret language' around the house when they want to confuse the kids. Now they will have to learn a new language. Which to choose? Perhaps Russian, he ventures.[46]

* * * *

Small nations can tell us a lot about larger nations' relationships with languages, but larger nations serve as a necessary reminder that the power of a state to impose order upon languages will only ever go so far. In thinking about the future of plural language use, it's also necessary to consider a new and potentially transformative force: communications technology, bridging languages as well as distances.

CHAPTER NINE

Possible Words

The future of language use will be shaped by both familiar factors and novel ones. It could be enriched by a recognition that languages brought together offer more than languages set against each other.

TAMING THE WEST

Raees drives his wife out beyond the city, bouncing through dirt and scrub in an open Jeep, to show her where he plans to make his dream come true. This is the site he has chosen for his world, 'Your World', the housing colony he wants to build for his people, the ones he grew up among, using the wealth he has amassed bootlegging liquor into 'dry' Gujarat. He points this way and that to show what will be where. Over there will be an English-medium school, 'where kids are speaking perfect English,' he tells Aasiyah, in Hindi. 'Good morning,' he adds, by way of illustration, in English and with a bow.[1]

It's another box-office success for Shah Rukh Khan, the Bollywood superstar who ranks among the world's highest-earning screen actors. The film is set in the 1980s, but the idea of an English-medium school as the key to achieving aspirations in India is entirely current. Seventy years after the British quit the subcontinent, their language represents the summit of a dream in a Bollywood movie. Across the border, Pakistani schools are said to be in the grip of 'English-medium fever', an epidemic also reported from Africa, China and South-East Asia. World domination for English seems as inevitable as the plot trajectory that ensures Raees's world will never be built. People saw it coming long before the advent of the technology that seems to assure its triumph. Back in 1923, a Welsh schoolteacher and bilingualism researcher called David Saer wrote of 'the powerful and penetrating English tongue, which in every part of the world has proved itself to be all-conquering among the languages of the earth'.[2]

Conquering is not the same as replacing, though. English could never win more than a fraction of the language franchises in a country as populous, segmented and stratified as India. It may indeed be developing a cross-border role as a home language for middle-class children whose parents come from different caste or religious back-grounds, in large cities such as Bengaluru and Hyderabad, but that will always be a niche market. Among university-educated people in Hyderabad, there are signs that the use of it is increasing outside the most intimate circles of friendship and family, but that still leaves the mass of the city's five million inhabitants, as well as the heart of the personal sphere, to Telugu, the most extensively spoken language, and Dakkhini, the Urdu dialect spoken by the city's Muslim minority. It is true that India is likely to lose many languages: the People's Linguistic Survey of India, working its way through 50 planned volumes to cover the 780 tongues it has identified, estimates that 220 others have gone extinct in the last 50 years, and warns that more than half of the remainder may disappear in the next 50. But India will always be multilingual. Millions of Indians will continue to speak more than one language, and often several, using different ones in different domains of their lives. Indian languages are not existentially threatened by the prestige of English, any more than they were when it was the language of what even its British rulers called the Raj.[3]

Whereas small states like Latvia and Singapore can apply language policies with results that are as diagrammatic as the real world gets, India is the world's greatest reminder of the limits to design. With a few signal exceptions such as airports, everything will always be a compromise between the plans and the populace, the latter modifying the former to its own myriad requirements. The variety of those needs and demands will sustain the variety of the languages, within individuals as well as across communities. If people acquire their various language repertoires in a patchwork of settings, as so many in India do, they end up with a mosaic of competences. 'In certain domains, I speak English well,' says the neurologist Suvarna Alladi. 'If it's groceries, it's Telugu. If it's animals, it's Telugu. But if it's objects, it's English. If you give me a list of twenty objects to name, I say them all in English, but I can't do that in Telugu. Glass, computer, book, glasses, telephone, window, door – they're all in English.' For people who have more than one language at their disposal, however, such divisions are not an impediment to communication. In a mosaic, the pieces work together. At one point in a conversation with Dr Alladi and her colleagues Vasanta Duggirala and Bapiraju Surampudi, which ranges broadly across different aspects of language and research into it, I ask them what language they would be speaking if I weren't there. English, they tell me, and also Telugu. Towards the end of the conversation they do indeed begin to combine the two languages.

It may be true that the ability to combine an Indian language with English is largely the preserve of the elites, the upper middle classes, and the striving lower middle classes who send their children to English-medium schools. It may also be true that the global language on which people draw when they want to say 'telephone' or 'computer' is better adapted to the modern world than its regional neighbours. But prestige is not the same as dominance, and Western languages do not turn their speakers into Westerners. In the domain of language research, Dr Alladi and her colleagues do not find that Western ideas satisfactorily reflect their experience or that of their compatriots, who comprise 1.3 billion of the 7.5 billion people on the planet. Linguistic theory like that of Chomsky, 'concerned primarily with an ideal speaker-listener, in a completely homogeneous speech community', is far removed from the everyday hubbub of Indian speakers who are less than ideal, but more than adequate within their various domains. Suvarna Alladi sees little use for the Western – or more particularly American – model of bilingualism in which a person has a fixed mother tongue, neatly labelled L1 by the linguists, and then learns a clear-cut second language, the L2, usually in a classroom. 'That doesn't work for us,' she says.[4]

It certainly doesn't work as a model of her own language history, or that of her family. 'My mother-in-law spoke Bengali and Hindi fluently and some English, and my Hindi was not so good, so for seven years my mother-in-law and I were speaking to each other in a broken Hindi,' she recalls. 'Hindi was not her mother tongue, my Hindi was not so good either, but I had Bengali surrounding me. Then my daughter was born, and in seven days, I don't know how, I was speaking fluent Bengali, and I haven't stopped since.'

Seven years of broken Hindi, then fluent Bengali within seven days: there could hardly be a clearer illustration of the role of incentive in language proficiency. Realising that her daughter would grow up speaking Bengali, she claimed her place in that language community without further delay. The story also illustrates how intimately languages can mix in India: people may encounter a variety of them not just in the marketplace, the workplace or the school, but within their own families.

Yet while India offers countless examples of plural, flexible and adaptive language use, language is also implicated in the country's many divisions of religion, ethnic identity, caste and class. The language most widely spoken in various forms across the north of the subcontinent is even divided within itself. In India it is called Hindi;

it is called Urdu in Pakistan, and in India when identified with Muslim communities. The major difference between the two is that Hindi is written in the Devanagari script, while Urdu is written in a script of Arabic and Persian derivation. In a city marketplace the two branches may be indistinguishable to the ear; in other settings, they may be mutually incomprehensible. They have diverged with increasing speed since the partition of the subcontinent. High-status forms of Hindi were infused with more Sanskrit influences, their Urdu counterparts with Persian. India's first prime minister, Jawaharlal Nehru, spoke Hindi but often called it Urdu. He would complain that he could not understand the Hindi broadcast on All-India Radio – including reports of his own speeches.[5]

Hindi has been seen as a threat in states to the south of the great Hindi belt. In 1965 plans to make it the country's sole official language provoked two months of rioting in what is now the state of Tamil Nadu, despite provisions for the continuing use of English that had been introduced in the face of earlier opposition. More than fifty years later, a leading Tamil Nadu politician referred to the 'tradition of martyrdom' in such protests when he denounced Hindi-promoting measures taken by the current central government, including the replacement of English by Hindi on highway milestones. M.K. Stalin – born in the week of the Soviet dictator's death, and named after him – warned against the central government's 'manoeuvres to push India into becoming Hindia'.[6]

Pushing a country is one thing, though; pushing a subcontinent is another matter. Politicians recognise that if they press down on it, it will well up around them. The viaducts built to carry metro railway lines through cities like Hyderabad stride on concrete pylons at heights that could almost be described as altitudes, as if the traffic below might rise like floodwater to multi-storey levels. In Kochi, the largest city in Kerala, the station names are presented in three different languages and scripts: Malayalam, Kerala's main language, the arcs and loops of its script suggesting a calisthenic kind of harmony; Hindi, in the Devanagari script that looks like rails with utensils hanging from them; and English, which looks like it does all over the world. The same formula – main state language, in this case Kannada, Hindi, English – was prescribed for the metro in Bengaluru, capital of Karnataka, but the authorities took a second look at it in the face of protests against the inclusion of Hindi. At last the cities are getting public transport capable of travelling unimpeded in straight lines from one stop to another, but language choices are rarely so straightforward.[7]

This variation on the international phenomenon of the tram conflict, with the dispute here revolving around the system's language choices rather than those of the passengers, illustrates that the global advance of English is not the only big story in language power politics. In states like Karnataka and Tamil Nadu, English plays the part of the overseas great power on which a smaller nation can draw to offset the might of the neighbouring regional power. That does not imply becoming a cultural vassal, though, any more than the use of English by individual Indians implies assimilation into Western culture. On the billboards advertising women's fashions along the roads in Kerala, the text is entirely in English, and the styles exclusively Indian.

Like individuals, organisations combine languages in varied, vigorous and sometimes curious ways. Kerala's TV channels report domestic news and foreign football matches using Malayalam captions headlined by English exclamations – 'Flash', 'Live', 'Breaking News'. And where media English is used at length, in newspapers, it is written in a distinctively Indian journalistic idiom that bears traces of how the British spoke English when they ruled India. When several thousand young men brought Kochi traffic to a standstill, hoping to catch a glimpse of a celebrity who had come to town to open a mobile phone showroom, the *Times of India* reported that police charged the crowd wielding canes 'to restrain the infatuated youths, lest their collective ogling take a different, less innocuous shape'.

Although Sunny Leone was 'demurely but fetchingly clad' for her engagement in Kochi, her fame is based not on her Bollywood movie appearances, but on her previous overseas career as a pornographic performer – a trajectory that is determined by the balance of forces between globalisation and India's capacity to recast foreign culture in its own image. India is more powerful than the internet, through which Leone built her Indian fan base. It absorbed the challenge to its mores that she represented. Now she is 'demurely clad' in public, and features in a movie whose leading actors swerve at the last moment in romantic scenes to avoid 'lip lock'.[8]

India is unique, but it is compelling in part because it seems to encompass all humankind. Its dialogues with globalisation suggest that in culture, the West's dominance will never be as pervasive as Westerners fancy. That may prove to be the case for language too.

AUTOMATED BARRIERS

Writing in the 1920s, David Saer understood political power to be the main force driving language shift. The 'powerful and penetrating English tongue' had proved 'all-conquering' because Britain had conquered so much of the planet's land and could boast of ruling its waves as well. Saer contemplated the process not just in lands of the Empire overseas but also in his own native land, Wales. 'Under British rule there are many peoples who speak other tongues,' he observed, 'and, consciously or unconsciously, the English language is coming to prevail in the subject-states of Britain, the natives during the process passing through various stages of bilingualism.'[9]

These stages, however, would be prolonged by the natives' reluctance to abandon their language. Shifts would resemble steps rather than slopes, each downward step arousing 'patriotic emotions' that might prompt measures to counter the decline. In Wales the statistics would go on to give broad support to this account, with the percentage of Welsh speakers continuing to fall over the subsequent fifty years, but then picking up somewhat in the last decades of the century. The uptick reflected a shift in the balance of political power towards Welsh, which achieved equality with English as a public and official language through the Welsh Language Act of 1993.[10]

By then, of course, the British Empire had all but vanished. The onward global advance of English was now being fuelled by America's economic might, and its cultural soft power, rather than its political dominance. Electronic technology was an increasingly salient vehicle for projecting English across continents and borders, lighting up the skies with American scenes and filling the air with American choruses. In the very last years of the century, early internet adopters began to realise that digital technology had untapped potential to support languages, particularly marginal or struggling ones, by bringing their speakers together. But it was not until the internet had demonstrated itself to be an even more commanding global phenomenon than English that technology began to emerge as an active agent, as distinct from a vehicle or medium, in the interplay of languages. As computers have acquired the ability to translate, transferring meaning not just between places but between languages themselves, they have introduced a potent new factor into processes hitherto dominated by politics and economics.

The idea of automating translation emerged from political conflict, between the powers that emerged strongest from the Second World War, and both sides' need for intelligence about each other's military capabilities. Its founding text, a memorandum written in 1949 by Warren Weaver of the Rockefeller Foundation, was informed by the author's wartime experience of computer design and awareness of cryptography. Weaver related an anecdote from the war in which a

mathematician asked a colleague for a coded message to test a deci-
phering method that he had devised. His colleague wrote a message
in Turkish and then encrypted it as a column of digits. The would-be
codebreaker came back the next day, reporting that he had failed to
decipher the message. In fact he had, but did not realise that it was in
Turkish.[11]

It occurred to Weaver that if a codebreaker could decode a message
without knowing what language it was in, a machine might be able to
translate from one language to another. Having guessed that new
mechanized codebreaking methods had been developed, he wondered
'if the problem of translation could conceivably be treated as a problem
in cryptography'. This would entail treating foreign languages as
codes, and foreign texts as English ones that had been encrypted:
'When I look at an article in Russian, I say "This is really written in
English, but it has been coded in some strange symbols. I will now
proceed to decode."'

His fictive assumption of deceit goes with the cryptographic territory, but it speaks of the dual nature of language, shutter as well as
window. The notion of concealment contrasts with the vision of
transparency that animates the memorandum. Weaver regarded the
existence of multiple languages as an obstacle to cultural interchange
and international understanding. He wanted to reverse the confusion
of Babel, to which he implicitly alluded in his image of languages as
a set of tall towers that are closed, but built on a common foundation.
People struggle to communicate by shouting from one tower to
another, but if they descend to below the surface, they find themselves
in a 'great open basement', where they can meet and communicate
freely with each other.

A few years later, having inspired a major research effort to make
machine translation a reality in America, he hailed the linguists, logi-
cians and electronic engineers who were 'engaged in erecting a new
Tower of Anti-Babel'. One of them was the young Noam Chomsky,

hired to work on machine translation at the Massachusetts Institute of Technology despite declaring at his job interview that the project 'had no intellectual interest and was also pointless'. He and Weaver did share a deep conceptual interest, though. Weaver's image of a deep universal foundation to language, beneath the differences that set languages apart, anticipated Chomsky's notion of Universal Grammar. And Weaver's quest for 'the real but as yet undiscovered universal language' channelled thinkers from an earlier age such as John Dee, as charismatic and baffling in his own way as Chomsky is in his, who believed that deep linguistic study could lead them back towards the original divine tongue, of which human languages were corrupted forms. Codes, ciphers, secret knowledge and the notion of an undiscovered universal language have an imaginative affinity.[12]

Spies and associated seekers of hidden knowledge warmed to the idea of machine translation, as the information front of the Cold War became increasingly active. The front extended far beyond military secrets and political intelligence. Scientists and engineers needed to read scientific and technical texts published on the other side, so that they knew what their opposite numbers knew and were doing. In 1954 IBM and Georgetown University staged a demonstration in which a computer, occupying an area the size of a tennis court, translated a set of sentences from Russian into English. Most of them were about chemistry.[13]

The demonstration was instigated by Léon Dostert, a French émigré who had interpreted for General Eisenhower during the war, and installed the simultaneous interpretation system at the Nuremberg trials afterwards. He had worked for the Office of Strategic Services, the predecessor of the Central Intelligence Agency, the CIA, and was friends with Allen Dulles, its director. The Agency took a keen interest in machine translation, and funded subsequent research into it at Georgetown. Dulles affirmed the need to keep up with the ever-expanding volume of technical literature from the USSR – and also invoked the goal that Warren Weaver hoped to attain in that great open basement beneath the towers. 'In addition,' he told the director of the National Science Foundation, 'many of us feel that the degree of human understanding that could be accomplished if language barriers could be lowered without sacrificing linguistic integrity might well be a major step towards peace.' One of his colleagues quoted those words to a Congressional committee in May 1960, a day after the Soviet leader Nikita Khrushchev threatened to attack the United States with atomic bombs if the Americans continued to fly spy planes over its territory. Khrushchev's forces had marked May Day by shooting one down and capturing its pilot.[14]

Weaver had suggested that translation could be achieved by statistical methods, mapping one language to another by identifying patterns within texts. The researchers whom he inspired took a different approach, seeking to equip computers with sets of rules defining how the languages worked. This strategy failed to live up to the hopes placed in it, and in 1966 the research programme folded after an expert report advised the US government not to fund it further. The report also dealt a hammer blow to the American programme's mirror image in the USSR, because 'for the Soviet bureaucracy, an American opinion on scientific, economic or military problems was of the highest authority'.[15]

Though the cold warriors set machine translation aside, governments elsewhere became increasingly interested in it as a technology for harmonisation. Canada needed to translate between the two languages, English and French, to which it accorded official status in 1969. The European Community started off with six countries and four official languages; by 1993, when the Maastricht Treaty elevated it into the European Union, it had twelve members, and the Treaty was set down in ten languages. Brussels was becoming the global capital of translation data.[16]

At the end of the 1980s, texts from the Canadian parliamentary record, known as Hansard after its British prototype, provided the data for a project offering proof of a new machine translation concept – or rather, the vindication of Warren Weaver's original concept. The IBM team behind the Candide system argued that Weaver's idea of using statistical methods had failed not because the idea was wrong, but because early machine translation projects lacked sufficient computing power to do the statistical analysis, and sufficient data to do it on. Now they had the means and the material. The system could proceed by calculating the probability that if a word appears in a text, it will also appear at a corresponding location in a translated version of the text. By learning the associations between words on the left-hand page and words on the right, so to speak, it would become able to make translations of its own.[17]

This was how Google Translate subsequently established itself, training on vast bodies – the term of art is corpora – of text generated by translation hothouses such as the European Parliament. For most languages, it achieved in the early twenty-first century what Allen Dulles and the CIA hoped machine translation would achieve for Russian in the 1950s. It might be inelegant and erratic, but it gave readers the gist – and that, as Dulles anticipated, has proved immensely useful. With compatible language pairs between which there is particularly heavy traffic, such as Spanish and English, computers demonstrate that they are capable of producing texts that would take editors less time to tidy up than much of the native copy they might get from human contributors. Performance will improve as the volumes of translated text swell ever larger, giving the systems more and more data to learn from, and as new learning programs are installed. Google Translate began with a system that tackled texts phrase by phrase; ten years later, it graduated to a 'neural machine translation' system that could handle entire sentences.[18]

The really transformative possibilities lie in live speech translation, which Skype introduced in 2014. It was immediately obvious to onlookers where this technology should go: into the ear, like Babel fish, the imaginary creatures thought up by the humorous writer Douglas Adams in the 1970s, which could translate any language in the universe. Prototype earpiece versions duly began to emerge. Once the technology has achieved truly comprehensive coverage, it will offer the promise of a world without language barriers. Wherever you go in the world, you will hear what people say to you in your own tongue, no matter what language they are actually speaking. In a perfect world, that is.[19]

Even in an imperfect world, ubiquitous and immediate speech translation looks like a very realistic prospect. So where will that leave English? Two headline possibilities suggest themselves. One is that English will be drastically devalued as a currency. The other is that English monoglots will decide that they no longer need to worry about their monolingual condition. These possibilities are mutually consistent.

Once stocked with artificial Babel fish, the world will have much less need of linguae francae. For everyday practical purposes, an earpiece will do the job. The value of learning English, or any other lingua franca, will diminish correspondingly. So will the value to monoglots of learning a foreign language. But the economic impact will be greater upon English than on most other languages, since it has so much more value to lose.

The effects may be both less dramatic and more ambivalent, however. Smartphones are already making it easier for travellers in need of local information to consult the internet rather than ask a local. By the time Babel fish have become universal, travellers' interest in speaking to the people around them may have declined considerably. The same may go for migrants who would prefer not to speak the surrounding language if they can possibly avoid it. Speech translation would be just another stage in the erosion by technology of incentives to use different languages.

Those incentives are not the only ones, though, and not necessarily the most important ones. They relate to commodity-level speech, limited to practical information and instrumental functions. At the premium end of the language market, and also in the private realms of life that don't have prices put on them, it may be the social and emotional dimensions of language that add the most value.

Perhaps the most intriguing question about earpiece translators is how people will warm to each other with electronic intermediation when they are face to face in person. One of the most remarkable and least anticipated phenomena of modern communication is how readily limited channels support sociability and intimacy. People form friendships, conduct courtships and share feelings via fragmentary text exchanges, pocket-sized screens and images labouring to avoid disintegration. They need very little bandwidth for their deepest connections. But these are all ways to communicate at a distance. In each other's presence, people may feel electronic mediation to be an inferior substitute for direct speech. They may dislike the perceptual dissonance between the face they see and the voice they hear. Even if the translator simulates the sound of the speaker's voice, it won't match the moving lips. People will look, and may well feel, like actors in dubbed movies.

That might not deter some of them from relationships with spouses or children based on communication via headsets. But the very existence of such an option will highlight the value of a shared language, which derives from the investment required to attain it. Because learning a language requires time, effort and often expense, it is a reliable signal of commitment, and reliable signals promote trust. They work both for deep relationships, such as those between intimate partners or between parents and children, and for shallow interactions of the passing kind that make up much of everyday life. Immigrant shopkeepers who learn their customers' language do not just make sales and purchases easier. They show that they are making an effort to draw closer to their customers' community. At the same time, they are also politely asserting their place in the speech community and the territory which that community occupies.

Up above street level, people in business, the professions and elite domains in general will likewise use their investment in languages to powerful but intangible effect. They will understand the monoglots they encounter better than the monoglots will understand them, which will give them an advantage in their business or political dealings. In international relations, monolinguals will be able to get computers to provide them with clear translations of what the other side's media are saying about them. (With some of the most heavily translated languages, they already can.) They won't get the jokes, though. Tone and nuance will escape them. Nor will they really get the importance of understanding the other side's point of view, because they have not been encouraged into the habit of doing so by using other languages. Among the many asymmetries that worked to Britain's disadvantage in its negotiations to leave the European Union was the twenty-seven other nations' fluent grasp of the *Daily Telegraph* and the *Daily Mail,* unmatched by any corresponding British familiarity with the *Frankfurter Allgemeine Zeitung* or *Bild.*

Wherever they go, the multilingual cosmopolitans will feel and seem at home. They will sound as though they have a right to be there. And they will also enjoy the advantages of being able to make friends without having to rely on a synthesised voice in the ear. So will those who recognise that a little knowledge can go a long way. Possessing that knowledge is what matters. A phone may be able to handle foreign languages better than you can, and it is far better at arithmetic than you can ever be, but you will use a foreign language more fruitfully if you have made even a small part of it your own, in the same way that a person who can do sums in their head will have an advantage in transactions with a person who has to reach for a calculator in order to find out where they stand. You may only need a few words to make a friend. Possessing those words makes them part of your world, too. Unlike the ones that you rely upon your phone to deliver, they are not entirely foreign – and the people who possess the language comprehensively will not seem so foreign to you either.

The value of language will separate into two tiers, commodity and premium. Machine-translated speech will become a commodity product, delivering basic information not dissimilar in character to the kind of technical material that the CIA hoped to obtain from the systems they backed in the 1950s. Human speech will enjoy a premium arising from its power to bring people together, to make them comfortable with each other, and to promote trust. Shared language will add value to services, making them pleasant to experience, and promoting those feelings of trust that commercial enterprises have come to recognise as vital to success under light-speed trading conditions. The international hotel will still have receptionists, and they will have translation earpieces, but guests will be happiest when greeted by a voice that is in synch with the lips. For many of them, that will require a lingua franca, and English has the advantage of global incumbency.

Meanwhile, just a few blocks away, the grocery shopkeeper may very well be sitting behind a security screen and a language screen too, with a microphone and a chip to keep the channel as narrow as possible. In an unequal world, machine translation will lower language barriers in some quarters, and keep them raised in others.

SHINING IN EACH OTHER'S LIGHT

The question is whether the twenty-first century world is like that of the two previous centuries but faster, or whether it is different in quality from previous worlds. Its driving force is as described in the Communist Manifesto of 1848, only even more so: 'Constant revolutionising of production, uninterrupted disturbance of all social conditions, everlasting uncertainty and agitation ... All that is solid melts into air ...' In the late twentieth century that extraordinary pronouncement, from an age of iron and steam, reappeared like a prophecy that could not be understood until it had come to pass. With the onset of the twenty-first century, the metaphor seemed to have anticipated the idea of the sublimation of the physical into the virtual. It had been there ready for 150 years, waiting to define how the internet would transform the human condition.[20]

Contemporary prophets of the Great Sublimation – most of whom are anything but communists – broadly share a vision of speed, fluidity and mobility. As in the economy, so in the self: 'fixed, fast-frozen relations' are a thing of the past; all is accessible and all can be combined; identities are fluid and categories melt into each other. These would seem to be highly favourable conditions for the free and flexible use of language. Some scholars affirm that goal by speaking of 'translanguaging', which refers to the use of language without regard for boundaries, rules or standard forms. They use the term in order to challenge the very idea that there are such entities as languages, definable by rules and identifiable by names.[21]

In this radically self-centred perspective, nobody speaks languages: everybody speaks their own idiolect, or repertoire of words and ways of combining them. But to deny that languages are linguistic entities is not to deny that they are social entities. It is to mount a challenge to their political power, and in particular the power of national and state languages. In form and intent the manoeuvre resembles the largely successful challenge mounted against the idea that race is a biological reality, rather than a social one. The rejection of categories hitherto taken for granted, like Spanish and English, also parallels the more recent movement to sideline the two previously unquestioned gender categories, male and female, in favour of fluidity.

A world in which all relations seem to be in flux certainly has a different quality to its predecessors. But this is not the whole world, nor even most of it. And what works for issues of gender may not work for questions of language use. Demands for the right to define one's gender as one wishes, or for people to be able to marry each other regardless of gender, can win broad assent in modern liberal societies because they invoke generally shared beliefs that individuals should be able to shape their identities and live their lives as they choose. Language choices may also be fundamental to an individual's identity, but society at large is likely to put its own idea of its collective interests first.

That leaves languages in the world they have inhabited for the past couple of centuries, bound to nations and nation states. Historians divide the era since the Middle Ages into the early modern period and the late modern period, the former giving way to the latter as the eighteenth century gave way to the nineteenth. When Johann Gottfried Herder lived in Rīga, during the 1760s, early modern order prevailed over the city and its hinterland. Rīga was part of the Russian empire, but local power remained in the hands of the Baltic German nobility. The lands to the south and west were under the rule, direct or indirect, of the Polish-Lithuanian Commonwealth. That great amoeba of the eastern European flatlands, enclosing an assortment of languages, religions and clans, represented fluidity of an early modern kind. Its days were numbered, though, and its dismemberment began a few years after Herder left Rīga. With it went a pluralistic notion of belonging, based on allegiance rather than on identity. The state had been embodied and defined by its ruling elite. Its subjects were part of it by virtue of their subjecthood, regardless of whether they were Catholic, Protestant, Orthodox or Jewish, whether they spoke Lithuanian, Yiddish or a Slavic tongue.

As a more modern modernity took shape, the assumption that a state could be defined solely by its dominant class was challenged by the Herderian idea that a nation is embodied in its common people, or Volk. It readily followed that states should correspond to nations, in the sense of peoples, and that each nation ought ideally to have a state of its own. But what made the common people into a people?

The obvious answer was a common tongue. Claims to statehood were to be based on nationhood, and nationhood was to be based on language. As Wilhelm von Humboldt nearly said, every language should draw about the people that possesses it a border.[22]

In practice, and especially in those eastern tracts where natural borders are among the scarcest of natural resources, states have tended to harbour more than one language within their territories. Poland today is the exception that proves the rule, most dreadfully: its unnatural homogeneity was achieved by Nazi genocide and post-war ethnic cleansing in which many millions of people were forced across its redrawn frontiers. Rīga has become the capital of a state that is devoted to a single language and the people who speak it, but has had to reconcile its raison d'être with the presence of a large minority who speak a different language. Its solution has been to mitigate ethnic nationalism with a civic nationalism that accords citizenship to members of the minority who can demonstrate an ability to speak the national language.

Although Latvia's institutional preoccupation with language makes it look unusual among nations, not to say eccentric, its underlying assumption is shared by many other countries around the world. If people want to become part of a nation, they are expected to achieve a grasp of its language, and they may have to pass a test of their ability in order to be granted citizenship. Latvia differs from other countries in imposing such conditions upon people who were born there, rather than on immigrants, but the principle is the same: one nation, one language. Most countries that embrace this principle apply a modernised version of the nineteenth-century model, in which the idea of a national language is detached from ideas of 'native stock' and anything else that smacks of race. They believe in assimilation instead.

The apparent vigour of the national idea does not necessarily imply that the era of the nation state, as conceived in the nineteenth century, is set to continue throughout the twenty-first. Contemporary nationalism is a reaction against globalisation, off which it is feeding hungrily. It may not prevail against its worldwide enemy. The noise it has been making in the early part of the century might be a final hurrah, as it rallies to its flags one last time. It faces the inevitability of mass migration, drawn from east to west and south to north by the growing demand for labour in developed countries with ageing populations, and the competitive advantages of globally organised enterprise. Behind national borders it is already starting to find itself in competition with alternative identities, asserted by large cities that differ in character and outlook from the surrounding provinces. The vernaculars that flourish in the metropolises, sampling and remixing the various languages spoken in them, are the sound of those differences. Yet the national idea remains politically compelling, in large measure precisely because it defies the rising seas of economics and demography. And its power is not confined to the reactionary nationalist camp. Across populations as a whole, it remains emotionally compelling as the basis of a collective sense of self. Nation-states will continue to inspire loyalty on the basis of national identity for the foreseeable future. Forced by their own needs to accept migrants, they may well compensate with flagship assimilation policies, in which language will be central.

Alternatively, they might evolve more pluralistic ideas of themselves and their citizens. They might start to see languages not as threatening identities, but as valuable assets.

* * * *

Here is a synopsis of the future, based on reasonable assumptions, realistic expectations, and things that are likely to happen. Some of these things are highly likely. Others are all too likely. There are also one or two developments that depend on big ifs.

The world will keep turning, and people will keep moving around it. They will also move across shorter distances, continuing human-kind's exodus from the country to the city. This constant circulation and mixture will bring speakers of different languages into contact more intensely than ever before. The areas in which many languages are simultaneously spoken will steadily increase in size.

In many parts of the world, several languages or more will co-exist indefinitely. No single language will become so politically powerful or economically valuable that it sends all the other languages around it into irreversible decline. Some languages will prosper more than others, however. A country, city or neighbourhood may remain unshakeably multilingual, but the mix of languages spoken in it may alter as time goes by. Across the Indian subcontinent the balances between the stronger languages will not shift dramatically. In emerging foci of multi-lingualism, such as African megacities, the outcomes will depend on the pace and variety of immigration. Languages spoken by small numbers of people will succumb to competition in these busy marketplaces. They will fare no better where they came from. Rates of language extinction will increase, though specimens will be better preserved thanks to tech-nology and the dedication of supporters in the face of the inevitable.

The more that wealthy and ageing nations depend on migration, the more they will insist on competence in the national language, and the more pressure they will place on immigrants to abandon their family languages for the dominant one. Some of them will, however, become readier to promote regional languages, such as Occitan or Breton in France, that are regarded as part of the country's indigenous heritage. Such languages will no longer be seen as a threat to national unity, having declined to levels at which official patronage will do little to empower them. They will serve to enhance the contrast between native and foreign.

That simple contrast will be subverted in the cities – as it is now, but to an ever greater extent. Migration and trade will accentuate the contrasts between metropolitan areas and provincial centres. Major cities will become yet more major, in size, economic importance, and as political actors with wills of their own. Although they will remain within nation-states, many will become increasingly autonomous. By nature readier than nation-states to live with diversity, they will be readier to adopt pluralistic attitudes towards language.

Among migrants and their descendants, the three-generation rule will continue to operate. Children of migrants will speak the language of the old country to their parents and the language of the new country to their own children, who will mostly speak no other tongue. The United States will continue to be a language graveyard. But the rule will not be as powerful and general as it has been in the past. Communications will keep families together across continents, enabling them to maintain traditional levels of involvement in each other's lives. Cousin conversations will sustain family languages across borders and generations. Bollywood movies and music from south of the Rio Grande will also play their part. The status of Spanish within US society will be strengthened by the growth of Mexico as an economic power, which will increase the language's international prestige and commercial value.

The tongues themselves will be kept together as well. People emigrate from a time as well as a place: in the past, with limited channels of communication to the old country, they would continue to speak the language as it was when they left. In the homeland, meanwhile, the language would move on. Emigrant communities would become preservation societies for quaint turns of phrase. With twenty-first century bandwidth, however, innovations will be able to spread throughout the larger language community, regardless of distance. They will go back as well as forth, conveying influences from the new lands to the homeland, and so the pattern of diversity within a language will change. There will be fewer diaspora varieties, or at least less marked divergence between them and those of the homeland, but the language as a whole will gain a richer variety of influences.

Artificial translation will do for phrasebook-level exchanges what the pocket calculator did for arithmetic. It will enable communication at a basic level of understanding between almost any pair of individuals on the planet. In doing so it will also enhance the value of language skills, by highlighting how much more richly and effectively people connect with each other when they enter each other's speech communities in person, or meet on common ground via a lingua franca. High levels of fluency will continue to command a premium. Among elite cosmopolitans – in business, science, knowledge and various forms of authority – near-native competence in important languages will always maintain its value. Automation will reduce the capability gap between monolinguals and high-level bilinguals. Both groups will be able to understand texts or speech in the language of interest accurately and comprehensively, but the bilinguals will enjoy the advantages of understanding idiom, grasping nuance, and being able to make themselves at home in the language. These may not always be overwhelming advantages, but the runaway logic of elite pay will apply. Enterprises pay hyperbolic amounts to secure the services of individuals with capabilities, such as scoring goals or conducting negotiations, that might just give them the crucial edge over their rivals. Super-accomplished individuals whose skill-sets include the ability to dispel language boundaries without artificial assistance will be very much the kind of people they are looking for.[23]

English will continue to be the world's second language. It will retain its value because the United States will continue to be one of the world's most important economies, because the world has standardised upon it, and because in many parts of the world people have invested their hopes for the future in it. The costs of changing would be immense, even if there were any good reason to do so, and agreement could be reached on an alternative. It will retain its political usefulness in some parts of the world that were once ruled by Britain, where it is not identified with any local ethnic group and can thus be employed as a neutral common language. The European Union will continue to favour it for similar reasons, despite and indeed because of the United Kingdom's departure. Under the influence of its speakers' legion other languages, English will become ever more diverse. There will be fewer living tongues, but more Englishes.

While the world will continue to appreciate the value of English, native English speakers will continue to fail to appreciate the value of learning other languages. As the world keeps turning, and speakers of different languages encounter each other more intensely than ever before, the Americans and the British will remain onlookers.

* * * *

Of all the reasons to avoid other languages, the very worst is the fear of rootlessness. In a modern open society, any public jibe against cosmopolitans, however oblique or superficially moderate in tone, should trigger a visceral pang of alarm. The figure uttering it should thereafter be regarded with deep suspicion, however unexceptionable their stated views on any other issue may subsequently be.

The unspoken half of the expression is 'rootless', as in the denunciatory Stalinist phrase 'rootless cosmopolitan'. People who appear to be rootless meet with hostility because loyalty is understood to require bonds. Those who are not rooted to a country are assumed to be incapable of loyalty to it. They are seen as potential traitors, and also as a threat to a country's own roots: those it already has, or those it is striving to grow. It is a matter not so much of people but of peoples – and one people in particular. For that reason alone, any citizen of an open society, aware of what happened in Germany, the Soviet Union and elsewhere when the word 'cosmopolitan' was used as a malign incantation, should experience at the very minimum a shudder and a chill when they hear this trope in its contemporary codes.

The idea of roots is itself rooted in the nineteenth-century conception of nationhood, which, by identifying a nation with a particular people speaking a particular language, fixed the nation to the particular land in which the people lived. Their roots were in the soil – which cast doubt upon the nature of peoples less intimately or statically connected to the land, like town-dwelling Jews in eastern Europe, and the nomadic Roma. Insisting as it does upon a single locus, the underground hemisphere whose extent is indicated by the spread of the crown of the tree above, the metaphor of rootedness draws limits around peoples.

To sceptics, the very notion of cosmopolitanism is an oxymoron. The word combines two opposed Greek terms: 'kosmos', the universe, and 'polis', the city. It 'encapsulates the tension between global and local, the universal and the particular'. By integrating the two terms, it implies that the tension can be resolved, 'with the "cosmopolitan" – literally, "a citizen of the world" – serving as a mediator between the two'. Sceptics dismiss that possibility. In the words of Theresa May, who was at the time prime minister of the United Kingdom, 'If you believe you are a citizen of the world, you are a citizen of nowhere.'[24]

If I had not already committed myself to practising my first language every day, I would have reached for my Polish grammar book as soon as I heard those words. What I heard was, among other things, a denial of my identity, and those of countless others who understand that they have been formed by more than one country or culture. As May's government struggled towards the isolation of Brexit, I moved from simply practising my first language to using it, in a successful application to recover the citizenship that according to Polish law I was born with, and lost when my father became a British citizen. The determining principle was ius sanguinis, the right of blood, as distinct from ius soli, the right of soil: citizenship based on parental nationality, rather than on the territory in which one was born. Ius sanguinis can be used to deny people citizenship of a country although they have lived in it all their lives, but it can also serve to help affirm that the children of migrants may be 'from' a country they have never lived in, or even visited, as well as the one in which they have grown up. That requires the surrounding community to accept both those kinds of belonging as authentic and valid, eliminating the subtext from the question 'where are you from?' If the community is open to different senses of belonging, those children should find it easier to embrace the cultures associated with each of them, including their heritage languages.

Joe Appiah, a Ghanaian politician whose memoirs were entitled 'Autobiography Of An African Patriot', left his children an unfinished note in which he urged them: 'Remember you are a citizen of the world.' One of them, the philosopher Kwame Anthony Appiah, quoted it in an essay entitled 'Cosmopolitan Patriots', in which he argued that his father had believed in a rooted cosmopolitanism. Despite the 'favorite slander of the narrow nationalist' that cosmopolitans are rootless, rootedness is the normal cosmopolitan condition. It is perfectly possible to have roots in more than one place, and branches anywhere. After all, we are not plants. Human beings are indeed attached to their roots, but they are also capable of holding more than one affinity dear. That is potentially a source of great creative strength, for individuals and the society in which they live. Adding 'rooted' affirms the possibility embedded in the word 'cosmopolitan', that the individual can mediate between the local and the global – and can be committed to both. It also points towards a precious resource, the knowledge embedded in roots, that individuals can draw upon to make their mediation fruitful. Rooted cosmopolitanism encourages people to harness the particular for the benefit of the universal. It assures them that what is distinctively theirs is an asset that they should value rather than a liability they should shed, and it encourages them to draw upon such assets for the common good. Joe Appiah, an African and Ghanaian patriot who also loved Asante, his ancestral homeland, told his children that being a citizen of the world meant that wherever in it they went to live, they should make sure they left the place 'better than you found it'.[25]

That is always going to be easier if you speak the language of the place, or if the people there speak yours. The most obvious advantage is mutual comprehension in everyday public encounters. Although that particular asset is likely to diminish in value as translation devices come to play the role of intermediaries, the value of deeper mutual understanding will endure. So will the power of using more than one language, a power that is knowledge. It comes in a variety of forms. One is the knowledge of other cultures to which other languages open access; another is the knowledge of other cultures that is embedded in the languages themselves, such as the awareness that Russian speakers must testify to the strength of their friendships by choosing from three or four words when they want to speak of a friend. Perhaps most important of all is the understanding that different languages are not the same language in different codes: that each has its own way of organising thought and communication, and therefore that other words are always possible.

Although this awareness does not automatically make a person more sympathetic or open to others, it should at minimum enhance the intuitive understanding that others have different perspectives. That is something to build on. It can be used to promote critical self-reflection, helping remind an individual that their own perspective is not the whole of the scene, that it applies its own filters, and that it may contain distortions. Given goodwill, the knowledge of the possibility of other words should encourage people to model other people's perspectives. A knowledge of another person's language may make a reasonable approximation of their perspective attainable. You can put yourself in their place.

Learning another language may also change the place that you are in. For the movie gangster Raees, the 'World' of his dreams is the smallest of possible worlds: a colony planted in dust, containing only the people he grew up with. His imagined community is the community in which he locates his roots, transplanted. And yet he dreams of bilingualism, of children speaking perfect English. If 'Your World' was built and its children emerged fluently bilingual from the jewel in its crown, the English-medium school, it would become a different, more open world. It would probably retain a sullen defensive solidarity, given its origins, but its perimeter would become more permeable, and its young people would be gazing towards the horizon.

Where populations are diverse, the overlapping of languages may allow mosaic communities to be imagined into being. People who share a culture can imagine themselves as constituting a community, even though the vast majority of its members will never meet or even know of each other. Overlapping languages allow cultures to be shared. If people come to feel that as well as having their own culture, they also have an emotionally significant degree of access to those of others, they will be able to imagine themselves as part of a mosaic community enfolding a wealth of diversity. Bilingualism is the essential enabler here. People don't have to be able to speak all the languages of the community; they just have to speak more than one. You only need one or two connections to become part of a network that can be indefinitely large. Given an indefinite supply of goodwill, it could cover the whole world.[26]

That is not what is likely to happen, but it illustrates a strategy that would help us to leave the world a better place than we found it. A world in which people are able to make the most of using more than one language is possible. But people will have to make it happen, by affirming that a world in which languages illuminate each other is preferable to one in which languages strive to outshine each other. The model and the basis for that world is the mind that has become a home for more than one language, each sparkling in the other's light.

Acknowledgements

I began planning this book towards the end of 2014, as I became increasingly disturbed by the swelling roar of xenophobia, nativism and belligerent nationalism from so many quarters. I decided that from then on I wanted to commit my writing to promoting values that stand in opposition to those baleful giants and their legion of trolls: openness, inclusiveness, harmony, unity in diversity. The use of more than one language, which had become a growing personal preoccupation, seemed to me a uniquely appropriate subject through which to pursue this aim.

Things duly proceeded to get worse: choosing a moment that would prove to be sadly apt, I flew to Rīga the morning after the British general election that set in train the referendum on whether to remain in the European Union. Latvia was a trove of insights into the relationships between language, nationhood, identity, and everyday lived lives. I'm most grateful to Ammon Cheskin for enabling me to arrive well-briefed and with a schedule of appointments that proved outstandingly fruitful; and to Ina Druviete and her husband Jānis for taking me to the spiritual heartland of the country. I'm also grateful to everybody else I met there: Lina Ovčiņņikova, who arranged for me to meet her colleagues at Rīga's Russian Theatre, Olga Dragiļeva, Maria Golubeva, Nora Krevneva, Elizabete Krivcova, Māra Laizāne, Alexander Malikov, Olga Procevska, Elmars

Senkovs, Līga Sudare and Svetlana Voronetskaya; Irina Frolova and her colleagues at Rīgas 74.vidusskola (Rīga Secondary School No. 74); Agris Timuška and his colleagues at the Valsts valodas centrs (State Language Centre); and Jānis Valdmanis and his colleagues at the Latviešu valodas aģentūra (Latvian Language Agency).

My other international excursion was very different, but likewise wonderfully rewarding, thanks to Suvarna Alladi, who 'removed all obstacles' for me in Hyderabad, in the spirit of the deity Lord Ganesha, during whose festival I arrived; to her family, who welcomed me to their Ganesha Chathurthi celebration; and to her colleagues Vasanta Duggirala and Bapiraju Surampudi, whom she brought together for an engrossing conversation about how the science of bilingualism looks from an Indian perspective.

Closer to home, I also encountered openness, generosity and readiness to engage with what I was trying to do – which was all the more welcome as qualities of that kind continued to lose ground in the wider world. I'm especially grateful to Thomas Bak, who introduced me to the community of bilingualism researchers at the University of Edinburgh, and started exactly the conversations I hoped to have; I have appreciated my continuing dialogue with him since. My thanks are also due to his colleagues Madeleine Long, Antonella Sorace and Mariana Vega-Mendoza. I am likewise grateful to researchers elsewhere who discussed or corresponded about their work with me: Panos Athanasopoulos, Manne Bylund, Maria Polinsky, Monika Schmid and Sümeyra Tosun.

My editor Julian Loose has been immensely supportive, responsive and helpful from the moment he set eyes on the proposal for the book. His understated determination to realise this project has deepened my confidence in it greatly, and working with him on the text as it has taken shape has been a pleasure throughout. That goes for everybody else involved with editing and publishing the book too, thanks to their engagement, enthusiasm and good humour.

I owe special thanks to Simon Ings; thanks also for one thing and another to A.M. Bakalar, Neil Belton, Alice Jahanpour, Antonia Lloyd-Jones, Judith Phillips, Peter Tallack, Boyd Tonkin, Jyotsna Vaid and Malcolm Wolf. I am grateful – genuinely! – to the anonymous readers who commented on the proposal and the manuscript for their encouraging, constructive and stimulating observations.

In addition I'd like to thank my Polish friends who have supported my efforts to use our common first language, despite the indignities they have had to hear me inflict on it; especially Magda Raczyńska, whose unilateral (and initially unnerving) decision that we should converse at length in Polish made me realise how deeply rewarding it is to be back in the language. That was also the decisive moment when I realised the first step was to start talking, and keep going.

Most of all, I thank my wife Sue Matthias Kohn and our son Teo for their love and support; Sue for her unfailing encouragement and patience, Teo for his keen interest and good questions. I should also acknowledge the efforts of my parents Czesław and Joyce Kohn to sustain a language in a home far from its homeland. They had a more profound effect than might have appeared at the time.

Notes

1 Other Words Are Possible

1. Erard, 2013.
2. Kristeva, 1991, 15.
3. Jakobson, 1959.
4. Michael Erard, Are We Really Monolingual? 14 January 2012, http://www.nytimes.com/2012/01/15/opinion/sunday/are-we-really-monolingual.html; Ryan, 2013.
5. Peal and Lambert, 1962; Grosjean, 2010, 4.
6. Mackey, 2013, 707–8; Council of Europe, 2001, 4–6.
7. Sheela Banerjee, How Should I Talk To My Daughter? 23 December 2017, https://www.theguardian.com/lifeandstyle/2017/dec/23/bilingual-english-bengali-children-speak-two-languages; Polish television series, *Londyńczycy*, 2008–2009, Telewizja Polska.
8. One excellent source of guidance about language questions is the Bilingualism Matters website, http://www.bilingualism-matters.ppls.ed.ac.uk/.
9. Berlin, 2013, 208; Ingrid Piller, Herder: an explainer for linguists, 4 March 2016, http://www.languageonthemove.com/herder-an-explainer-for-linguists/; Language Dispute Blocks Path Out of Crisis in Northern Ireland, 3 November 2017, https://www.nytimes.com/2017/11/03/world/europe/northern-ireland-language.html; http://www.sinnfein.ie; Equal Rights For Irish Speakers, http://www.sinnfein.ie/equal-rights-for-irish-speakers; Statement by DUP Leader Arlene Foster MLA, 14 February 2018, http://www.mydup.com/news/article/statement-by-dup-leader-arlene-foster-mla.
10. Central Statistics Office (Republic of Ireland / Poblacht na hÉireann), 2016; Northern Ireland Statistics and Research Agency, 2013.
11. Meet Taylor Mason (Asia Kate Dillon) | Billions | Season 2, https://www.youtube.com/watch?v=Ow6VVQO2Q-o (0.40); Déclaration de l'Académie française sur l'écriture dite 'inclusive', 26 October 2017, http://www.academie-francaise.fr/actualites/declaration-de-lacademie-francaise-sur-lecriture-dite-inclusive.
12. Singer and Harris, 2016.
13. Snyder, 2004, 36–7.
14. Neeley, 2013; Jenkins, 2017; Modiano, 2017.
15. See for example, Club Europ Express #7, https://www.youtube.com/watch?v=GqCKiZh_vkA&t=8s, (0.35).
16. Dina Mehmedbegovic, 'Don't Speak to Me in our Language, when you Pick Me up from School', 18 December 2017, http://www.meits.org/blog/post/dont-speak-to-me-in-our-language-when-you-pick-me-up-from-school.

2 Babel: The Conspiracy Theory

1. Volodarsky, 2014, 379.
2. Andrew and Mitrokhin, 1999, 465–6.
3. Abrahamsson and Hyltenstam, 2009.
4. The Holy Bible: King James Version, Judges 12: 5–6.
5. Lynd, Lynd and Bahour, 1994, 101; Chaucer, 1966, 205; Spindler, 2012.
6. Spindler, 2012.
7. Schmid, 2011; Flege, 1984.
8. Bongaerts et al., 1997.
9. Abrahamsson and Hyltenstam, 2008; Abrahamsson and Hyltenstam, 2009.
10. Leeuw, 2009.
11. Hakuta, 1989.
12. Leopold, 1959.
13. Klusmeyer and Papademetriou, 2009, 69–70; Davies, 1981, 513.
14. Ethnologue: Languages of the World, https://www.ethnologue.com/world; Pagel, 2009.
15. Whitfield, 2008.
16. Laycock, 2001a, 41–3.
17. Laycock, 2001b; von Humboldt, 1999, 60.
18. Kulick, 1997, 2.
19. Romaine, 2000, 8.
20. Nettle, 1998.
21. Bowern et al., 2011.
22. Laycock, 2001b.
23. Singer and Harris, 2016.
24. McConvell and Thieberger, 2001; Aikhenvald, 2004a.
25. Fennell, 2001, 129; Crystal, 2003, 32; Philip Durkin, Middle English – An Overview, http://public.oed.com/aspects-of-english/english-in-time/middle-english-an-overview/; Baugh and Cable, 2002, 94; Bentz and Christiansen, 2010.
26. Velupillai, 2012, 200.
27. Bentz and Winter, 2013.
28. Fennell, 2001, 129.
29. Lupyan and Dale, 2015; Bates and Macwhinney, 1989.
30. Richerson and Boyd, 2010.
31. Dunbar, 2003; Pagel, 2009.
32. Atkinson et al., 2008; Greenberg, 2004, 2–3, 119, 122.
33. Mairs, 2011.
34. Karttunen, 1994, 1–23.
35. Tokarczuk, 2010, 199–200. Translated by MK. Published in English in 2017 as *Flights*, translated by Jennifer Croft, Fitzcarraldo Editions.

3 The Rising Din

1. Quoted in Krashen, 1983.
2. Gervain, 2015; Mampe et al., 2009.
3. DeCasper and Fifer, 1980; Voegtline et al., 2013.
4. Vouloumanos and Werker, 2007; Werker and Byers-Heinlein, 2008; Byers-Heinlein, Burns and Werker, 2010.
5. Balari and Lorenzo, 2015.
6. Mintz et al., 2018.
7. Werker and Byers-Heinlein, 2008; Pons, Bosch and Lewkowicz, 2015.
8. Sebastián-Gallés et al., 2012; Kuhl, 2011; Weikum et al., 2012; Werker and Tees, 1984.
9. Pallier, 2007; Kuhl, 2011; Byers-Heinlein and Lew-Williams, 2013; Vanhove, 2013; Balari and Lorenzo, 2015; Werker and Hensch, 2015; Thiessen, Girard and Erickson, 2016.

10. Mayberry and Lock, 2003.
11. DeKeyser, Alfi-Shabtay and Ravid, 2010; Granena and Long, 2013.
12. Norrman and Bylund, 2016; The Irreversibility of Sensitive Period Effects in Language Development (Video Abstract), https://www.youtube.com/watch?v=1J9X50aePeU&feature=youtu.be.
13. Byers-Heinlein and Lew-Williams, 2013, answers parents' frequently asked questions about bilingualism in children's early years.
14. Blom and Paradis, 2016; Blom and Bosma, 2016.
15. Houwer, 2007.
16. Houwer, Bornstein and Putnick, 2014.
17. Hoff et al., 2012; Hoff and Core, 2013; Hoff et al., 2014.
18. Hoff et al., 2014; Houwer, 2007; Gathercole and Thomas, 2009; Welsh Government and Welsh Language Commissioner, 2015.
19. Hammer et al., 2009; Hoff and Core, 2013.
20. Byers-Heinlein and Garcia, 2015.
21. Fan et al., 2015; Yow and Markman, 2015; Liberman et al., 2017.
22. Grice, 1989, 26–7; Siegal, Iozzi and Surian, 2009; Siegal et al., 2010.
23. DeKeyser, Alfi-Shabtay and Ravid, 2010.
24. Stansfield and Reed, 2004; Carroll, 1962.
25. Stansfield and Reed, 2004; John B. Carroll in Whorf, 2012, 5–6.
26. Carroll, 1962; Wen, Biedroń and Skehan, 2017.
27. Baddeley, 1992; Baddeley, Gathercole and Papagno, 1998; Royal Mail Reveals Why We Never Forget a Postcode, 57 Years After its Introduction, 4 June 2016, https://www.royalmailgroup.com/royal-mail-reveals-why-we-never-forget-postcode-57-years-after-its-introduction.
28. Twain, The awful German language, 1880, available at https://www.cs.utah.edu/~gback/awfgrmlg.html.
29. Baddeley, 1992; Just and Carpenter, 1992; Kempe and Brooks, 2011; Yoo and Dickey, 2017; Linck and Weiss, 2015; Linck et al., 2013.
30. Morgan-Short et al., 2014; Ullman and Lovelett, 2018.
31. Macnamara and Conway, 2016.
32. Mamiya et al., 2016; Chandrasekaran et al., 2015; Hernandez et al., 2015; Vaughn and Hernandez, 2018.
33. Kempe and Brooks, 2011.

4 It Must Still Be In There Somewhere

1. Hobsbawm, 2002, 98–9.
2. Hobsbawm, 2002, 167.
3. Schmid, 2002, 54.
4. Schmid, 2002; 2004.
5. Hobsbawm, 2002, 78.
6. Schmid, 2002, 177, 192; Schmid, 2009.
7. O'Grady, 2018.
8. Schmid, 2007; 2012; Linck, Kroll and Sunderman, 2009.
9. Use it or Lose it? https://languageattrition.org/use-or-lose/; Seton and Schmid, 2016; Bylund and Ramírez-Galan, 2016.
10. Schmid, 2007; 2012.
11. Montrul, 2010.
12. Kim, 2010, 22, 25; Pallier et al., 2003.
13. Pierce et al., 2014; 2015.
14. Ventureyra, Pallier and Yoo, 2004; Oh, Au and Jun, 2010; Bowers, Mattys and Gage, 2009; Singh et al., 2011.
15. Montrul, 2012.

16. Rumbaut, Massey and Bean, 2006; Ryan, 2013; Lopez, Gonzalez-Barrera and López, 2017; Rasinger, 2013.
17. Polinsky, 2006.
18. Polinsky, Fathers and Sons: Do All Russians in the USA Speak the Same Language?, https://vimeo.com/58100438 (15.10, 41.55).
19. Polinsky, 2006; 2016.
20. Polinsky, 2008.
21. As note 18 (20.30, 22.50).
22. Polinsky, Heritage language, https://www.youtube.com/watch?v=PKtSAirA_T8 (4.40).
23. As note 22 (7.20); Polinsky, 2015; as note 18 (1.08.21); correspondence with Maria Polinsky.
24. First Peoples' Cultural Council, 2018; Programs & Projects, http://fpcf.ca/programs-projects/; FPCC Success Story: the Silent Speaker Pilot Project, First Peoples' News, Summer 2017, http://www.fpcc.ca/files/PDF/General/FPCC_Newsletter_Summer_2017_-_WEB.pdf.
25. Tannenbaum and Abugov, 2010.
26. Lopez, Gonzalez-Barrera and López, 2017.
27. Bourdieu, 1977.
28. Conor Williams, The Intrusion of White Families into Bilingual Schools, 28 December 2017, https://www.theatlantic.com/education/archive/2017/12/the-middle-class-take-over-of-bilingual-schools/549278/.

5 Two Languages In One Head

1. Comment by Falcom on article by Ben Spencer, Being Bilingual May Keep Brain Sharp in Old Age: Learning Extra Languages Can Help Prevent Onset of Dementia, Study Claims, 2 June 2014, http://www.dailymail.co.uk/sciencetech/article-2645741/Being-bilingual-brain-sharp-old-age-learning-extra-languages-help-prevent-onset-dementia.html.
2. Eddie Izzard, Dress To Kill – Languages, https://www.youtube.com/watch?v=wxGHK7EnYVg (2.04).
3. Peal and Lambert, 1962; Hakuta and Diaz, 1985; Bialystok, 2011; Diamond, 2013; Titone et al., 2017.
4. Online demos of these tests are available at http://www.psytoolkit.org/experiment-library/.
5. Emmorey et al., 2008; Emmorey, Giezen and Gollan, 2016.
6. Thierry and Wu, 2007.
7. Costa et al., 2017; Titone et al., 2017; Olulade et al., 2016; Baum and Titone, 2014; Byers-Heinlein and Lew-Williams, 2013.
8. Hartanto, Yang and Yang, 2018.
9. Bialystok, 2016; Perani et al., 2017.
10. Bialystok, Craik and Freedman, 2007; Valenzuela and Sachdev, 2006; Snowdon, 1997.
11. Stern, 2009, 2012; Zhu et al., 2014.
12. Bialystok, Craik and Freedman, 2007; Craik, Bialystok and Freedman, 2010.
13. Schweizer et al., 2012; Luk et al., 2011; Abutalebi et al., 2015; Olsen et al., 2015; Grundy, Anderson and Bialystok, 2017.
14. Deary et al., 2007; Bak et al., 2014; Corley, Cox and Deary, 2018; Gow et al., 2012.
15. Bak et al., 2016; About us, Bilingualism Matters, http://www.bilingualism-matters.ppls.ed.ac.uk/.
16. Zahodne et al., 2014; Lawton et al., 2015; Fuller-Thomson, 2015; Gold, 2015; Paap, Johnson and Sawi, 2015, and responses; Bak, 2016a, 2016b; Bialystok, 2016; García-Pentón et al., 2016; Calvo et al., 2016; Bialystok, Craik and Freedman, 2007; Chertkow et al., 2010; Freedman et al., 2014; Valian, 2015, and responses.
17. Fuller-Thomson and Kuh, 2014; Alladi et al., 2013.

18. Alladi et al., 2013; Bialystok, Craik and Freedman, 2007.
19. Alladi et al., 2011; Nussbaum and Ellis, 2003; Abridged Life Tables 2010–14, Office of the Registrar General and Census Commissioner, India.
20. Iyer et al., 2014.
21. Alladi et al., 2013; Bak and Alladi, 2016; Ramakrishnan et al., 2017.
22. Nair, Biedermann and Nickels, 2017; Santillán and Khurana, 2018; Calvo and Bialystok, 2014; Engel de Abreu et al., 2012; Morton and Harper, 2007.
23. Open Science Collaboration, 2015; Zwaan et al., 2017; Baker, 2016.
24. Head et al., 2015; John, Loewenstein and Prelec, 2012; Paap, Johnson and Sawi, 2015.
25. Elizabeth Church, A Researcher's Journey Begins with the Smallest Steps, 13 April 2010, https://beta.theglobeandmail.com/news/national/a-researchers-journey-begins-with-the-smallest-steps/article4352711/.
26. Higginson and Munafò, 2016; de Bruin and Della Sala, 2015.
27. de Bruin, Treccani and Della Sala, 2015.
28. Paap, Johnson and Sawi, 2015; García-Pentón et al., 2016; Klein, 2015.
29. Fuller-Thomson, 2015; Valian, 2015; Mukadam, Sommerlad and Livingston, 2017; Woumans et al., 2017.
30. Paap, Johnson and Sawi, 2016; Alladi et al., 2013.
31. Alladi et al., 2016.
32. Bak, 2016a.
33. Bak, 2016b.
34. Thomas Bak, Education is Much More Than Just Going to School and Bilingualism is an Important Part of it, 4 October 2017, https://forwardthinking.ppls.ed.ac.uk/2017/10/04/education-is-much-more-than-just-going-to-school-and-bilingualism-is-an-important-part-of-it/.
35. Paap, Johnson and Sawi, 2015; Paap, Johnson and Sawi, 2016; Gathercole, 2015.
36. As note 1.

6 Speakers In Search Of An Endpoint

1. Bono, 1995, 55, 20; Laycock, 2001a, 19–64; Parry, 2011, 174–6.
2. Bylund and Athanasopoulos, 2014; Młynarczyk, 2004, Ch. 1.
3. Bylund and Athanasopoulos, 2015a.
4. Athanasopoulos et al., 2015a.
5. Stutterheim and Nüse, 2003; Müller, 2008.
6. Schmiedtová, Stutterheim and Carroll, 2011; Stutterheim et al., 2012.
7. Athanasopoulos et al., 2015a; Athanasopoulos et al., 2015b; Bylund and Athanasopoulos, 2014; Bylund and Athanasopoulos, 2015b.
8. Slobin, 1987.
9. Flecken, Stutterheim and Carroll, 2014.
10. Flecken et al., 2015.
11. Athanasopoulos and Bylund, 2013.
12. Dorfman, 2005.
13. Cunningham, Vaid and Chen, 2011.
14. Fausey and Boroditsky, 2011.
15. Fausey et al., 2010.
16. Filipović, 2007, 2013.
17. Detailed Languages Spoken at Home and Ability to Speak English for the Population 5 Years and Over for States: 2009–2013, https://www.census.gov/data/tables/2013/demo/2009-2013-lang-tables.html.
18. Sümeyra Tosun: Psi Chi/APA Edwin B. Newman Graduate Research Award, 2014, *American Psychologist* 69 (8):793–5.
19. Slobin, 2016.
20. Friedman, 2003.

21. Tosun, 2014; Tosun, Vaid and Geraci, 2013.
22. Aikhenvald, 2004b, 1–35; Slobin, 2016; Aikhenvald, 2013.
23. Slobin and Aksu, 1982; Batuman, 2017, 53–4.
24. Slobin, 2016.
25. Whorf, 1944, 1950; Levinson, 2012; Pavlenko, 2014, 30; Deutscher, 2010; McWhorter, 2014.
26. Montero-Melis et al., 2017.
27. Pinker, 2007, 135, 148.
28. Pinker, 2007, 148.
29. Berlin and Kay, 1969.
30. Winawer et al., 2007; Franklin et al., 2008.
31. Franklin et al., 2008; Mazoyer et al., 2014; Regier and Kay, 2009.
32. Grandin, 1995; About Temple Grandin, http://www.templegrandin.com/.
33. Chomsky, 2000, 7; Knight, 2016, 17–18, Ch. 5.
34. Chomsky, 2002, 76; Knight, 2016, 156.
35. Pinker and Jackendoff, 2005.
36. Forder, He and Franklin, 2017; Pavlenko, 2014, 2–3.
37. Miller, 1968, 21; Berlin, 2013, 208.
38. Crystal, 2004, 310; Leigh, 1997, 104–7.
39. Wierzbicka, 1997, 57–71.
40. James, 2007, 511–12; Lupyan, 2012.
41. Wierzbicka, 1997, 63.
42. Firmat, 2003, 13.

7 Being Somebody Else

1. Dewaele and Pavlenko, n.d.; Pavlenko, 2006.
2. McWhorter, 2014, 163; Polinsky, 2006.
3. Dewaele, 2016.
4. Harris, Ayçiçegi and Gleason, 2003.
5. Pavlenko, 2006; Panicacci and Dewaele, 2017.
6. Pavlenko, 2006; Panicacci and Dewaele, 2017.
7. Kahneman, 2011; Costa, Vives and Corey, 2017.
8. Kahneman, 2011, 368–9; Keysar, Hayakawa and An, 2012; Costa et al., 2014.
9. Keysar, Hayakawa and An, 2012; Gao et al., 2015.
10. Hadjichristidis, Geipel and Surian, 2018; Hayakawa and Keysar, 2018.
11. Hadjichristidis, Geipel and Savadori, 2015.
12. Costa et al., 2014; Hayakawa et al., 2017.
13. Geipel, Hadjichristidis and Surian, 2016; Geipel, Hadjichristidis and Surian, 2015a; Geipel, Hadjichristidis and Surian, 2015b; Harris, Ayçiçegi and Gleason, 2003; Hayakawa et al., 2016.
14. Ramírez-Esparza et al., 2006.
15. Veltkamp et al., 2012.
16. Ramírez-Esparza, Gosling and Pennebaker, 2008.
17. Eurobarometer, 2012, 147.
18. Dewaele, 2016; Ożańska-Ponikwia, 2012.
19. Dewaele, 2016.
20. de Courtivron, 2003, 5; Vassilis Alexakis, From 'Paris–Athens', March 2009, https://www.wordswithoutborders.org/article/from-paris-athens-andriana-mastor; Stavans, 2002, 224; Huston, in de Courtivron, 2003, 55; Lesser, 2005, 31–7; Firmat, 2003, 13.
21. Steiner, 1998, 120; Firmat, 2003, 8–9; Schmid, 2004.
22. About Gustavo Pérez Firmat, http://www.gustavoperezfirmat.com/gpf_about.php; Steiner, 1998, 121.
23. Pousada, 1994.

8 One Nation, One Language

1. Woman Wanted over Racist Rant on Train between Embankment and Plaistow, 28 April 2015, http://www.newhamrecorder.co.uk/news/crime-court/video-woman-wanted-over-racist-rant-on-train-between-embankment-and-plaistow-1-4052468; 'You Can Only Speak English while You're on this Train', 28 March 2015, http://www.dailymail.co.uk/news/article-3016170/Woman-filmed-hurling-racist-abuse-two-men-Tube.html.
2. London Germans Told 'Don't Speak German in Public after Brexit Vote', 27 October 2016, https://www.standard.co.uk/news/politics/dont-speak-german-in-london-after-brexit-lawyer-tells-germans-a3380136.html; UK Student Stabbed in Neck for Speaking Polish Describes Brutal Post-Brexit Assault in Telford, 20 September 2016, http://www.independent.co.uk/news/uk/crime/uk-student-stabbed-in-neck-for-speaking-polish-brutal-post-brexit-assault-telford-donnington-park-a7319181.html.
3. For their Sake, Immigrants Must Speak the Language of Shakespeare, 8 March 2015, http://www.telegraph.co.uk/news/uknews/immigration/11457877/For-their-sake-immigrants-must-speak-the-language-of-Shakespeare.html; Farage 'Felt Awkward' on Train, 28 February 2014, https://www.standard.co.uk/panewsfeeds/farage-felt-awkward-on-train-9158785.html.
4. 'Di hoam uns ned richtig verstanden tuen', 8 December 2014, http://www.spiegel.de/politik/deutschland/yallacsu-deutsch-pflicht-sorgt-fuer-spott-auf-twitter-a-1007177.html; Merkel Allies want Immigrants to Speak German at Home, 7 December 2014, http://uk.reuters.com/article/uk-germany-immigration/merkel-allies-want-immigrants-to-speak-german-at-home-idUKKBN0JL0C620141207; Peter Tauber, 5 December 2014, https://twitter.com/petertauber/status/540938231777619968.
5. Prof. Jerzy Kochanowski pobity w warszawskim tramwaju. Powód: mówił po niemiecku, 9 September 2015, https://www.polityka.pl/tygodnikpolityka/kraj/1675200,1,prof-jerzy-kochanowski-pobity-w-warszawskim-tramwaju-powod-mowil-po-niemiecku.read; Kraków. Happening w tramwaju linii 22 – czytali na głos, po niemiecku, 12 September 2015, http://krakow.naszemiasto.pl/artykul/krakow-happening-w-tramwaju-linii-22-czytali-na-glos-po,3854926,artgal,t,id,tm.html; Kara dla motorniczego tramwaju, w którym pobito profesora, 12 September 2016, http://tvnwarszawa.tvn24.pl/informacje,news,kara-dla-motorniczego-tramwaju-w-ktorym-pobito-profesora,211422.html; Bo rozmawiał po niemiecku. Wyrok za pobicie profesora w tramwaju, 13 March 2017, https://tvnwarszawa.tvn24.pl/informacje,news,bo-rozmawial-po-niemiecku-wyrok-za-pobicie-profesora-w-tramwaju,226446.html.
6. Vassilis Alexakis, From 'Paris–Athens', March 2009, https://www.wordswithoutborders.org/article/from-paris-athens-andriana-mastor.
7. Ločmele, Procevska and Zelče, 2011.
8. Faces in the Crowd, 12 May 2015, https://meduza.io/en/feature/2015/05/12/faces-in-the-crowd.
9. Biography: http://kustu.com/w2/en:biography; Drang nach Osten Performance, 8 May 2015, https://www.youtube.com/watch?v=vGxPc78V3Ho (5.40–8.40).
10. Security Message for U.S. Citizens: Riga (Latvia), May 8–9 Events in Riga, https://www.osac.gov/pages/ContentReportDetails.aspx?cid=17622; Cheskin, 2013.
11. Anatoly Korolev, Dmitry Kosyrev, RIA Novosti Commentators, National Symbolism in Russia: the Old and the New, 11 June 2007, https://sputniknews.com/analysis/2007061166883914/; For victory day, post-soviets show their colors – just not orange and black, 7 May 2015, https://www.rferl.org/a/victory-day-st-george-ribbon-orange-and-black/26999911.html.
12. 9. maijs: kā uzvara kļuva par Krievijas ideoloģiju, 10 May 2015, http://ltv.lsm.lv/lv/raksts/10.05.2015-9.-maijs-ka-uzvara-kluva-par-krievijas-ideologiju.id49064/.
13. Latvian Centre for Human Rights, 2013.
14. The Programme of the Social Democratic Party Concord, www.saskana.info/about-concord/programm/; Saskaņa Quietly Ditches Putin Party Agreement, 9 October 2017,

https://eng.lsm.lv/article/politics/politics/saskana-quietly-ditches-putin-party-agreement.a252983/.

15. Latvia Grapples with EU over Euro, 14 January 2006, http://news.bbc.co.uk/1/hi/world/europe/4578806.stm.
16. Rozenvalds, 2010.
17. Druviete and Strelēvica-Ošiņa, 2008.
18. Basic Facts about Citizenship and Language Policy of Latvia and Some Sensitive History-Related Issues, http://www.mfa.gov.lv/en/policy/society-integration/citizenship-in-latvia/citizenship-policy-in-latvia/basic-facts-about-citizenship-and-language-policy-of-latvia-and-some-sensitive-history-related-issues.
19. Security Police, 2014.
20. Households in Riga Mostly Use Latvian in Bieriņi and Buļļi Neighbourhood, 15 May 2015, http://www.csb.gov.lv/en/notikumi/households-riga-mostly-use-latvian-bierini-and-bulli-neighbourhood-42813.html.
21. 'Hipster' Enters Latvian, 21 September 2015, http://eng.lsm.lv/article/society/society/hipster-enters-latvian.a146586/.
22. Riga Mayor off the Hook for Russian-Language Speech, 22 May 2015, http://www.lsm.lv/en/article/societ/society/riga-mayor-off-the-hook-for-russian-language-speech.a130703/.
23. Data on the State Language Law compliance in 2014, Valsts valodas centrs.
24. Latvian Centre for Human Rights, 2013.
25. Leonid Raihman v. Latvia, Communication No. 1621/2007, U.N. Doc. CCPR/C/100/D/1621/2007, 30 November 2010, http://hrlibrary.umn.edu/undocs/1621-2007.html; Déclaration de l'Académie française sur l'écriture dite 'inclusive', 26 October 2017, http://www.academie-francaise.fr/actualites/declaration-de-lacademie-francaise-sur-lecriture-dite-inclusive; Jean-Michel Blanquer, 15 November 2017, https://twitter.com/jmblanquer/status/930813255211208707.
26. Riekstiņš, 2012, 127.
27. Noyes, 2015, 48; Herder, 1992, 29–34.
28. Jaremko-Porter, 2008, 84; Herder and Bohlman, 2017, 25, 37–8.
29. Rīgas 74.vidusskola, http://www.r74vsk.lv/.
30. Rozenvalds, 2010; Address by President of the Russian Federation, 18 March 2014, http://en.kremlin.ru/events/president/news/20603; Information regarding the transition to instruction in the state language in general education institutions offering education programmes for minorities, http://www.izm.gov.lv/en/highlights/2762-information-regarding-the-transition-to-instruction-in-the-state-language-in-general-education-institutions-offering-education-programmes-for-minorities.
31. Laizāne, Putniņa and Mileiko, 2015; Latvia's Russian-Speakers Belong to Latvia, say Schoolkids, 6 May 2015, http://eng.lsm.lv/article/society/society/latvias-russian-speakers-belong-to-latvia-say-schoolkids.a128445/.
32. Balodis et al., 2012, 19.
33. Rīgas Krievu teātris, http://www.trd.lv/.
34. John McWhorter, Where Do Languages Go to Die? 10 September 2015, https://www.theatlantic.com/international/archive/2015/09/aramaic-middle-east-language/404434/?utm_source=SFFB.
35. Transcript of Minister Mentor Lee Kuan Yew's Interview with Seth Mydans of New York Times and IHT on 1 September 2010 (National Archives of Singapore).
36. Leimgruber, 2013; Speech By Mr S. Iswaran, 15 August 2009, http://www.nas.gov.sg/archivesonline/speeches/view-html?filename=20090824002.htm.
37. Leimgruber, 2013.
38. Speak Mandarin Campaign: About the Campaign, http://mandarin.org.sg/en/about.
39. Leimgruber, 2013; Singlish – The Native Language, https://www.youtube.com/watch?v=LMMzDAg4VvI.
40. Speech by Mr S. Iswaran, 15 August 2009, as note 36; Singapore Department of Statistics, 2011.

41. Speak Good English Movement, http://eresources.nlb.gov.sg/infopedia/articles/SIP_575_2004-12-23.html; Speech by Prime Minister Goh Chok Tong, 29 August 1999, http://www.nas.gov.sg/archivesonline/speeches/view-html?filename=1999082905.htm; Wee, 2010.
42. Singaporean Blunders, https://www.goodenglish.org.sg/resources/grammar-rules/singaporean-blunders.
43. Singlish – The Native Language, https://www.youtube.com/watch?v=LMMzDAg4VvI.
44. Wong, 2004.
45. Icons of SG, https://www.sg/ICON.aspx.
46. Tessa Wong, The Rise of Singlish, 6 August 2015, http://www.bbc.co.uk/news/magazine-33809914.

9 Possible Words

1. *Raees*, 2017, directed by Rahul Dholakia. Red Chillies Entertainment.
2. Manan, Dumanig and David, 2017; Saer, Smith and Hughes, 1924, 13.
3. Sajith Pai, Say Hello to India's Newest and Fastest-Growing Caste, 24 January 2018, https://medium.com/@sajithpai/say-hello-to-indias-newest-and-fastest-growing-caste-2e6bd822687b; Vasanta et al., 2010; More Than Half of India's Languages May Die out in 50 Years – Survey, http://peopleslinguisticsurvey.org/news-details.aspx?id=255.
4. Chomsky, 1965, 3.
5. King, 2001.
6. MK Stalin – About Stalin, https://web.archive.org/web/20170923185625/; M.K. Stalin, https://twitter.com/mkstalin/status/855701465335287808.
7. No Hindi on Bengaluru Metro, Karnataka Chief Minister Siddarmaiah Tells Centre, 28 July 2017, https://www.ndtv.com/bangalore-news/no-hindi-on-bengaluru-metro-karnataka-chief-minister-siddarmaiah-tells-centre-1730482.
8. What's it with Sunny Leone and Malayali men? 18 August 2017, https://timesofindia.indiatimes.com/city/kochi/whats-it-with-sunny-leone-and-malayali-men/articleshow/60112757.cms; *Raees*, 2017.
9. Saer, Smith and Hughes, 1924, 13; Saer, 1923.
10. Jones, 2012.
11. Weaver, 1949; Hutchins, 2000.
12. Knight, 2016, 55; Barsky, 1998, 86.
13. Hutchins, 2004.
14. Paul Robert Walker, The Trials and Triumphs of Leon Dostert '28, Fall 2015, https://www.oxy.edu/magazine/fall-2015/trials-triumphs-leon-dostert-28; Borel, 1960.
15. Piotrowski and Romanov, 1999.
16. Hutchins, 2010.
17. Brown et al., 1990.
18. V. Le Quoc and Mike Schuster, A Neural Network for Machine Translation, at Production Scale, 27 September 2016, https://research.googleblog.com/2016/09/a-neural-network-for-machine.html.
19. Skype Translator Preview – An Exciting Journey to a New Chapter in Communication, 15 December 2014, https://blogs.skype.com/stories/2014/12/15/skype-translator-preview-an-exciting-journey-to-a-new-chapter-in-communication/?eu=true.
20. Manifesto of the Communist Party, Chapter I, Bourgeois and Proletarians, https://www.marxists.org/archive/marx/works/1848/communist-manifesto/ch01.htm; Berman, 1983.
21. Otheguy, García and Reid, 2015.
22. Snyder, 2004, Chapters 1, 2.
23. Frank and Cook, 1995.
24. Miller and Ury, 2010; Theresa May: Speech to Conservative Party Conference 2016, https://www.youtube.com/watch?time_continue=17&v=08JN73K1JDc (12.47).
25. Appiah, 1997.
26. Anderson, 2006, 6.

Bibliography

Abrahamsson, Niclas, and Hyltenstam, Kenneth. 2008. 'The Robustness of Aptitude Effects in Near-Native Second Language Acquisition', *Studies in Second Language Acquisition*, 30 (4):481–509.

Abrahamsson, Niclas, and Hyltenstam, Kenneth. 2009. 'Age of Onset and Nativelikeness in a Second Language: Listener Perception versus Linguistic Scrutiny', *Language Learning*, 59 (2):249–306.

Abutalebi, Jubin et al. 2015. 'Bilingualism Provides a Neural Reserve for Aging Populations', *Neuropsychologia*, 69:201–10.

Aikhenvald, Alexandra Y. 2004a. 'Language Endangerment in the Sepik Area of Papua New Guinea', in *Lectures on Endangered Languages: 5. Endangered Languages of the Pacific Rim*, edited by O. Sakiyama and F. Endo, ELPR, Osaka Gakuin University, 97–142.

Aikhenvald, Alexandra Y. 2004b. *Evidentiality*, Oxford University Press.

Aikhenvald, Alexandra Y. 2013. 'Shifting Language Attitudes in North-West Amazonia', *International Journal of the Sociology of Language*, 222:195–216.

Alladi, Suvarna et al. 2013. 'Bilingualism Delays Age at Onset of Dementia, Independent of Education and Immigration Status', *Neurology*, 81:1938–44.

Alladi, Suvarna et al. 2016. 'Impact of Bilingualism on Cognitive Outcome After Stroke', *Stroke*, 47.

Alladi, Suvarna et al. 2011. 'Subtypes of Dementia: A Study from a Memory Clinic in India', *Dementia and Geriatric Cognitive Disorders*, 32 (1):32–38.

Anderson, Benedict. 2006. *Imagined Communities*, Verso, London and New York.

Andrew, Christopher, and Mitrokhin, Vasili. 1999. *The Mitrokhin Archive: The KGB in Europe and the West*, Allen Lane, London.

Appiah, Kwame Anthony. 1997. 'Cosmopolitan Patriots', *Critical Inquiry*, 23 (3):617–39.

Athanasopoulos, Panos, and Bylund, Emanuel. 2013. 'Does Grammatical Aspect Affect Motion Event Cognition? A Cross-Linguistic Comparison of English and Swedish Speakers', *Cognitive Science*, 37 (2):286–309.

Athanasopoulos, Panos et al. 2015a. 'Two Languages, Two Minds: Flexible Cognitive Processing Driven by Language of Operation', *Psychological Science*, 26 (4):518–26.

Athanasopoulos, Panos et al. 2015b. 'Learning to Think in a Second Language: Effects of Proficiency and Length of Exposure in English Learners of German', *Modern Language Journal*, 99 (S1):138–53.

Atkinson, Quentin D. et al. 2008. 'Languages Evolve in Punctuational Bursts', *Science*, 319 (5863):588.

Baddeley, Alan. 1992. 'Working Memory', *Science*, 255 (5044):556–59.

Baddeley, Alan, Gathercole, Susan, and Papagno, Costanza. 1998. 'The Phonological Loop as a Language Learning Device', *Psychological Review*, 105 (1):158–73.

Bak, Thomas H. 2016a. 'The Impact of Bilingualism on Cognitive Ageing and Dementia: Finding a Path through a Forest of Confounding Variables', *Linguistic Approaches to Bilingualism*, 6 (1–2):205–26.

Bak, Thomas H. 2016b. 'Cooking Pasta in La Paz', *Linguistic Approaches to Bilingualism*, 6 (5):699–717.

Bak, Thomas H., and Alladi, Suvarna. 2016. 'Bilingualism, Dementia and the Tale of Many Variables: Why We Need to Move beyond the Western World. Commentary on Lawton et al. (2015) and Fuller-Thomson (2015)', *Cortex*, 74:315–17.

Bak, Thomas H. et al. 2014. 'Does Bilingualism Influence Cognitive Aging?' *Annals of Neurology*, 75 (6):959–63.

Bak, Thomas H. et al. 2016. 'Novelty, Challenge, and Practice: The Impact of Intensive Language Learning on Attentional Functions', *PLOS ONE*, 11 (4):e0153485.

Baker, Monya. 2016. 'Is there a Reproducibility Crisis?' *Nature*, 533 (7604):452–54.

Balari, Sergio, and Lorenzo, Guillermo. 2015. 'Should it Stay or Should it Go? A Critical Reflection on the Critical Period for Language', *Biolinguistics*, 9:8–42.

Balodis, Pauls et al. 2012. *Language Situation in Latvia: 2004–2010*, Latviešu valodas aģentūra, Rīga.

Barsky, Robert F. 1998. *Noam Chomsky: A Life of Dissent*, MIT Press, Cambridge MA.

Bates, Elizabeth, and Macwhinney, Brian. 1989. 'Functionalism and the Competition Model', in *The Crosslinguistic Study of Sentence Processing*, edited by B. MacWhinney and E. Bates, Cambridge University Press, 3–76.

Batuman, Elif. 2017. *The Idiot*, Jonathan Cape, London.

Baugh, Albert C., and Cable, Thomas. 2002. *A History of the English Language*, Routledge, Abingdon-on-Thames.

Baum, Shari, and Titone, Debra. 2014. 'Moving toward a Neuroplasticity View of Bilingualism, Executive Control, and Aging', *Applied Psycholinguistics*, 35 (5):857–94.

Bentz, Christian, and Christiansen, Morten H. 2010. 'Linguistic Adaptation: The Trade-Off Between Case Marking and Fixed Word Orders in Germanic and Romance Languages', in *The Evolution of Language: Proceedings of the 8th International Conference (EVOLANG8)*, edited by A.D.M. Smith et al., World Scientific Publishing, Singapore, 26–33.

Bentz, Christian, and Winter, Bodo. 2013. 'Languages with More Second Language Learners Tend to Lose Nominal Case', *Language Dynamics and Change*, 3:1–27.

Berlin, Isaiah. 2013. *Three Critics of the Enlightenment: Vico, Hamann, Herder*, Princeton University Press.

Berlin, Brent, and Kay, Paul. 1969. *Basic Color Terms: Their Universality and Evolution*, University of California Press.

Berman, Marshall. 1983. *All That is Solid Melts into Air: The Experience of Modernity*, Verso, London and New York.

Bialystok, Ellen. 2011. 'Reshaping the Mind: The Benefits of Bilingualism', *Canadian Journal of Experimental Psychology/Revue Canadienne de Psychologie Expérimentale*, 65 (4):229–35.

Bialystok, Ellen. 2016. 'The Signal and the Noise', *Linguistic Approaches to Bilingualism*, 6 (5):517–34.

Bialystok, Ellen, Craik, Fergus I.M., and Freedman, Morris. 2007. 'Bilingualism as a Protection against the Onset of Symptoms of Dementia', *Neuropsychologia*, 45 (2):459–64.

Blom, Elma, and Bosma, Evelyn. 2016. 'The Sooner the Better? An Investigation into the Role of Age of Onset and its Relation with Transfer and Exposure in Bilingual Frisian-Dutch Children', *Journal of Child Language*, 43 (3):581–607.

Blom, Elma, and Paradis, Johanne. 2016. 'Introduction: Special Issue on Age Effects in Child Language Acquisition', *Journal of Child Language*, 43 (3):473–78.

Bongaerts, Theo et al. 1997. 'Age and Ultimate Attainment in the Pronunciation of a Foreign Language', *Studies in Second Language Acquisition*, 19 (4):447–65.

Bono, James J. 1995. *The Word of God and the Languages of Man: Interpreting Nature in Early Modern Science and Medicine: Ficino to Descartes,* University of Wisconsin Press.

Borel, Paul A. 1960. 'Machine Translation', Central Intelligence Agency, Washington DC.

Bourdieu, Pierre. 1977. 'The Economics of Linguistic Exchanges', *Social Science Information*, 16 (6):645–88.

Bowern, Claire et al. 2011. 'Does Lateral Transmission Obscure Inheritance in Hunter-Gatherer Languages?' *PLOS ONE*, 6 (9):e25195.

Bowers, Jeffrey S., Mattys, Sven L., and Gage, Suzanne H. 2009. 'Preserved Implicit Knowledge of a Forgotten Childhood Language', *Psychological Science*, 20 (9):1064–69.

Brown, Peter F. et al. 1990. 'Statistical Approach to Machine Translation', *Computational Linguistics*, 16 (2):79–85.

Bruin, Angela de, and Sala, Sergio Della. 2015. 'The Decline Effect: How Initially Strong Results Tend to Decrease over Time', *Cortex*, 73:375–77.

Bruin, Angela de, Treccani, Barbara, and Sala, Sergio Della. 2015. 'Cognitive Advantage in Bilingualism: An Example of Publication Bias?' *Psychological Science*, 26 (1):99–107.

Byers-Heinlein, Krista, Burns, Tracey C., and Werker, Janet F. 2010. 'The Roots of Bilingualism in Newborns', *Psychological Science*, 21 (3):343–48.

Byers-Heinlein, Krista, and Garcia, Bianca. 2015. 'Bilingualism Changes Children's Beliefs About What Is Innate', *Developmental Science*, 18 (2):344–50.

Byers-Heinlein, Krista, and Lew-Williams, Casey. 2013. 'Bilingualism in the Early Years: What the Science Says', *Early Childhood Education: Successes and Challenges*, 7 (1):95–112.

Bylund, Emanuel, and Athanasopoulos, Panos. 2014. 'Linguistic Relativity in SLA: Toward a New Research Program', *Language Learning*, 64 (4):952–85.

Bylund, Emanuel, and Athanasopoulos, Panos. 2015a. 'Introduction: Cognition, Motion Events, and SLA', *Modern Language Journal*, 99 (S1):1–13.

Bylund, Emanuel, and Athanasopoulos, Panos. 2015b. 'Televised Whorf: Cognitive Restructuring in Advanced Foreign Language Learners as a Function of Audiovisual Media Exposure', *Modern Language Journal*, 99 (S1):123–37.

Bylund, Emanuel, and Ramírez-Galan, Pedro. 2016. 'Language Aptitude in First Language Attrition: A Study on Late Spanish-Swedish Bilinguals', *Applied Linguistics*, 37 (5):621–38.

Calvo, Alejandra, and Bialystok, Ellen. 2014. 'Independent Effects of Bilingualism and Socioeconomic Status on Language Ability and Executive Functioning', *Cognition*, 130 (3):278–88.

Calvo, Noelia et al. 2016. 'Bilingualism and Cognitive Reserve: A Critical Overview and a Plea for Methodological Innovations', *Frontiers in Aging Neuroscience*, 7: 249.

Carroll, John B. 1962. 'The Prediction of Success in Intensive Foreign Language Training', in *Training Research and Education*, edited by R. Keyser, University of Pittsburgh Press, 87–136.

Chandrasekaran, B. et al. 2015. 'Enhanced Procedural Learning of Speech Sound Categories in a Genetic Variant of FOXP2', *Journal of Neuroscience*, 35 (20): 7808–12.

Chaucer, Geoffrey. 1966. 'The Nun's Priest's Tale', in *The Works of Geoffrey Chaucer*, edited by F.N. Robinson. Oxford University Press, 205: 3395–6.

Chertkow, Howard et al. 2010. 'Multilingualism (But Not Always Bilingualism) Delays the Onset of Alzheimer Disease: Evidence from a Bilingual Community', *Alzheimer Disease & Associated Disorders*, 24 (2):118–25.

Cheskin, Ammon M. 2013. 'Identity, Memory, Temporality and Discourse: The Evolving Discursive Positions of Latvia's Russian-Speakers', PhD thesis, University of Glasgow.

Chomsky, Noam. 1965. *Aspects of the Theory of Syntax*, MIT Press, Cambridge MA.

Chomsky, Noam. 2000. *New Horizons in the Study of Language*, Cambridge University Press.

Chomsky, Noam. 2002. *On Nature and Language*, Cambridge University Press.

Corley, J., Cox, S.R., and Deary, I.J. 2018. 'Healthy Cognitive Ageing in the Lothian Birth Cohort Studies: Marginal Gains not Magic Bullet', *Psychological Medicine*, 48 (2):187–207.

Costa, Albert et al. 2014. 'Your Morals Depend on Language', *PLOS ONE*, 9 (4):e94842.

Costa, Albert et al. 2017. 'Do Bilinguals Automatically Activate Their Native Language When They Are Not Using It?' *Cognitive Science*, 41 (6):1629–44.

Costa, Albert, Vives, Marc-Lluís, and Corey, Joanna D. 2017. 'On Language Processing Shaping Decision Making', *Current Directions in Psychological Science*, 26 (2):146–51.

Council of Europe. 2001. 'Common European Framework of Reference for Languages: Learning, Teaching, Assessment', Cambridge University Press.

Courtivron, Isabelle de. 2003. *Lives in Translation: Bilingual Writers on Identity and Creativity*, Palgrave Macmillan, New York.

Craik, Fergus I.M., Bialystok, Ellen, and Freedman, Morris. 2010. 'Delaying the Onset of Alzheimer Disease: Bilingualism as a Form of Cognitive Reserve', *Neurology*, 75 (19):1726–29.

Crystal, David. 2003. *Cambridge Encyclopedia of the English Language*, Cambridge University Press.

Crystal, David. 2004. *The Stories of English*, Overlook Press, New York.

Cunningham, Debbie S., Vaid, Jyotsna, and Chen, Hsin-Chin. 2011. 'Yo no lo tire, se cayo solito, I Did not Throw it, it Just Fell Down': Interpreting and Recounting Accidental Events in Spanish and English', in *Language and Bilingual Cognition*, edited by V. Cook and B. Bassetti, Psychology Press, New York and Hove, 407–29.

Davies, Norman. 1981. *God's Playground: A History of Poland*, Volume II, Oxford University Press.

Deary, Ian J. et al. 2007. 'The Lothian Birth Cohort 1936: A Study to Examine Influences on Cognitive Ageing from Age 11 to Age 70 and beyond', *BMC Geriatrics*, 7 (1):28.

DeCasper, Anthony J., and Fifer, William P. 1980. 'Of Human Bonding: Newborns Prefer their Mothers' Voices', *Science*, 208 (4448):1174–76.

DeKeyser, Robert, Alfi-Shabtay, Iris, and Ravid, Dorit. 2010. 'Cross-Linguistic Evidence for the Nature of Age Effects in Second Language Acquisition', *Applied Psycholinguistics*, 31 (3):413–38.

Deutscher, Guy. 2010. *Through the Language Glass: Why the World Looks Different in Other Languages*, Metropolitan Books, New York.

Dewaele, Jean-Marc. 2016. 'Why Do so Many Bi- and Multilinguals Feel Different When Switching Languages?' *International Journal of Multilingualism*, 13 (1):92–105.

Dewaele, Jean-Marc, and Pavlenko, Aneta. n.d. 'Web Questionnaire Bilingualism and Emotions', University of London.

Diamond, Adele. 2013. 'Executive Functions', *Annual Review of Psychology*, 64: 135–68.

Dorfman, Ariel. 2005. 'Footnotes to a Double Life', in *The Genius of Language*, edited by W. Lesser, Anchor Books, New York, 206–17.

Druviete, Ina, and Strelēvica-Ošiņa, Dace. 2008. 'Some Aspects of the Sociolinguistic Situation in Latvia: Causes and Effects', *Suvremena Lingvistika*, 34 (1):89–114.

Dunbar, Robin I.M. 2003. 'The Origin and Subsequent Evolution of Language', in *Language Evolution*, edited by M.H. Christiansen and S. Kirby, Oxford University Press, 219–34.

Emmorey, Karen, Giezen, Marcel R., and Gollan, Tamar H. 2016. 'Psycholinguistic, Cognitive, and Neural Implications of Bimodal Bilingualism', *Bilingualism*, 19 (2):223–42.

Emmorey, Karen et al. 2008. 'The Source of Enhanced Cognitive Control in Bilinguals: Evidence from Bimodal Bilinguals', *Psychological Science*, 19 (12):1201–6.

Engel de Abreu, Pascale M.J. et al. 2012. 'Bilingualism Enriches the Poor: Enhanced Cognitive Control in Low-Income Minority Children', *Psychological Science*, 23 (11):1364–71.

Erard, Michael. 2013. *Mezzofanti's Gift: The Search for the World's Most Extraordinary Language Learners*, Duckworth Overlook, London.

Eurobarometer. 2012. 'Europeans and Their Languages', *Special Eurobarometer 386*.

Fan, Samantha P. et al. 2015. 'The Exposure Advantage: Early Exposure to a Multilingual Environment Promotes Effective Communication', *Psychological Science*, 26 (7):1090–97.

Fausey, Caitlin M., and Boroditsky, Lera. 2011. 'Who Dunnit? Cross-Linguistic Differences in Eye-Witness Memory', *Psychonomic Bulletin & Review*, 18 (1):150–57.

Fausey, Caitlin et al. 2010. 'Constructing Agency: The Role of Language', *Frontiers in Psychology*, 1:162.

Fennell, Barbara A. 2001. *A History of English: A Sociolinguistic Approach*, Blackwell, Oxford.

Filipović, Luna. 2007. 'Language as a Witness: Insights from Cognitive Linguistics', *International Journal of Speech, Language and the Law*, 14:245–67.

Filipović, Luna. 2013. 'The Role of Language in Legal Contexts: A Forensic Cross-Linguistic Viewpoint', in *Law and Language: Current Legal Issues*, Volume 15, edited by M. Freeman and F. Smith, Oxford University Press.

Firmat, Gustavo Pérez. 2003. *Tongue Ties: Logo-Eroticism in Anglo-Hispanic Literature*, Palgrave Macmillan, New York.

First Peoples' Cultural Council (FPCC). 2018. 'Report on the Status of B.C. First Nations Languages', Brentwood Bay, B.C.

Flecken, Monique et al. 2015. 'On the Road to Somewhere: Brain Potentials Reflect Language Effects on Motion Event Perception', *Cognition*, 141:41–51.

Flecken, Monique, Stutterheim, Christiane von, and Carroll, Mary. 2014. 'Grammatical Aspect Influences Motion Event Perception: Findings from a Cross-Linguistic Non-Verbal Recognition Task', *Language and Cognition*, 6 (1):45–78.

Flege, James Emil. 1984. 'The Detection of French Accent by American Listeners', *The Journal of the Acoustical Society of America*, 76 (3):692.

Forder, Lewis, He, Xun, and Franklin, Anna. 2017. 'Colour Categories Are Reflected in Sensory Stages of Colour Perception When Stimulus Issues Are Resolved', *PLOS ONE*, 12 (5):e0178097.

Frank, Robert H., and Cook, Philip J. 1995. *The Winner-Take-All Society: How More and More Americans Compete for Ever Fewer and Bigger Prizes, Encouraging Economic Waste, Income Inequality, and an Impoverished Cultural Life*, Free Press, New York.

Franklin, A. et al. 2008. 'Categorical Perception of Color Is Lateralized to the Right Hemisphere in Infants, but to the Left Hemisphere in Adults', *Proceedings of the National Academy of Sciences*, 105 (9):3221–25.

Freedman, Morris et al. 2014. 'Delaying Onset of Dementia: Are Two Languages Enough?' *Behavioural Neurology*, 2014: 808137.

Friedman, Victor A. 2003. 'Evidentiality in the Balkans with Special Attention to Macedonian and Albanian', in *Studies in Evidentiality*, edited by A.Y. Aikhenvald and R.M.W. Dixon, John Benjamins, Amsterdam, 189–218.

Fuller-Thomson, Esme. 2015. 'Emerging Evidence Contradicts the Hypothesis That Bilingualism Delays Dementia Onset. A Commentary on "Age of Dementia Diagnosis in Community Dwelling Bilingual and Monolingual Hispanic Americans" by Lawton et al., 2015', *Cortex*, 66:170–72.

Fuller-Thomson, Esme, and Kuh, Diana. 2014. 'The Healthy Migrant Effect May Confound the Link between Bilingualism and Delayed Onset of Alzheimer's Disease', *Cortex*, 52 (1):128–30.

Gao, Shan et al. 2015. 'Second Language Feedback Abolishes the 'Hot Hand' Effect During Even-Probability Gambling', *Journal of Neuroscience*, 35 (15):5983–89.

García-Pentón, Lorna et al. 2016. '"Hazy" or "Jumbled"? Putting Together the Pieces of the Bilingual Puzzle', *Language, Cognition and Neuroscience*, 31 (3):353–60.

Gathercole, Virginia C. Mueller. 2015. 'Are We at a Socio-Political and Scientific Crisis?' *Cortex*, 73:345–46.

Gathercole, Virginia C. Mueller, and Thomas, Enlli M. 2009. 'Bilingual First-Language Development: Dominant Language Takeover, Threatened Minority Language Take-Up', *Bilingualism: Language and Cognition*, 12 (2):213–37.

Geipel, Janet, Hadjichristidis, Constantinos, and Surian, Luca. 2015a. 'How Foreign Language Shapes Moral Judgment', *Journal of Experimental Social Psychology*, 59:8–17.

Geipel, Janet, Hadjichristidis, Constantinos, and Surian, Luca. 2015b. 'The Foreign Language Effect on Moral Judgment: The Role of Emotions and Norms', *PLOS ONE*, 10 (7):e0131529.

Geipel, Janet, Hadjichristidis, Constantinos, and Surian, Luca. 2016. 'Foreign Language Affects the Contribution of Intentions and Outcomes to Moral Judgment', *Cognition*, 154:34–39.

Gervain, Judit. 2015. 'Plasticity in Early Language Acquisition: The Effects of Prenatal and Early Childhood Experience', *Current Opinion in Neurobiology*, 35:13–20.

Gold, Brian T. 2015. 'Lifelong Bilingualism and Neural Reserve against Alzheimer's Disease: A Review of Findings and Potential Mechanisms', *Behavioural Brain Research*, 281:9–15.

Gow, Alan J. et al. 2012. 'Reverse Causation in Activity-Cognitive Ability Associations: The Lothian Birth Cohort 1936', *Psychology and Aging*, 27 (1):250–55.

Grandin, Temple. 1995. 'How People with Autism Think', in *Learning and Cognition in Autism*, edited by E. Schopler and G.B. Mesibov, Plenum, New York, 137–56.

Granena, Gisela, and Long, Michael H. 2013. 'Age of Onset, Length of Residence, Language Aptitude, and Ultimate L2 Attainment in Three Linguistic Domains', *Second Language Research*, 29 (3):311–43.

Greenberg, Robert D. 2004. *Language and Identity in the Balkans: Serbo-Croatian and its Disintegration*, Oxford University Press.

Grice, H. Paul. 1989. *Studies in the Way of Words*, Harvard University Press.

Grosjean, François. 2010. *Bilingual: Life and Reality*, Harvard University Press.

Grundy, John G., Anderson, John A.E., and Bialystok, Ellen. 2017. 'Neural Correlates of Cognitive Processing in Monolinguals and Bilinguals', *Annals of the New York Academy of Sciences*, 1396:183–201.

Hadjichristidis, Constantinos, Geipel, Janet, and Savadori, Lucia. 2015. 'The Effect of Foreign Language in Judgments of Risk and Benefit: The Role of Affect', *Journal of Experimental Psychology: Applied*, 21 (2):117–29.

Hadjichristidis, Constantinos, Geipel, Janet, and Surian, Luca. 2018. 'Breaking Magic: Foreign Language Suppresses Superstition', *Quarterly Journal of Experimental Psychology*, 39 (1).

Hakuta, Kenji. 1989. 'An Interview with Werner F. Leopold', *Bilingual Research Group Working Paper*, 89–07, University of California, Santa Cruz.

Hakuta, Kenji, and Diaz, Rafael M. 1985. 'The Relationship between Degree of Bilingualism and Cognitive Ability: A Critical Discussion and Some New Longitudinal Data', in *Children's Language*, Volume 5, edited by K.E. Nelson, Lawrence Erlbaum, Hillsdale NJ, 319–44.

Hammer, Carol Scheffner et al. 2009. 'The Effect of Maternal Language on Bilingual Children's Vocabulary and Emergent Literacy Development during Head Start and Kindergarten', *Scientific Studies of Reading*, 13 (2):99–121.

Harris, Catherine L., Ayçiçegi, Ayse, and Gleason, Jean Berko. 2003. 'Taboo Words and Reprimands Elicit Greater Autonomic Reactivity in a First Language than in a Second Language', *Applied Psycholinguistics*, 24 (4):561–79.

Hartanto, Andree, Yang, Hwajin, and Yang, Sujin. 2018. 'Bilingualism Positively Predicts Mathematical Competence: Evidence from Two Large-Scale Studies', *Learning and Individual Differences*, 61:216–27.

Hayakawa, Sayuri et al. 2016. 'Using a Foreign Language Changes Our Choices', *Trends in Cognitive Sciences*, 20 (11):791–93.

Hayakawa, Sayuri et al. 2017. 'Thinking More or Feeling Less? Explaining the Foreign-Language Effect on Moral Judgment', *Psychological Science*, 28 (10):1387–97.

Hayakawa, Sayuri, and Keysar, Boaz. 2018. 'Using a Foreign Language Reduces Mental Imagery', *Cognition*, 173:8–15.

Head, Megan L. et al. 2015. 'The Extent and Consequences of P-Hacking in Science', *PLOS Biology*, 13 (3):e1002106.

Herder, Johann Gottfried. 1992. *Johann Gottfried Herder: Selected Early Works, 1764–1767: Addresses, Essays, and Drafts; Fragments on Recent German Literature*, edited by E.A. Menze and K. Menges, Pennsylvania State University Press.

Herder, Johann Gottfried, and Bohlman, Philip V. 2017. *Song Loves the Masses: Herder on Music and Nationalism*, University of California Press.

Hernandez, Arturo E. et al. 2015. 'Beyond the Bilingual Advantage: The Potential Role of Genes and Environment on the Development of Cognitive Control', *Journal of Neurolinguistics*, 35:109–19.

Higginson, Andrew D., and Munafò, Marcus R. 2016. 'Current Incentives for Scientists Lead to Underpowered Studies with Erroneous Conclusions', *PLOS Biology*, 14 (11):e2000995.

Hobsbawm, Eric. 2002. *Interesting Times: A Twentieth-Century Life*, Allen Lane, London.

Hoff, Erika et al. 2012. 'Dual Language Exposure and Early Bilingual Development', *Journal of Child Language*, 39 (1):1–27.

Hoff, Erika, and Core, Cynthia. 2013. 'Input and Language Development in Bilingually Developing Children', *Seminars in Speech and Language*, 34 (4):215–26.

Hoff, Erika et al. 2014. 'Expressive Vocabulary Development in Children from Bilingual and Monolingual Homes: A Longitudinal Study from Two to Four Years', *Early Childhood Research Quarterly*, 29 (4):433–44.

Houwer, Annick De. 2007. 'Parental Language Input Patterns and Children's Bilingual Use', *Applied Psycholinguistics*, 28:411–24.

Houwer, Annick De, Bornstein, Marc H., and Putnick, Diane L. 2014. 'A Bilingual–Monolingual Comparison of Young Children's Vocabulary Size: Evidence from Comprehension and Production', *Applied Psycholinguistics*, 35 (6):1189–1211.

Humboldt, Wilhelm von. 1999. *On Language: On the Diversity of Human Language Construction and its Influence on the Mental Development of the Human Species*, Cambridge University Press.

Hutchins, John. 2000. 'Warren Weaver and the Launching of MT. Brief Biographical Note', in *Early Years in Machine Translation*, edited by W.J. Hutchins, John Benjamins, Amsterdam, 17–20.

Hutchins, W. John. 2004. 'The Georgetown–IBM Experiment Demonstrated in January 1954', *Proceedings of the 6th Conference of the Association for Machine Translation in the Americas (AMTA 2004)*, 102–14.

Hutchins, W. John. 2010. 'Machine Translation: A Concise History', *Journal of Translation Studies*, 13 (1–2):29–70.

Iyer, Gowri K. et al. 2014. 'Dementia in Developing Countries: Does Education Play the Same Role in India as in the West?' *Dementia & Neuropsychologia*, 8 (2):132–40.

Jakobson, Roman. 1959. 'On Linguistic Aspects of Translation', in *On Translation*, edited by A. Fang and R.A. Brower, Harvard University Press, 232–39.

James, William. 2007. *The Principles of Psychology*, Volume 1, Cosimo, New York.

Jaremko-Porter, Christina. 2008. 'Johann Gottfried Herder and the Latvian Voice', PhD thesis, University of Edinburgh.

Jenkins, Jennifer. 2017. 'An ELF Perspective on English in the Post-Brexit EU', *World Englishes*, 36 (3):343–46.

John, Leslie K., Loewenstein, George, and Prelec, Drazen. 2012. 'Measuring the Prevalence of Questionable Research Practices with Incentives for Truth Telling', *Psychological Science*, 23 (5):524–32.

Jones, Hywel M. 2012. *A Statistical Overview of the Welsh Language*, Welsh Language Board.

Just, Marcel A., and Carpenter, Patricia A. 1992. 'A Capacity Theory of Comprehension: Individual Differences in Working Memory', *Psychological Review*, 99 (1):122–49.

Kahneman, Daniel. 2011. *Thinking, Fast and Slow*, Allen Lane, London.

Karttunen, Frances E. 1994. *Between Worlds: Interpreters, Guides, and Survivors*, Rutgers University Press.

Kempe, Vera, and Brooks, Patricia J. 2011. 'Individual Differences in Adult Second Language Learning: A Cognitive Perspective', *Scottish Languages Review*, 23: 15–22.

Keysar, Boaz, Hayakawa, Sayuri L., and An, Sun Gyu. 2012. 'The Foreign-Language Effect: Thinking in a Foreign Tongue Reduces Decision Biases', *Psychological Science*, 23 (6):661–68.

Kim, Eleana J. 2010. *Adopted Territory: Transnational Korean Adoptees and the Politics of Belonging*, Duke University Press.

King, Robert D. 2001. 'The Poisonous Potency of Script: Hindi and Urdu', *International Journal of the Sociology of Language*, 150 (1):43–59.

Klein, Raymond M. 2015. 'On the Belief that the Cognitive Exercise Associated with the Acquisition of a Second Language Enhances Extra-Linguistic Cognitive Functions: Is 'Type-I Incompetence' at Work Here?' *Cortex*, 73:340–41.

Klusmeyer, Douglas B., and Papademetriou, Demetrios G. 2009. *Immigration Policy in the Federal Republic of Germany: Negotiating Membership and Remaking the Nation*, Berghahn, New York and Oxford.

Knight, Chris. 2016. *Decoding Chomsky: Science and Revolutionary Politics*, Yale University Press.

Krashen, Stephen D. 1983. 'The Din in the Head, Input, and the Language Acquisition Device', *Foreign Language Annals*, 16 (1):41–4.

Kristeva, Julia. 1991. *Strangers to Ourselves*, Harvester Wheatsheaf, New York.

Kuhl, Patricia. 2011. 'Early Language Learning and Literacy: Neuroscience Implications for Education', *Mind Brain Education*, 5, 3:128–42.

Kulick, Don. 1997. *Language Shift and Cultural Reproduction: Socialization, Self and Syncretism in a Papua New Guinean Village*, Cambridge University Press.

Laizāne, Māra, Putniņa, Aivita, and Mileiko, Ilze. 2015. 'Mazākumtautību Skolu Skolēnu Identitāte Un Piederība Latvijai', Prezi, Rīga.

Latvian Centre for Human Rights. 2013. 'Second Alternative Report on the Implementation of the Council of Europe Framework Convention for the Protection of National Minorities in Latvia', Rīga.

Lawton, Deborah M., Gasquoine, Philip G., and Weimer, Amy A. 2015. 'Age of Dementia Diagnosis in Community Dwelling Bilingual and Monolingual Hispanic Americans', *Cortex*, 66:141–5.

Laycock, Donald C. 2001a. *The Complete Enochian Dictionary: A Dictionary of the Angelic Language as Revealed to Dr. John Dee and Edward Kelley*, Weiser, Red Wheel/Weiser, York Beach ME.

Laycock, Donald C. 2001b. 'Linguistic Diversity in Melanesia: A Tentative Explanation', in *Ecolinguistics Reader: Language, Ecology and Environment*, edited by A. Fill and P. Mühlhäusler, Continuum, London and New York, 167–71.

Leeuw, Esther de. 2009. 'When Your Native Language Sounds Foreign: A Phonetic Investigation into First Language Attrition', PhD thesis, Queen Margaret University, Edinburgh.

Leigh, Dick. 1997. *A Social History of English*, Routledge, London.

Leimgruber, Jakob R.E. 2013. 'The Management of Multilingualism in a City-State: Language Policy in Singapore', in *Multilingualism and Language Contact in Urban Areas: Acquisition, Development, Teaching, Communication*, edited by P. Siemund et al., John Benjamins, Amsterdam, 227–56.

Leopold, Werner F. 1959. 'The Decline of German Dialects', *Word*, 15 (1):130–53.

Lesser, Wendy. 2005. *The Genius of Language: Fifteen Writers Reflect on their Mother Tongue*, Anchor, New York.

Levinson, Stephen C. 2012. 'The Original Sin of Cognitive Science', *Topics in Cognitive Science*, 4 (3):396–403.

Liberman, Zoe et al. 2017. 'Exposure to Multiple Languages Enhances Communication Skills in Infancy', *Developmental Science*, 20:e12420.

Linck, Jared A. et al. 2013. 'Hi-LAB: A New Measure of Aptitude for High-Level Language Proficiency', *Language Learning*, 63 (3):530–66.

Linck, Jared A., Kroll, Judith F., and Sunderman, Gretchen. 2009. 'Losing Access to the Native Language While Immersed in a Second Language: Evidence for the Role of Inhibition in Second-Language Learning', *Psychological Science*, 20 (12):1507–15.

Linck, Jared A., and Weiss, Daniel J. 2015. 'Can Working Memory and Inhibitory Control Predict Second Language Learning in the Classroom?' *SAGE Open*, 5 (4).

Ločmele, Klinta, Procevska, Olga, and Zelče, Vita. 2011. 'Celebrations, Commemorative Dates and Related Rituals: Soviet Experience, its Transformation and Contemporary Victory Day Celebrations in Russia and Latvia', in *The Geopolitics of History in Latvian-Russian Relations*, edited by N. Muižnieks, Academic Press of the University of Latvia, 109–37.

Lopez, Mark Hugo, Gonzalez-Barrera, Ana, and López, Gustavo. 2017. 'Hispanic Identity Fades Across Generations as Immigrant Connections Fall Away', Pew Research Center.

Luk, Gigi et al. 2011. 'Lifelong Bilingualism Maintains White Matter Integrity in Older Adults', *Journal of Neuroscience*, 31 (46):16808–13.

Lupyan, Gary. 2012. 'What Do Words Do? Toward a Theory of Language-Augmented Thought', in *Psychology of Learning and Motivation – Advances in Research and Theory*, Volume 57, edited by B.H. Ross, Academic Press, San Diego CA, 255–97.

Lupyan, Gary, and Dale, Rick. 2015. 'The Role of Adaptation in Understanding Linguistic Diversity', in *Language Structure and Environment: Social, Cultural, and Natural Factors*, edited by R. De Busser and R.J. Lapolla, John Benjamins, Amsterdam, 289–316.

Lynd, Staughton, Lynd, Alice, and Bahour, Sam. 1994. *Homeland: Oral Histories of Palestine and Palestinians*, Olive Branch Press, New York.

Mackey, William F. 2013. 'Bilingualism and Multilingualism in North America', in *The Handbook of Bilingualism and Multilingualism*, edited by T.K. Bhatia and W.C. Ritchie, Blackwell, Oxford, 707–24.

Macnamara, Brooke N., and Conway, Andrew R.A. 2016. 'Working Memory Capacity as a Predictor of Simultaneous Language Interpreting Performance', *Journal of Applied Research in Memory and Cognition*, 5 (4):434–44.

Mairs, Rachel. 2011. '*Translator, Traditor*: The Interpreter as Traitor in Classical Tradition', *Greece & Rome*, 58 (1):64–81.

Mamiya, Ping C. et al. 2016. 'Brain White Matter Structure and COMT Gene Are Linked to Second-Language Learning in Adults', *Proceedings of the National Academy of Sciences*, 113 (26):7249–54.

Mampe, Birgit et al. 2009. 'Newborns' Cry Melody Is Shaped by their Native Language', *Current Biology*, 19 (23):1994–7.

Manan, Syed A., Dumanig, Francisco P., and David, Maya K. 2017. 'The English-Medium Fever in Pakistan: Analyzing Policy, Perceptions and Practices through Additive Bi/multilingual Education Lens', *International Journal of Bilingual Education and Bilingualism*, 20 (6):736–52.

Mayberry, Rachel I., and Lock, Elizabeth. 2003. 'Age Constraints on First versus Second Language Acquisition: Evidence for Linguistic Plasticity and Epigenesis', *Brain and Language*, 87 (3):369–84.

Mazoyer, Bernard et al. 2014. 'Gaussian Mixture Modeling of Hemispheric Lateralization for Language in a Large Sample of Healthy Individuals Balanced for Handedness', *PLOS ONE*, 9 (6):e101165.

McConvell, Patrick, and Thieberger, Nicholas. 2001. 'State of Indigenous Languages in Australia – 2001', Environment Australia.

McWhorter, John H. 2014. *The Language Hoax: Why the World Looks the Same in Any Language*, Oxford University Press.

Miller, Michael L., and Ury, Scott. 2010. 'Cosmopolitanism: The End of Jewishness?' *European Review of History*, 17 (3):337–59.

Miller, Robert L. 1968. *The Linguistic Relativity Principle and Humboldtian Ethnolinguistics: A History and Appraisal*, Mouton, The Hague.

Mintz, Toben H. et al. 2018. 'Infants' Sensitivity to Vowel Harmony and its Role in Segmenting Speech', *Cognition*, 171:95–107.

Młynarczyk, Anna K. 2004. 'Aspectual Pairing in Polish', PhD thesis, Universiteit Utrecht.

Modiano, Marko. 2017. 'English in a Post-Brexit European Union', *World Englishes*, 36:313–27.

Montero-Melis, Guillermo et al. 2017. 'Satellite- vs. Verb-Framing Underpredicts Nonverbal Motion Categorization: Insights from a Large Language Sample and Simulations', *Cognitive Semantics*, 3 (1):36–61.

Montrul, Silvina. 2010. 'Current Issues in Heritage Language Acquisition', *Annual Review of Applied Linguistics*, 30:3–23.

Montrul, Silvina A. 2012. 'Is the Heritage Language like a Second Language?' in *EUROSLA Yearbook:* Volume 12, edited by L. Roberts et al., John Benjamins, Amsterdam, 1–29.

Morgan-Short, Kara et al. 2014. 'Declarative and Procedural Memory as Individual Differences in Second Language Acquisition', *Bilingualism: Language and Cognition*, 17 (1):56–72.

Morton, J. Bruce, and Harper, Sarah N. 2007. 'What Did Simon Say? Revisiting the Bilingual Advantage', *Developmental Science*, 10 (6):719–26.

Mukadam, Naaheed, Sommerlad, Andrew, and Livingston, Gill. 2017. 'The Relationship of Bilingualism Compared to Monolingualism to the Risk of Cognitive

Decline or Dementia: A Systematic Review and Meta-Analysis', *Journal of Alzheimer's Disease*, 58 (1):45–54.

Müller, Torsten. 2008. 'An Important Type of Unplanned Spoken Language: A Brief History of Football Commentary in England and Germany', *Brno Studies in English*, 34:63–78.

Nair, Vishnu K.K., Biedermann, Britta, and Nickels, Lyndsey. 2017. 'Effect of Socio-Economic Status on Cognitive Control in Non-Literate Bilingual Speakers', *Bilingualism: Language and Cognition*, 20 (5):999–1009.

Neeley, Tsedal B. 2013. 'Language Matters: Status Loss and Achieved Status Distinctions in Global Organizations', *Organization Science*, 24 (2):476–97.

Nettle, Daniel. 1998. 'Explaining Global Patterns of Linguistic Diversity', *Journal of Anthropological Archaeology*, 17 (4):354–74.

Norrman, Gunnar, and Bylund, Emanuel. 2016. 'The Irreversibility of Sensitive Period Effects in Language Development: Evidence from Second Language Acquisition in International Adoptees', *Developmental Science*, 19 (3):513–20.

Noyes, John K. 2015. *Herder: Aesthetics against Imperialism*, University of Toronto Press.

Nussbaum, Robert L., and Ellis, Christopher E. 2003. 'Alzheimer's Disease and Parkinson's Disease', *New England Journal of Medicine*, 348 (14):1356–64.

O'Grady, William. 2018. 'The Linguistics of Language Revitalization: Problems of Acquisition and Attrition', in *Oxford Handbook of Endangered Languages*, edited by K. Rehg and L. Campbell, Oxford University Press, 490–509.

Oh, Janet S., Au, Terry Kit-Fong, and Jun, Sun-Ah. 2010. 'Early Childhood Language Memory in the Speech Perception of International Adoptees', *Journal of Child Language*, 37 (5):1123–32.

Olsen, Rosanna K. et al. 2015. 'The Effect of Lifelong Bilingualism on Regional Grey and White Matter Volume', *Brain Research*, 1612:128–39.

Olulade, O.A. et al. 2016. 'Neuroanatomical Evidence in Support of the Bilingual Advantage Theory', *Cerebral Cortex*, 26 (7):3196–204.

Open Science Collaboration. 2015. 'Estimating the Reproducibility of Psychological Science', *Science*, 349 (6251):aac4716.

Otheguy, Ricardo, García, Ofelia, and Reid, Wallis. 2015. 'Clarifying Translanguaging and Deconstructing Named Languages: A Perspective from Linguistics', *Applied Linguistics Review*, 6 (3):281–307.

Ożańska-Ponikwia, Katarzyna. 2012. 'What Has Personality and Emotional Intelligence to Do with "Feeling Different" While Using a Foreign Language?' *International Journal of Bilingual Education and Bilingualism*, 15 (2):217–34.

Paap, Kenneth R., Johnson, Hunter A., and Sawi, Oliver. 2015. 'Bilingual Advantages in Executive Functioning Either Do Not Exist or Are Restricted to Very Specific and Undetermined Circumstances', *Cortex*, 69:265–78.

Paap, Kenneth R., Johnson, Hunter A., and Sawi, Oliver. 2016. 'Should the Search for Bilingual Advantages in Executive Functioning Continue?', *Cortex*, 74:305–14.

Pagel, Mark. 2009. 'Human Language as a Culturally Transmitted Replicator', *Nature Reviews. Genetics*, 10 (6):405–15.

Pallier, Christophe et al. 2003. 'Brain Imaging of Language Plasticity in Adopted Adults: Can a Second Language Replace the First?' *Cerebral Cortex*, 13 (2):155–61.

Pallier, Christophe. 2007. 'Critical Periods in Language Acquisition and Language Attrition', in *Language Attrition: Theoretical Perspectives*, edited by B. Köpke et al., John Benjamins, Amsterdam, 155–68.

Panicacci, Alessandra, and Dewaele, Jean-Marc. 2017. "A Voice from Elsewhere": Acculturation, Personality and Migrants' Self-Perceptions across Languages and Cultures', *International Journal of Multilingualism*, 14 (4):419–36.

Parry, Glyn. 2011. *The Arch Conjuror of England: John Dee*, Yale University Press.

Pavlenko, Aneta. 2006. 'Bilingual Selves', in *Bilingual Minds: Emotional Experience, Expression and Representation*, edited by A. Pavlenko, Multilingual Matters, Clevedon, 1–33.

Pavlenko, Aneta. 2014. *The Bilingual Mind, And What It Tells Us About Language and Thought*, Cambridge University Press.

Peal, Elizabeth, and Lambert, Wallace E. 1962. 'The Relation of Bilingualism to Intelligence', *Psychological Monographs*, 76 (27):1–23.

Perani, Daniela et al. 2017. 'The Impact of Bilingualism on Brain Reserve and Metabolic Connectivity in Alzheimer's Dementia', *Proceedings of the National Academy of Sciences*, 114 (7):1690–95.

Pierce, Lara J. et al. 2014. 'Mapping the Unconscious Maintenance of a Lost First Language', *Proceedings of the National Academy of Sciences*, 111 (48): 17314–19.

Pierce, Lara J. et al. 2015. 'Past Experience Shapes Ongoing Neural Patterns for Language', *Nature Communications*, 6: 10073.

Pinker, Steven. 2007. *The Stuff of Thought: Language as a Window into Human Nature*, Allen Lane, London.

Pinker, Steven, and Jackendoff, Ray. 2005. 'The Faculty of Language: What's Special about It?' *Cognition*, 95 (2):201–36.

Piotrowski, Rajmund, and Romanov, Yourij. 1999. 'Machine Translation in the Former Soviet Union and in the Newly Independent States (NIS)', *Histoire Épistémologie Langage*, 21 (1):105–17.

Polinsky, Maria. 2006. 'Incomplete Acquisition: American Russian', *Journal of Slavic Linguistics*, 14 (2):191–262.

Polinsky, Maria. 2008. 'Gender under Incomplete Acquisition: Heritage Speakers' Knowledge of Noun Categorization', *Heritage Language Journal*, 6 (1):40–71.

Polinsky, Maria. 2015. 'When L1 Becomes an L3: Do Heritage Speakers Make Better L3 Learners?' *Bilingualism: Language and Cognition*, 18:163–78.

Polinsky, Maria. 2016. 'Bilingual Children and Adult Heritage Speakers: The Range of Comparison', *International Journal of Bilingualism*, doi: 10.1177/ 1367006916656048.

Pons, Ferran, Bosch, Laura, and Lewkowicz, David J. 2015. 'Bilingualism Modulates Infants' Selective Attention to the Mouth of a Talking Face', *Psychological Science*, 26 (4):490–98.

Pousada, Alicia. 1994. 'Joseph Conrad's Multilingualism: A Case Study of Language Planning in Literature', *English Studies*, 75 (4):335–49.

Ramakrishnan, Subasree et al. 2017. 'Comparative Effects of Education and Bilingualism on the Onset of Mild Cognitive Impairment', *Dementia and Geriatric Cognitive Disorders*, 44 (3–4):222–31.

Ramírez-Esparza, Nairán et al. 2006. 'Do Bilinguals Have Two Personalities? A Special Case of Cultural Frame Switching', *Journal of Research in Personality*, 40 (2):99–120.

Ramírez-Esparza, Nairán, Gosling, Samuel D., and Pennebaker, James W. 2008. 'Paradox Lost: Unraveling the Puzzle of Simpatía', *Journal of Cross-Cultural Psychology*, 39 (6):703–15.

Rasinger, Sebastian M. 2013. 'Language Shift and Vitality Perceptions amongst London's Second-Generation Bangladeshis', *Journal of Multilingual and Multicultural Development*, 34 (1):46–60.

Regier, Terry, and Kay, Paul. 2009. 'Language, Thought, and Color: Whorf Was Half Right', *Trends in Cognitive Sciences*, 13 (10):439–46.

Richerson, Peter J., and Boyd, Robert. 2010. 'Why Possibly Language Evolved', *Biolinguistics*, 4:289–306.

Riekstiņš, Jānis. 2012. *In Defence of the Latvian Language: Against Russification: Documents from 1944–1989*, Latviešu valodas aģentūra, Rīga.

Romaine, Suzanne. 2000. *Language in Society: An Introduction to Sociolinguistics*, Oxford University Press.

Rozenvalds, Juris. 2010. 'The Soviet Heritage and Integration Policy Development Since the Restoration of Independence', in *How Integrated Is Latvian Society? An Audit of Achievements, Failures and Challenges*, edited by N. Muižnieks, University of Latvia Press, 33–59.

Rumbaut, Rubén G., Massey, Douglas S., and Bean, Frank D. 2006. 'Linguistic Life Expectancies: Immigrant Language Retention in Southern California', *Population and Development Review*, 32 (3):447–60.

Ryan, Camille. 2013. 'Language Use in the United States: 2011', United States Census Bureau.

Saer, David J. 1923. 'The Effect of Bilingualism on Intelligence', *British Journal of Psychology*, 14 (1):25–38.

Saer, David J., Smith, Frank, and Hughes, John. 1924. *The Bilingual Problem: A Study Based Upon Experiments and Observations in Wales*, Hughes & Son, Wrexham.

Santillán, Jimena, and Khurana, Atika. 2018. 'Developmental Associations between Bilingual Experience and Inhibitory Control Trajectories in Head Start Children', *Developmental Science*, 21 (4):e12624.

Schmid, Monika S. 2002. *First Language Attrition, Use and Maintenance: The Case of German Jews in Anglophone Countries*, John Benjamins, Amsterdam.

Schmid, Monika S. 2004. 'Identity and First Language Attrition: A Historical Approach', *Estudios de Sociolingüística: Linguas, Sociedades e Culturas*, 5 (1):41–58.

Schmid, Monika S. 2007. 'The Role of L1 Use for L1 Attrition', in *Language Attrition: Theoretical Perspectives*, edited by B. Köpke et al., John Benjamins, Amsterdam, 135–53.

Schmid, Monika S. 2009. 'On L1 Attrition and the Linguistic System', in *EUROSLA Yearbook: Volume 9*, edited by L. Roberts et al., John Benjamins, Amsterdam, 212–44.

Schmid, Monika S. 2011. 'Treacherous Shibboleths Language as an Indicator of Origin', Rijksuniversiteit Groningen.

Schmid, Monika S. 2012. 'Attrition and Multilingualism', in *The Encyclopedia of Applied Linguistics*, edited by C.A. Chapelle, Wiley Blackwell.

Schmiedtová, Barbara, Stutterheim, Christiane von, and Carroll, Mary. 2011. 'Language-Specific Patterns in Event Construal of Advanced Second Language Speakers', in *Thinking and Speaking in Two Languages*, edited by A. Pavlenko, Multilingual Matters, Bristol, 66–107.

Schweizer, Tom A. et al. 2012. 'Bilingualism as a Contributor to Cognitive Reserve: Evidence from Brain Atrophy in Alzheimer's Disease', *Cortex*, 48 (8):991–96.

Sebastián-Gallés, Núria et al. 2012. 'A Bilingual Advantage in Visual Language Discrimination in Infancy', *Psychological Science*, 23 (9):994–99.

Security Police (Drošības policija). 2014. 'Annual Report 2013', Rīga.

Seton, Bregtje, and Schmid, Monika S. 2016. 'Multi-Competence and First Language Attrition', in *The Cambridge Handbook of Linguistic Multi-Competence*, edited by V. Cook and L. Wei, Cambridge University Press, 338–54.

Siegal, Michael et al. 2010. 'Bilingualism Accentuates Children's Conversational Understanding', *PLOS ONE*, 5 (2):e9004.

Siegal, Michael, Iozzi, Laura, and Surian, Luca. 2009. 'Bilingualism and Conversational Understanding in Young Children', *Bilingualism*, 110:115–22.

Singer, Ruth, and Harris, Salome. 2016. 'What Practices and Ideologies Support Small-Scale Multilingualism? A Case Study of Warruwi Community, Northern Australia', *International Journal of the Sociology of Language*, 2016 (241):163–208.

Singh, Leher et al. 2011. 'Rapid Reacquisition of Native Phoneme Contrasts after Disuse: You Do Not Always Lose What You Do Not Use', *Developmental Science*, 14 (5):949–59.

Slobin, Dan I. 2016. 'Thinking for Speaking and the Construction of Evidentiality in Language Contact', in *Exploring the Turkish Linguistic Landscape: Essays in Honor of Eser Erguvanlı-Taylan*, edited by M. Güven et al., John Benjamins, Amsterdam, 105–20.

Slobin, Dan I. 1987. 'Thinking For Speaking', in *Proceedings of the Thirteenth Annual Meeting of the Berkeley Linguistics Society*, 435–45.

Slobin, Dan I., and Aksu, Ayhan A. 1982. 'Tense, Aspect, and Modality in the Use of the Turkish Evidential', in *Tense-Aspect: Between Semantics and Pragmatics*, edited by P.J. Hopper, John Benjamins, Amsterdam, 185–200.

Snowdon, David A. 1997. 'Aging and Alzheimer's Disease: Lessons From the Nun Study', *The Gerontologist*, 37 (2):150–56.

Snyder, Timothy. 2004. *The Reconstruction of Nations: Poland, Ukraine, Lithuania, Belarus, 1569–1999*, Yale University Press.

Spindler, Erik. 2012. 'Flemings in the Peasants' Revolt, 1381', in *Contact and Exchange in Later Medieval Europe: Essays in Honour of Malcolm Vale*, edited by H. Skoda, P. Lantschner, and R.L.J. Shaw, Boydell Press, Woodbridge, 59–78.

Stansfield, Charles W., and Reed, Daniel J. 2004. 'The Story Behind the Modern Language Aptitude Test: An Interview with John B. Carroll (1916–2003)', *Language Assessment Quarterly*, 1 (1):43–56.

Stavans, Ilan. 2002. *On Borrowed Words: A Memoir of Language*, Penguin, London.

Steiner, George. 1998. *After Babel: Aspects of Language and Translation*, Oxford University Press.

Stern, Yaakov. 2009. 'Cognitive Reserve', *Neuropsychologia*, 47 (10):2015–28.

Stern, Yaakov. 2012. 'Cognitive Reserve in Ageing and Alzheimer's Disease', *Lancet Neurology*, 11 (11):1006–12.

Stutterheim, Christiane von et al. 2012. 'How Grammaticized Concepts Shape Event Conceptualization in Language Production: Insights from Linguistic Analysis, Eye Tracking Data, and Memory Performance', *Linguistics*, 50 (4): 833–67.

Stutterheim, Christiane von, and Nüse, Ralf. 2003. 'Processes of Conceptualization in Language Production: Language-Specific Perspectives and Event Construal', *Linguistics*, 41 (5):851–81.

Tannenbaum, Michal, and Abugov, Netta. 2010. 'The Legacy of the Linguistic Fence: Linguistic Patterns among Ultra-Orthodox Jewish Girls', *Heritage Language Journal*, 7 (1):117–47.

Thierry, Guillaume, and Wu, Yan J. 2007. 'Brain Potentials Reveal Unconscious Translation during Foreign-Language Comprehension', *Proceedings of the National Academy of Sciences*, 104 (30):12530–35.

Thiessen, Erik D., Girard, Sandrine and Erikson, Lucy C. 2016. 'Statistical Learning and the Critical Period: How a Continuous Learning Mechanism Can Give Rise to Discontinuous Learning', *WIREs Cognitive Science*, 7 (4):276–88.

Titone, Debra et al. 2017. 'History-Inspired Reflections on the Bilingual Advantages Hypothesis', in *Growing Old with Two Languages: Effects of Bilingualism on Cognitive Aging*, edited by E. Bialystok and M. Sullivan, John Benjamins, Amsterdam, 265–95.

Tokarczuk, Olga. 2010. *Bieguni*, Wydawnictwo Literackie, Kraków.

Tosun, Sümeyra. 2014. 'Source vs. Stance? On the Interpretation and Use of Evidential Utterances by Turkish- vs. English-Speaking Adults', doctoral dissertation, Texas A&M University.

Tosun, Sümeyra, Vaid, Jyotsna, and Geraci, Lisa. 2013. 'Does Obligatory Linguistic Marking of Source of Evidence Affect Source Memory? A Turkish/English Investigation', *Journal of Memory and Language*, 69 (2):121–34.

Ullman, Michael T., and Lovelett, Jarrett T. 2018. 'Implications of the Declarative/ Procedural Model for Improving Second Language Learning: The Role of Memory Enhancement Techniques', *Second Language Research*, 34 (1):39–65.

Valenzuela, Michael J., and Sachdev, Perminder. 2006. 'Brain Reserve and Dementia: A Systematic Review', *Psychological Medicine*, 36 (4):441–54.

Valian, Virginia. 2015. 'Bilingualism and Cognition', *Bilingualism: Language and Cognition*, 18 (1):3–24.

Vanhove, Jan. 2013. 'The Critical Period Hypothesis in Second Language Acquisition: A Statistical Critique and a Reanalysis', *PLOS ONE*, 8 (7):e69172.

Vasanta, Duggirala et al. 2010. 'Language Choice and Language Use Patterns among Telugu–Hindi/Urdu–English Speakers in Hyderabad, India', in *International Conference on Language, Society, and Culture in Asian Contexts (LSCAC) Proceedings*, 57–67.

Vaughn, Kelly A., and Hernandez, Arturo E. 2018. 'Becoming a Balanced, Proficient Bilingual: Predictions from Age of Acquisition & Genetic Background', *Journal of Neurolinguistics*, 46:69–77.

Veltkamp, G. Marina et al. 2012. 'Is Personality Modulated by Language?' *International Journal of Bilingualism*, 17 (4):496–504.

Velupillai, Viveka. 2012. *An Introduction to Linguistic Typology*. John Benjamins, Amsterdam.

Ventureyra, Valérie A.G., Pallier, Christophe, and Yoo, Hi-Yon. 2004. 'The Loss of First Language Phonetic Perception in Adopted Koreans', *Journal of Neurolinguistics*, 17 (1):79–91.

Voegtline, Kristin M. et al. 2013. 'Near-Term Fetal Response to Maternal Spoken Voice', *Infant Behavior and Development*, 36 (4):526–33.

Volodarsky, Boris. 2014. *Stalin's Agent: The Life and Death of Alexander Orlov*, Oxford University Press.

Vouloumanos, Athena, and Werker, Janet F. 2007. 'Listening to Language at Birth: Evidence for a Bias for Speech in Neonates', *Developmental Science*, 10 (2):159–64.

Weaver, Warren. 1949. 'Translation', report to the Rockefeller Foundation, New York.

Wee, Lionel. 2010. ' "Burdens" and "Handicaps" in Singapore's Language Policy: On the Limits of Language Management', *Language Policy*, 9:97–114.

Weikum, Whitney M. et al. 2012. 'Prenatal Exposure to Antidepressants and Depressed Maternal Mood Alter Trajectory of Infant Speech Perception', *Proceedings of the National Academy of Sciences*, 109 (Supplement 2):17221–27.

Welsh Government & Welsh Language Commissioner. 2015. 'Welsh Language Use in Wales, 2013–15'.

Wen, Zhisheng (Edward), Biedroń, Adriana, and Skehan, Peter. 2017. 'Foreign Language Aptitude Theory: Yesterday, Today and Tomorrow', *Language Teaching*, 50 (1):1–31.

Werker, Janet F., and Byers-Heinlein, Krista. 2008. 'Bilingualism in Infancy: First Steps in Perception and Comprehension', *Trends in Cognitive Sciences*, 12 (4):144–51.

Werker, Janet F., and Hensch, Takao K. 2015. 'Critical Periods in Speech Perception: New Directions', *Annual Review of Psychology*, 66 (1):173–96.

Werker, Janet F., and Tees, Richard C. 1984. 'Cross-Language Speech Perception: Evidence for Perceptual Reorganization during the First Year of Life', *Infant Behavior and Development*, 7 (1):49–63.

Whitfield, John. 2008. 'Across the Curious Parallel of Language and Species Evolution', *PLOS Biology*, 6 (7):e186.

Whorf, Benjamin Lee. 1944. 'The Relation of Habitual Thought and Behavior to Language', *ETC: A Review of General Semantics*, 1 (4):197–215.

Whorf, Benjamin Lee. 1950. 'An American Indian Model of the Universe', *International Journal of American Linguistics*, 16 (2):67–72.

Whorf, Benjamin Lee. 2012. *Language, Thought, and Reality*, MIT.

Wierzbicka, Anna. 1997. *Understanding Cultures Through their Key Words: English, Russian, Polish, German, and Japanese*, Oxford University Press.

Winawer, Jonathan et al. 2007. 'Russian Blues Reveal Effects of Language on Color Discrimination', *Proceedings of the National Academy of Sciences of the United States of America*, 104 (19):7780–85.

Wong, Jock. 2004. 'The Particles of Singapore English: A Semantic and Cultural Interpretation', *Journal of Pragmatics*, 36 (4):739–93.

Woumans, Evy et al. 2017. 'Bilingualism and Cognitive Decline: A Story of Pride and Prejudice', *Journal of Alzheimer's Disease*, 60 (4):1237–39.

Yoo, Hyunsoo, and Dickey, Michael Walsh. 2017. 'Aging Effects and Working Memory in Garden-Path Recovery', *Clinical Archives of Communication Disorders*, 2 (2):91–102.

Yow, W. Quin, and Markman, Ellen M. 2015. 'A Bilingual Advantage in How Children Integrate Multiple Cues to Understand a Speaker's Referential Intent', *Bilingualism: Language and Cognition*, 18 (3):391–99.

Zahodne, Laura B. et al. 2014. 'Bilingualism Does Not Alter Cognitive Decline or Dementia Risk among Spanish-Speaking Immigrants', *Neuropsychology*, 28 (2):238–46.

Zhu, Na et al. 2014. 'Cardiorespiratory Fitness and Cognitive Function in Middle Age: The CARDIA Study', *Neurology*, 82 (15):1339–46.

Zwaan, Rolf A. et al. 2017. 'Making Replication Mainstream', *Behavioral and Brain Sciences*, 41:e120.

Index